Synthetic Panics

Philip Jenkins

SYNTHETIC
PANICS

THE SYMBOLIC
POLITICS OF
DESIGNER DRUGS

New York University Press

New York and London

NEW YORK UNIVERSITY PRESS
New York and London

Library of Congress Cataloging-in-Publication Data
Jenkins, Philip, 1952–
Synthetic panics : the symbolic politics of designer drugs / by
Philip Jenkins.
p.   cm.
Includes bibliographical references and index.
ISBN 0-8147-4243-2 (alk. paper)
ISBN 0-8147-4244-0 (pbk. : alk. paper)
1. Narcotics, Control of—United States. 2. Designer
drugs—Government policy—United States. 3. Drug abuse—United
States.   I. Title.
HV5825 1999
363.45'0973—dc21   99-6057
CIP

New York University Press books are printed on acid-free paper,
and their binding materials are chosen for strength and durability.

Manufactured in the United States of America

10 9 8 7 6 5 4 3 2 1

CONTENTS

Acknowledgments   vii

Note on Usage   ix

Abbreviations   xi

ONE
Synthetic Panics   1

TWO
Speed Kills   29

THREE
Monsters: The PCP Crisis, 1975–85   54

FOUR
Suppressing Ecstasy: The Designer Drug Crisis   76

FIVE
The Menace That Went Away: The Ice Age, 1989–90   95

SIX
The CAT Attack, 1993–94   117

SEVEN
Redneck Cocaine: The Methamphetamine
Panic of the Nineties   132

EIGHT
Rave Drugs and Rape Drugs   160

NINE
The Next Panic   183

Contents

Abbreviations in Notes 199

Notes 201

Index 239

About the Author 247

ACKNOWLEDGMENTS

Portions of chapter five originally appeared in *Justice Quarterly*. I am grateful to the Academy of Criminal Justice Sciences for permission to use this material.

I thank my daughters, Alex and Cathy Jenkins, for their dedicated assistance in providing me with popular-culture references. Thanks also to Kathryn Hume for reading the manuscript and making many helpful comments.

NOTE ON USAGE

Throughout this book, I will emphasize the subjective and controversial nature of many of the terms used in the debates over drug use, including "designer drugs," the exact definitions of which will be discussed at the appropriate places in the text. In many instances such words should properly be qualified with quotation marks, such as "epidemic," "problem," "menace," and "crisis," but in practice, this is scarcely possible. In order to avoid weighing down the text, therefore, these words will generally be used without the quotation marks or qualifiers that they often merit.

Perhaps the most important word requiring explanation is "drug" itself, a term that has a complex history. As we will see in chapter 2, not until the early 1970s did the word "drugs" acquire its present meaning covering all illegal stimulants, and before that period there were important distinctions between "drugs" and "narcotics." Today, the word "drug" is often used in an overbroad and nonspecific sense: technically, for instance, marijuana is not a drug, but a plant that contains a drug, or a psychoactive substance. Moreover, "drug" is by no means a neutral term, since it has come to have such undesirable connotations. In the American context, it has a loaded legal meaning, since drugs are regulated according to stringent standards that do not apply, for instance, to foodstuffs.

Much of the debate over the legal status of drugs revolves around the question of what exactly is or should be classified as a "drug." At the time of writing, a bitter legal controversy is in progress over whether dietary supplements and herbal remedies that boast of healing qualities are in fact drugs, and if so, whether they should be regulated by federal authorities. In the case of one substance that will be discussed in this book, the chemical GHB, it is a matter of hot debate between advocates and critics whether it is a drug at all or whether it is a nutrient. A similar and far more significant controversy surrounds nicotine, which, if adjudged a drug, would become subject to stricter official regulation, so that cigarettes would be classified as drug-delivery devices. Once again, it is both pedantic and unnecessary to bracket the word "drug" with quotation marks at every use, but this qualifier should be borne in mind throughout.

The term "drug abuse" poses still more difficulties, for to speak of abuse implies a recognized standard of use, and that is a matter for subjective definition. Drinking a glass of wine every few days is generally seen as a careful and moderate use of alcohol, while drinking several bottles a day would constitute abuse by most standards. For a strict temperance advocate, however, even the occasional glass would constitute abuse, and there are religious groups that condemn caffeine in equally absolute terms. Similarly, if we describe any individual who occasionally smokes marijuana or takes an Ecstasy tablet as abusing a drug, we have already accepted the view that the substance is dangerous and harmful even in minute quantities, which is a matter open to debate.

ABBREVIATIONS

BNE   Bureau of Narcotics Enforcement (California)

CSA   Controlled Substances Act (1970)

DAWN   Drug Abuse Warning Network

DEA   Drug Enforcement Administration

DUF   Drug Use Forecasting System

FBN   Federal Bureau of Narcotics

FDA   Food and Drug Administration

NIDA   National Institute on Drug Abuse

ONE

Synthetic Panics

Literally, as people are playing with these designer drugs and making these analogues up, they are creating Frankensteins.
                                    —Senator Lawton Chiles, 1985[1]

Over the last century and a half, America's social problems have often
been blamed on the devastating effects of some harmful substance or
chemical, and at various times, different substances have been seen as
the major demon figures threatening the nation. In the early twentieth
century, alcoholic drinks were seen as the chief social scourge, while at
other times marijuana, heroin, and cocaine have been presented in this
way. Since the mid-1980s, the worst condemnations have been reserved for cocaine in its crack form. Some scares last a few months or a
year before dying away, but a phenomenon such as crack can provide a
focus of concern for a decade or more, causing a thorough reshaping
of both social policy and the criminal justice system. Remarkably
often, too, popular anxiety has focused on less celebrated drugs,
namely synthetic or manufactured chemicals, which have enjoyed a
rhetorical importance far greater than might be suggested by their
meager treatment in the vast literature on drugs and drug policy.[2] At
times of crisis, these drugs have been seen, however briefly, as national
menaces at least as daunting as heroin or cocaine, and in recent years,
drug scares have tended overwhelmingly to be what I call synthetic
panics.

On average over the last quarter-century, a new nightmare over synthetics has erupted every three or four years. In the late 1970s and early 1980s, PCP or angel dust was regularly presented as the "number one teen killer," provoking an alarmist campaign that presaged the massive outbreak over crack cocaine a few years later. The phrase "designer drugs" entered the media's vocabulary in 1985, during a spate of media exposés, congressional inquiries, and hyperbolic attacks on drugs such as fentanyl and its analogs, the so-called "serial killer of designer drugs." Yet another abortive epidemic raged briefly.

The pace of such panics accelerated during the 1990s. The decade began with frenzied warnings about the imminent new "ice age," in which the nation was on the verge of being swept by a devastating new form of smokable methamphetamine nicknamed ice, a drug that was "chilling" law-enforcement officials. Public fears about ice vanished more or less overnight in mid-1990, but soon afterward concerns arose about the supposed new superdrug methcathinone, or CAT. Like ice, CAT was said to be "more addictive than crack," a phrase that became a cliché in describing new synthetics, and CAT was likewise on the verge of "sweeping the nation." The magazine *U.S. News and World Report* called CAT "the new drug of choice" and spoke of a "scourge that federal officials now say could threaten the entire nation." Concerns about CAT vanished as swiftly as they had arisen, as the drug sank out of view in early 1995, but other drugs, both new and not so new, continued to incite alarm. In 1995 and 1996, concern shifted back to methamphetamine, or speed, this time in its standard (non-ice) form, so that a national "white storm warning" was issued for this next ultimate drug.[3] Speed was now identified as the drug of the nineties. Meanwhile, other chemical predators were coming to the fore in different parts of the country and were again billed as budding national epidemics; concerns about a special threat to women were aroused by Rohypnol, GHB, and other so-called rape drugs, said to be used to immobilize unsuspecting victims for sexual exploitation.

Because they have had so much impact on public policy, successive scares over substance abuse have attracted the attention of many contemporary scholars, who use what is called a constructionist approach to social problems.[4] These writers argue that the intensity of cultural reactions to a particular chemical does not necessarily reflect the actual social harm or individual damage it causes; rather, they argue, the degree of revulsion is an outcome of the drug's symbolic or political connotations. A panic may develop over a particular drug regardless of whether its actual usage and degree of dangerousness are rising, falling or remaining static, they point out. A ferocious scare can arise from a fringe substance such as CAT, for instance, which never had more than a minuscule following.

Attitudes toward drugs and substance abuse are socially constructed and liable to change significantly over time, as social constituencies themselves evolve. Before the 1970s, for instance, tobacco use attracted little stigma or condemnation, though it was commonly known to be a devastating public health menace linked to hundreds of thousands of deaths each year in North America alone. Not until the 1990s was there serious discussion of classifying nicotine as a drug for purposes of official regulation, and governments still subsidize its production. In contrast, far less pernicious substances such as marijuana have long been treated as prime public enemies, generating countless scare stories. As Aldous Huxley remarked in *The Doors of Perception,* though humanity has used many different "modifiers of consciousness" throughout its history, in recent years, "for unrestricted use, the West has permitted only alcohol and tobacco. All the other chemical Doors in the Wall are labeled Dope, and their unauthorized takers are Fiends."[5]

It is not easy to see much intrinsic difference between drugs that are legally approved and their strictly prohibited chemical cousins. One therapy drug such as Prozac becomes a vast commercial success, while another, nicknamed Ecstasy, is laden with sanctions just as severe as those surrounding heroin, though there is little evidence that Ecstasy is any more or less harmful than Prozac. One drug is banned because it is associated with some stigmatized ethnic or racial group, while another is tolerated, either because it is used and accepted by a social elite or because it becomes a profitable commodity for mainstream business. One is proscribed, while its near chemical relation is prescribed, and quite lavishly. The boundary between legal and illegal drugs, between medicine and dope, is shifting and arbitrary.

Drug prohibitions, then, are symbolic crusades, and constructionist scholars seek to determine which particular interest groups or bureaucratic agencies are responsible for labeling substances as uniquely dangerous or damaging. A series of revealing studies has applied this interpretation to the scares over marijuana in the 1930s, glue-sniffing in the 1960s, and of course crack since the mid-1980s.[6] The artificial quality of such outbreaks is well illustrated by scares over synthetic drugs such as CAT, GHB and fentanyl, where the phenomenon at the center of debate is authentically new, and yet virtually every aspect of the social reaction is derived from previous waves of concern about other substances. Though the product may be new, in other words, the rhetoric is timeless. Methamphetamine, for instance, becomes "the crack of the nineties," as critics apply the scripts previously applied to that better-known drug.

I am certainly not claiming that any of these illegal substances is harmless or (necessarily) that they should be considered socially acceptable. Methamphetamine and PCP can in some cases inspire the worst kinds of paranoid and self-destructive behavior. These and other drugs, legal and otherwise, can in some individuals create physical and psychological dependence, which is perhaps the worst form of mental slavery known to humanity. And if not used with extreme care, fentanyl and its relatives can indeed kill or maim. Yet in each case the extravagant claims made about the synthetics justify the term panic, because these reactions are so wildly disproportionate to the scale of the problem and the claims made about the prevalence and effects of the substances are generally so exaggerated. Anti-drug scares rapidly become what sociologists term moral panics, with all that this term implies about their origins and outcomes.

A moral panic is an incident of widespread social fear that appears seemingly out of nowhere and that grows in the space of a few months or years, then fades to nothing: the CAT scare of the early 1990s is a perfect example. As expressed by Stuart Hall and his colleagues, "When the official reaction to a person, groups of persons or series of events is *out of all proportion* to the actual threat offered, when 'experts,' in the form of police chiefs, the judiciary, politicians and editors *perceive* the threat in all but identical terms, and appear to talk 'with one voice' of rates, diagnoses, prognoses and solutions, when the media representations universally stress 'sudden and dramatic' increases (in numbers involved or events) and 'novelty,' above and beyond that which a sober, realistic appraisal could sustain, then we believe it is appropriate to speak of the beginnings of a *moral panic.*"[7]

From this perspective, then, the degree of panic associated with a social problem depends upon the wider cultural and political context rather than on any intrinsic qualities of the phenomenon itself. Issues ignite public concern when they successfully focus generalized public anxiety over matters such as race, gender, ethnicity, or generational tensions. In this sense, it is irrelevant whether the claims arising from a particular panic are well founded or wholly spurious: the panic is valuable in itself for what it suggests about the perceptions of a society as a whole and of its policymakers and legislators in particular. Exploring the fears and mythologies of a given society provides a valuable tool for understanding how that community defines its values and beliefs, as well as the means by which those values are expressed, contested, and redefined over time. Though we might assess the claims made during a particular panic—whether, for example, a particular drug was really enjoying a sudden upsurge of popularity—it is at least as significant to know why the mass media decided that this phenomenon was so important at the time in question and why the public accepted their judgment. What were the cultural implications of the drug? What did people fear? Why were they prepared to believe? How was the menace presented so as to appeal to existing ideas and prejudices? These questions have as much to do with rhetoric, history, and cultural studies as with law and pharmacology.

The fact that synthetic drugs have so often generated panic reactions suggests that the substances reflect powerful and enduring public anxieties and that these fears are distinct from those normally aroused by better-known drugs such as cocaine. Though some themes are common to different variants of anti-drug rhetoric, crucial and telling differences exist between the rhetorical assaults on heroin and cocaine and on synthetics such as Ecstasy and methamphetamine, ketamine and fentanyl. These distinctions are partly a matter of ethnicity and class—synthetics tend to be "white" drugs—but much of the alarm caused by so-called designer drugs arises from their very synthetic quality. They terrify precisely because they are manufactured by scientific processes, thus drawing on fears concerning the fearsome potential of unchecked experiment.

The concept of synthetic drugs itself is problematic, and the term "designer drug" has no precise scientific or sociological meaning. Generally, it refers to a substance synthesized in a laboratory, usually in an attempt to imitate some better-known chemical, to create an analogue; the imitation might be undertaken to make a drug cheaper, safer, more effective, or more readily available to a mass public, and the designer phrase is often used to refer to quite legal pharmaceuticals. The popular science press regularly refers to the promise of new designer hormones, designer estrogens, designer genes, and so on. A large portion of modern industry owes its origin to a botched quest for a designer drug, when in 1856, William H. Perkin unsuccessfully attempted to synthesize quinine. He accidentally discovered a mysterious, brightly colored substance, the first of the synthetic aniline dyes that became the basis for the subsequent development of industrial chemistry worldwide; it also made Perkin very rich. In view of the modern stereotype of clandestine drug laboratories run by irresponsible teenagers, it is ironic that this epoch-making innovation was the work of an eighteen-year-old, amateur chemist undertaking an unauthorized experiment.[8]

The discovery of synthetic chemicals marked a turning point in the history of science. Through the first half of the nineteenth century, scientists isolated valuable drugs from various plants, often from ones encountered during European explorations of distant lands. These new substances included morphine, strychnine, quinine, caffeine and codeine, and cocaine itself was isolated in 1844. From the 1860s onwards, a whole pharmacopoeia of revolutionary new synthetic drugs appeared as chemists sought to improve upon these naturally derived substances, as for example when the anesthetic procaine (Novocaine) was created to provide the beneficial effects of cocaine without its drawbacks. In 1898, a new synthetic derivative was claimed to offer the benevolent effects of morphine without the addictive side effects: this was diacetylmorphine, marketed under the trade name of Heroin. And in 1903, the first of the barbiturate drugs became commercially available as a sedative and hypnotic, replacing the alcoholic drinks previously recommended as the best means of calming nerves and sleeping soundly. All of these substances are synthetic or designer drugs, as are twentieth-century products such as LSD and the whole amphetamine group: all were made not by black-market chemists, but by European pharmaceutical corporations such as Merck, Bayer, Hoechst and Sandoz.[9] The impact of the new drugs was vastly enhanced by the introduction in 1853 of the hypodermic syringe, which permitted substances to be injected directly into the bloodstream.

Though the concept of designer drugs has deep roots, the term is of much more recent origin: it appeared around 1980, after the appearance of the term "designer jeans," and was initially applied to *outré* analog substances created and marketed as a kind of synthetic heroin. After this usage was publicized during congressional hearings in 1985, the term was more widely—and unsystematically—applied to other synthetic drugs that came into vogue over the next decade, including MDMA (Ecstasy), fentanyl, methcathinone, GHB and ketamine. Applying the designer label to the newer synthetics carried the implication that these substances were ipso facto as lethal as the most notorious synthetic heroins of the early eighties, which incontestably had caused brain damage and even death. The phrase was used quite capriciously: though it was not applied to most established drugs of abuse, such as heroin and LSD, this division was neither absolute nor consistent. In the late 1980s, a perceived surge in the use of methamphetamine led to this long-established drug (which dated back to 1919) being listed alongside other so-called designer synthetics such as Ecstasy and PCP. A typical news report of the 1990s might refer to the detection of a clandestine laboratory manufacturing "designer drugs like methamphetamine and Ecstasy." MDMA, which was first synthesized in 1912, joined the emerging canon of designer drugs, whereas LSD (which dated from 1943) did not.

Reasonably or otherwise, synthetic chemicals arouse deep-seated fears concerning the power of science and technology to reshape human nature and subvert or corrupt humanity in a well-intentioned quest for social betterment, and these ideas run through most recent debates over designer chemicals. These fears are customarily expressed in terms of mythology, but often borrow from the language of popular horror. The rhetoric is Promethean, portraying scientists as irresponsibly venturing into realms of knowledge not meant for human beings; critics also draw on the image of the new Prometheus, namely Dr. Frankenstein. In recent years, fears about "forbidden knowledge" and the proper limits of scientific inquiry have most often been expressed in the context of genetic engineering, particularly in reactions to the prospect of human cloning. These technologies threaten to create new types of human being that exist in a contested borderland, not wholly subject to the laws of either biology or technology.[10]

The Frankenstein image is so frequently cited in discussions of synthetic drugs because, as in the original tale, a quest for human improvement results instead in the creation of what are presented as terrifying figures, violent, remorseless, and predatory—in fact, as monsters. Even Allen Ginsberg, himself no foe of chemical experimentation, wrote a tirade against the amphetamine use of the early 1960s in which he lamented the proliferation of "the real horror monster Frankenstein speed freaks." Through chemical technologies, drug users abandon full humanity in a quest for a superior state, often losing their human selves in the process. The whole notion of addiction implies the loss of control over one's humanity in exchange for an enslavement to the products of technology, so that the heroic creature of technology, the evolutionary breakthrough, becomes instead the slavish zombie. The 1985 scare over designer drugs produced abundant metaphors of scientists as Dr. Frankenstein and drug users as zombies. As the mother of one synthetic drug victim remarked, "I shudder for what is going to happen to our country if this takes hold of our American people, our young people. They will just be a bunch of walking zombies." Zombie imagery pervaded accounts of PCP, some users of which experienced near-total dissociation from the body and its sensations, and the same concepts recurred during the methamphetamine scare of the mid-nineties. In 1997, an Associated Press (AP) wire story told how "[u]sers can become walking zombies, fueled by paranoid fantasies as they go days without sleep or food, only craving more of the drug [methamphetamine]." Reinforcing the supernatural imagery, one television program described the process of methamphetamine manufacture as "a high stakes game of alchemy," and a thriller about a designer-drug mastermind was called *The Alchemist.*[11]

Scientific rhetoric provides a thin veneer for an older and more superstitious worldview, one of foolhardy occult experimenters forfeiting their souls in misguided deals with the devil. Promethean images shade into Faustian as technophobia becomes a dread of supernatural evil. The scientists wielding these dark powers are portrayed as mysterious, evil geniuses, threatening to use the lights of perverted science to plunge humanity into a new dark age. During the 1985 congressional hearings, one expert suggested that recent innovations in designer drugs must be the work of a particularly brilliant innovator, one sufficiently clever to make these drugs without suffering lethal consequences: this phantom scientist was "world class . . . a mysterious genius . . . probably a chemist by profession."[12] The notion of outlaw science is continually reinforced when police report raiding the "laboratories" in which synthetics are made, though this term is usually far too grand for the tabletop chemistry sets normally found.

Many substances could potentially be used to harm or kill people, but unlike arsenic or opium, these newer chemicals are judged uniquely sinister precisely because they are products of human ingenuity. In more senses than one, synthetics arouse suspicion because they are unnatural. Two closely related concerns are at work here: either these advances in science will supplant ideas and aspirations that are fundamental to humanity, or else the new technologies will summon forth monstrous or demonic qualities hitherto latent in individuals. On the first theme, the abolition of man, the best literary example is found in the work of Aldous Huxley, who offers a frightening image of the fictional and benevolent-seeming drug Soma in his novel *Brave New World.* Huxley depicts a world in which scientists mold human behavior to promote peace and harmony and, through Soma, society offers unlimited pleasure on demand. Yet this world is ultimately hellish, because it destroys free will: all higher aspirations have been removed or reduced to a simplistic matter of behavioral conditioning. Soma offers "all the advantages of Christianity and alcohol; none of their defects. . . . Take a holiday from reality whenever you like, and come back without so much as a headache or a mythology."[13]

Discussions of chemically induced ecstasies often draw on related fears. If happiness or spiritual exaltation, aggression or passivity can all reliably be produced by a synthetic pharmaceutical product, is there anything more to human nature than a complex of electrochemical interactions in the brain? In Huxley's day, such an idea remained in the realm of science fiction, but following the neurochemical revolution of the 1970s, the concept seems much more feasible, and the popular antidepressant Prozac has been widely considered a real-life Soma. Can human happiness and spirituality be reduced to the manipulation of neurochemicals such as serotonin or dopamine?

The other potent theme resonant in warnings about scientific progress and synthetic drugs is that of the scientist as the maker of monsters, wittingly or otherwise. Here the literary precedent is *Dr. Jekyll and Mr. Hyde,* published in 1886 at the height of the boom in new synthetic drugs; its author may have been writing under the influence of cocaine. The famous story tells how Dr. Henry Jekyll searched for a miracle drug that would call forth his just and upright self, but he was instead transformed into a bestial, conscienceless killer. Accidentally he lets loose the "lower elements in [his] soul," the evil side of his nature, "the lethal side of man." This theme emerged more recently in the 1980 Ken Russell film, *Altered States,* which was based on the career of real-life LSD experimenter John Lilly, who was among other things an early pioneer of ketamine.[14] In this film, psychedelic drugs and sensory deprivation combine to transform an experimenter into a violent savage as his anatomy and even his genetic structure revert to a quasi-simian condition: he becomes a killer ape of the kind then imagined by anthropologists as the earliest proto-human ancestor.

The fantastic idea of science unleashing the monster within pervades anti-drug rhetoric, which often portrays the effects of illegal chemicals in wildly exaggerated form. Users can supposedly perform feats of amazing strength, ignoring pain or wounds while carrying out acts of extreme violence. During the marijuana panic of 1937, an oft-told tale reported how "an entire family was murdered by a youthful addict *[sic]* in Florida. When officers arrived at the home, they found the youth staggering about in a human slaughterhouse."[15] This berserker image reappeared in the campaigns against PCP in the late 1970s and methamphetamine in the 1990s. Given the near-total chemical illiteracy of legislators and media personnel, such extravagant claims are unlikely to face serious challenge. Moreover, many new drugs, legal and otherwise, genuinely have had catastrophic side effects, and we may recall that both heroin and cocaine were originally touted as safe alternatives to morphine. When information about such drugs is distributed through the Internet, another form of uncontrolled technology that legislators suspect and fear, the potential for technology-based panics is enormous.

Some popular-culture treatments are explicit in their supernatural implications. Robin Cook's bestselling 1994 novel *Acceptable Risk* concerns the creation of a miracle designer drug, Ultra, that exceeds the real-life Prozac in its ability to remove anxiety and create balanced, happy, motivated individuals: as a character remarks, "My God, what *doesn't* it do?" In fact, it is directly compared to Soma. But the substance has a dark side. An appalling "Mr. Hyde effect" turns users into ghouls and zombies—ravening, orgiastic monsters who commit evil deeds of which they have no recollection, such as killing and mutilating. Ultra is a magic potion of limitless power, instant possession in a pill. The book achieved phenomenal commercial success, because readers responded so readily to warnings about the dark underside of synthetic drugs. Following all the recent publicity about synthetics, the notion of literal demon drugs seemed all too plausible.[16]

The idea that drugs can reduce users to primitive savagery is inextricably bound up with the racial fears that have always been so critical an element of America's drug scares. Synthetics are more closely associated with white dealers and users than with minorities, and they are as likely to be found in rural or suburban contexts as in inner cities: thus they defy conventional stereotypes of the American drug problem. By bringing supposedly urban and minority habits into the white community, synthetics allow claims-makers to warn of racial contamination, a dangerous erosion of cultural and social boundaries. In this way synthetic drugs raise critical questions about the cultural meanings attached to whiteness.

Though the idea has older roots, conceiving of whiteness as a socially constructed category has been a critical intellectual insight of the last decade or so. When people of European descent encountered other racial groups, they developed an ideology that exalted the status of whiteness and elevated this white race to the summit of human creation: whites were superior in intellect, moral character, scientific innovation, and, in short, in everything that formed the basis of modern (white) civilization. By no means all of the newly designated white people came close to this ideal, and alternative explanations had to be found for the deviant, criminal and inferior. It was suggested that these groups had degenerated in biological terms, reverting to a more primitive evolutionary type, or that they had succumbed to the atavistic influences of some other group, some lesser breed. Not coincidentally, the first quarter of the twentieth century witnessed both the high point of American scientific racism and the outpouring of eugenic studies that delineated and condemned the pathetic caste of degenerate, poor whites. In the latter instance, the racial slide from full human status was viewed as being exacerbated by the sinister effects of substance abuse in the form of alcohol.[17] Mr. Hyde is a model of drug-induced atavism, a throwback to primitive savagery. The whole language of zombies derives from racial nightmares of Afro-Caribbean primitivism and voodoo, so that when the famous horror film *White Zombie* was released in 1932, its title was intended as a shocking oxymoron: how could a zombie be white? Yet throughout the designer-drug debates of the mid-eighties, it was always white users who were depicted as vulnerable to such zombyism.

Even when the connection is not explicit, older biological theories and racial stereotypes underlie much modern writing on the nature of crime, in which some races are presumed likely to commit certain types of offense. When white people commit offenses seen as characteristically non-white (which usually means black), this is considered peculiarly shocking and transgressive. When used by white elite groups, synthetic drugs symbolize the uniquely dangerous corruption of white creative genius and entrepreneurial skills; when popular with the lower classes, the drugs threaten to reduce users to the status of white trash, scarcely superior to minorities. In both cases, the implied threat of the drugs is enhanced by the perceived squandering of what are presumed to be the greater natural skills, strengths, virtues and talents of white users. In every sense, it seems whites simply have more to lose.

Drug prohibitions often represent the restatement of threatened ethnic boundaries, an assertion of the outer boundaries of "us-ness." Substances are condemned at least in part because of their symbolic association with a particular ethnic or racial group, and striking at the substance in question is a means of stigmatizing that particular group. David Musto's classic account argues,

> American concern with narcotics is more than a medical or legal problem—it is in the fullest sense a political problem. The energy that has given impetus to drug control and prohibition came from profound tensions among socioeconomic groups, ethnic minorities and generations. . . . The most passionate support for legal prohibition of narcotics has been associated with fear of a given drug's effect on a specific minority. . . . The occasion for legal prohibition of drugs for non-medical purposes appears to come at a time of social crisis between the drug-linked group and the rest of American society.[18]

Historical examples are not hard to find. Joseph Gusfield's book *Symbolic Crusade* explained the temperance movement in nineteenth-century America in terms of underlying conflicts between old-established elite groups, who were mainly Anglo-Saxon and Protestant, and newer Catholic populations, who were German and Irish. As Catholics viewed alcohol consumption more tolerantly than did Protestants, temperance laws became a symbolic means of reasserting WASP power and values. Other writers have suggested ethnic agendas for the campaigns to prohibit opium in the 1880s (as part of an anti-Chinese movement) and marijuana in the 1930s (which stigmatized a drug associated with African Americans and Mexicans).[19] Repeatedly, African Americans have been the primary targets of such movements, whether the drug in question was cocaine in the progressive era, heroin in mid-century, or crack in the 1980s. During the drug war launched by Presidents Reagan and Bush, for example, the crack cocaine favored by black users attracted savage penalties in the form of severe mandatory sentences for dealing and possession, while lesser sanctions were inflicted upon the mainly white users of cocaine in its powdered form.

Often the rhetorical portrayal of a particular drug draws upon the most vicious stereotypes of the racial category with which it is associated. Cocaine was feared in the early twentieth century because it was said to drive users to savage violence and wild sexual abandon, exactly the kind of primitive, jungle characteristics so fundamental to racist caricature. In 1914, at the height of the first national cocaine panic, an article in the *Literary Digest* alleged that "most of the attacks upon white women of the South are a direct result of a cocaine-crazed Negro brain."[20] Time and again, anti-drug campaigns warn that such appalling behaviors will cross over into the American mainstream, a barely veiled threat that whites will be infected by the most reprehensible characteristics attributed to blacks. In some periods, such racist alarms are sounded quite overtly, as when anti-marijuana activists of the 1930s and 1940s warned of the dangers facing white, middle-class youngsters who dabbled in the drug and thereby risked falling prey to jungle savagery themselves. According to popular stereotype, acute sexual dangers were said to face white girls who abandoned all inhibitions in the marijuana parlors. These fears recurred during the heroin boom of the 1960s as whites adopted the argot of the black drug subculture, and crossover notions formed part of the indictment of PCP in the following decade.

From the mid-1980s, drug policy was dominated by the fear of the next crack cocaine, a new chemical that could make white people fall prey to the problems that traditionally characterize blacks and Hispanics. In this scenario, "inner-city conditions"—namely, the problems afflicting minorities—could be visited upon "nice kids" in the suburbs, and the havoc wrought by drugs would reach the heartland, those rural and overwhelmingly white states of the West and Midwest. The racial codes are transparent. In recent years, methamphetamine has played the primary role in such rhetoric as the latest drug "invading the heartland." In 1996, the television news show *48 Hours* depicted a speed recovery group in Arizona, which it introduced with the line, "These people could be your neighbors, your friends, even your family." Presumably this referred to the fact that all of the group's members were white and Anglo, in contrast to the minority drug abusers who had become so familiar a media stereotype in the preceding decade. Methamphetamine is viewed ominously as a redneck cocaine, a drug that threatens the white group with the lowest status, "rednecks" and "trailer trash," who are already perilously near to sliding out of the privileged white racial order.

The fact that synthetics tend to be consumed by whites has always shaped public perceptions of these substances. For one thing, we know a lot less about the usage patterns for synthetics than we do about "minority" drugs such as heroin and cocaine, because most of the existing official measures are heavily weighted towards detecting problems in metropolitan areas rather than in suburban or rural areas or even in middling cities. It is in the big cities that officials regularly test arrested offenders for drug use and where emergency rooms report the number of admissions due to drug overdoses. Until the late 1980s, most of the reliable statistics and observations were drawn from just a few big cities where the leading medical and sociological researchers were based. As a consequence, findings from New York and Philadelphia, San Francisco and Los Angeles were all too likely to be read as if they accurately represented national conditions. Few available figures told us anything worthwhile about trends in areas in which white subcultures using amphetamine drugs have long predominated. This ethnic slant is reflected as well in the professional literature, in which countless textbooks on drug abuse provide only passing references to synthetics; before the mid-1990s, even a major drug like methamphetamine received only scant notice.[21] With so little material readily available on the synthetics, our perceptions of the history of the American experience with illegal narcotics are woefully incomplete.

The lack of reliable data also makes us dangerously vulnerable to successive panics concerning these "white" synthetics. As these drugs have remained almost invisible to official eyes, it is all too easy to make shocking and unsubstantiated claims about their explosive or epidemic growth. Though we can gather data about past usage patterns, these drugs effectively have no history, at least in the sense of a universally recognized narrative familiar to policymakers and journalists, so they are always seen as new and growing in popularity, even as surging epidemics. When the media make the apparently amazing discovery that young white people are dabbling extensively in these drugs, the habit is presumed both to be novel and to have come from some outside source. When drug problems are observed in the heartland—in Oklahoma or Iowa—the immediate (and false) assumption is that the infection has spread from the big cities of the East or West.

*

Apart from its racist implications, the idea that drug habits spread from blacks to whites like a contagion assumes a dubious model of drug usage in the United States and ignores the extremely local and particular qualities of subcultures. In drug matters, as in so much else, the United States is an exceedingly diverse nation with many different regional and ethnic communities, and it is only natural that particular drugs develop strong regional niches. Over the last ten or twenty years, methamphetamine has always been popular in the West and Southwest, and ice in Hawaii; among the newer drugs, Ecstasy developed its loyal local markets in Dallas, Austin and New Orleans, and GHB found its niche in Georgia, while the methcathinone problem was heavily concentrated in Michigan. Even within particular cities, a drug might appeal to one specific group and locale, such as the gay club scene, or to particular types of blue-collar workers. Contrary to media stereotypes, there really is no one continental market that can so easily be swept by some new drug across the boundaries of race, class and region.[22] Some drugs can achieve this kind of status, as marijuana did in the late 1960s, or as cocaine did a decade later, but even these events do not overwhelm existing local tastes. And just because a drug is not featured in media exposés and official reports does not mean that it has vanished from popular use: although media reporting of heroin use faded to almost nothing during the 1980s and 1990s, for instance, substantial usage continued in particular cities, permitting the media to comment about the supposed return of the drug every three or four years.

This regional emphasis is fundamental for understanding the means by which successive drug problems come to public notice. Though the public's common impression is that a new drug is sweeping the nation, what is usually happening is that the media or law enforcement officials have discovered a regional fad, then projected it onto the national stage. The best recent example of this was the reporting in 1985–86 of the vogue for crack, which at that time was an issue in sections of New York City and Los Angeles. An influential television documentary, CBS's *48 Hours on Crack Street,* presented the bicoastal issue as if it was already a national plague, implying that crack vials already littered the streets and parks of virtually every community across the country.[23] This tendentious account did much to generate fears of a national epidemic. Once the media present a problem in this way, congressional hearings follow, permitting the issue to be discussed in another national forum, generating national news coverage that reinforces perceptions of a widespread crisis. In the case of crack, such intense publicity actually assisted in the drug's spread, causing a destabilization of existing criminal networks, and the consequent violence helped drive up violent crime rates in the late 1980s. (Despite the media consensus, most of the violence resulted not from the qualities of the drug itself, but from its radical effects on established illegal markets.) Nor are such extrapolations from local phenomena confined to drug issues: witness the way that media reporting of Los Angeles's distinctive gang problems helped spread gang colors and customs throughout the nation. False reports of national spread can become self-fulfilling prophecies.

All of the recent synthetic panics resemble the experience with crack, albeit on a smaller scale. Whether we are looking at PCP in the 1970s, Ecstasy and ice in the 1980s, or CAT and speed in the 1990s, the panics follow very similar scripts. Reports of a vogue for a new drug automatically generate media claims that use of the substance will soon reach epidemic status. Though its dangers are duly stressed, the chemical also acquires a reputation for producing powerful and pleasurable effects, and its synthetic manufacture makes it appear a wonder drug, one that can raise the threshold of human experience far beyond what could be accomplished by a naturally occurring substance. This kind of exaggerated display of a synthetic drug's capacities often characterizes media reports of discoveries of legitimate pharmaceuticals and medicines used to treat conditions as diverse as cancer, AIDS, baldness and impotence. In the realm of illegal drugs, claims suggest that anything so potent will surely generate an epidemic, with predictable consequences such as vast illegal markets, criminal gangs, devastation of communities, addiction, personal degradation, and violent and bizarre behavior. The new drug is duly given some threatening tag, such as "the crack of the nineties."[24] After being force-fed drug-war rhetoric since the early 1980s, popular opinion has become so familiar with a package of stereotypical images about the parlous effects of drugs that these ideas are readily applied to emerging synthetics, especially when claims-makers draw overt linkages with well-established menaces. The potential audience is thoroughly prepared for new drug menaces even before these are explicitly identified, so that claims-makers need only fill in the appropriate nickname, whether it be ice, CAT or speed.

However unwittingly, the media ensure that the new drug gains a popularity it might never have acquired if it had simply been ignored. Instead, the substance is described in the most exaggerated terms, stressing its extremely powerful, pleasurable and enduring effects in a way that in other contexts would be seen as unabashed advertising. The media appear neither to know nor to care that such hyperbole can be counterproductive, encouraging drug users to add the new substance to their repertoires. The act of defining a new drug of choice, an ultimate high, a hot drug, may lead potential users to ask themselves why they are not sufficiently fashionable to have experienced it. In the early 1960s, this process of imitation caused the practice of glue-sniffing to spread at "incredible speed . . . the enemies of glue-sniffing popularized the custom all by themselves." One historical account of this episode is titled simply "How to launch a nationwide drug menace." In the 1980s, similarly, media portrayals of the effects of crack excited interest among users of powdered cocaine, who were suddenly made to feel staid and left behind. Even the most negative publicity can have effects quite different from those intended. Nothing could be starker than the warnings addressed to young people of the 1960s who were injecting methamphetamine, yet even these excited interest: as a Canadian investigation reported, "Some speed users . . . may actually be trying to test the truth of the slogan, 'Speed Kills.' The role of the doomed person who is at once a martyr sacrificing himself, a hero braving the confrontation with certain destruction and a gambler playing dice with death, is a role which seems to have a strong seductive pull for some young people who are morbidly hungry for compassion, admiration and excitement . . . the slogan may paradoxically carry more attractive than deterrent power."[25]

In each synthetic panic of the 1990s, the media have served as brilliantly successful public-relations workers, bringing local products to the national consciousness in a way that would excite huge professional envy if they were promoting soft drinks or fast food instead. As the *Journal of the American Medical Association* warned following the events of 1989–90, "News articles describing [ice] as like 'ten orgasms pronto' are working like paid ads. . . . If the media says it's an epidemic, drug adventurers say, everybody's using it, so I've got to try it." Ice was being "beautifully advertised by the media" to existing cocaine users, though users (fortunately) reported being disappointed with the results.[26] The warnings accompanying the advertising copy are universally ignored, stemming as they do from law-enforcement experts who have so thoroughly discredited themselves with decades of misleading panic statements about drugs like marijuana.

Apart from being heavily regionalized, patterns of drug use are also quite volatile, as much so as legitimate consumer goods such as clothing or toys: at any given time, literally dozens of drugs have some sort of a following across the country, and some are gaining rapidly in popularity in one locale or another. Why does one such substance rather than another come to be anointed as the next crack cocaine? What decides which particular drug will attract national attention, as signified by urgent congressional hearings, a spate of warning articles in newsmagazines, television movies and after-school specials, and features on such shows as *48 Hours* and *20/20?* And how does a drug habit become politically valuable? Much depends on the geographical niche that a particular drug happens to occupy and on the interest of the mass media in that region. Traditionally, the American media were disproportionately involved in the affairs of major bicoastal centers such as New York and Los Angeles, so a problem in one of those communities would be seen as a particularly hot property. For instance, the explosion of national PCP coverage in the late 1970s owed much to the drug's popularity in the Los Angeles metropolitan region. Once a story emerges in one center, it is disseminated via media syndication, a process which plays a vital (if little examined) role in forming national perceptions of crime and social problems. Within days, newspapers across the country are warning that California-based problems like PCP or synthetic heroin will arrive imminently in Tennessee or Connecticut.

More recently, other media centers have risen dramatically in importance, notably Atlanta, which is home to both the CNN cable network and the Centers for Disease Control, which offer an abundance of experts prepared to offer commentary on new threats to life and safety. In the mid-nineties, CNN took a leading role in the exposure of the drug GHB, which was enjoying a vogue in and around Atlanta: the initials were even taken to stand for Georgia Home Boy. Local instances of rape-drug use in the Atlanta region similarly gave CNN a basis on which to present a national menace. Once publicized, the rape-drug concept proved irresistible to talk shows and activists throughout the nation, perhaps also giving ideas to sex criminals who would not otherwise have contemplated using this method. Atlanta's new role as a media center both reflected and contributed to a geographical shift in the political and economic significance of the Sunbelt states from the 1970s onwards. Not surprisingly, major synthetic-drug scares of the 1990s concerned drugs with a southern and western focus, including methamphetamine (Arizona and California), Ecstasy (Texas and Louisiana), and GHB and Rohypnol (Texas, Florida and Georgia).

But media factors alone cannot provide a complete answer, as other recent panics have taken place in settings far removed from major media centers: most striking was the coverage of CAT, which was a fad drug in Michigan's remote Upper Peninsula when it was said to be on the verge of overrunning the nation. This instance, like others before and since, suggests the importance of national and local political agendas in shaping moral crusades. In large measure, CAT became a national problem because the issue was taken up by federal anti-drug officials, whose interests were directly served by a new drug problem in their current political environment.

Such activists are commonly described as moral entrepreneurs. Sociologist Howard Becker was studying the origins of American narcotics policy in the 1930s when he observed, "Wherever rules are created and applied we should be alive to the possible presence of an enterprising individual or group. Their activities can properly be called 'moral enterprise' for what they are enterprising about is the creation of a new fragment of the moral constitution of society, its code of right and wrong."[27] These moral entrepreneurs can be individual activists, but bureaucratic agencies can also expand their influence and resources by focusing public attention on issues that fall within their scope of activity. Becker's much-quoted case study shows how the Federal Bureau of Narcotics (FBN) manufactured out of whole cloth a national marijuana menace in order to save and ultimately enhance its dwindling resources in the middle of the Great Depression. The recent furor over methamphetamine fits neatly into this entrepreneurial model, as virtually all of the claims and rhetorical work involved in this movement stemmed from one highly visible federal agency, the Drug Enforcement Administration (DEA), the FBN's lineal descendant. In terms of social problem theory, the DEA was uniquely well placed in terms of the three essential requirements of a successful claim-maker: the agency had an overwhelming *interest* in promoting the problem; it had enormous *resources* in terms of public credibility and media contacts; and over the previous decade it had secured effective *ownership* of the issue, in the sense that its analysis of drug issues had become generally accepted as authoritative.[28]

Stressing the role of just one agency in creating drug panics can seem like a kind of conspiracy theory: surely no single group has such power to influence opinion, even a venerable and well-connected body like the FBI or DEA? Yet the case studies offered here confirm that law-enforcement agencies can indeed exercise such influence. When the DEA or a similar body declares that a given issue is a problem or an epidemic, most media outlets immediately report this as unadorned fact, virtually never challenging the story's significance. News reporting of drug issues over the last quarter century has largely consisted of reprinting or paraphrasing DEA press releases; it is sobering to observe how precisely phrases and concepts from official sources echo through subsequent accounts, whether in print or in television news segments. When the DEA declared, as it did in 1996, that methamphetamine was the poor man's cocaine, this exact phrase would be quoted hundreds of times in the national media. It is scarcely surprising that there is so much reluctance to consider alternatives to the militarized, drug-war approach to substance abuse.

In addition to their role in serving national agendas, drug panics have also emerged from local alignments. Several synthetic panics have arisen from activism by local officials with a pressing interest in portraying themselves as vigorously committed to fighting against the drug threat—and often against the racial menaces linked to it. Their efforts have been brought into the national arena through newsworthy congressional hearings, coupled with the astute manipulation of a media ever in quest of a plausible social menace. In 1980, Philadelphia attracted the label "speed capital of the world" on the strength of entrepreneurial campaigns by suburban Pennsylvania legislators anxious about the spillover of urban crime problems into their neighborhoods. In 1989, the key activists on the ice issue were Hawaiian legislators campaigning to outdo one another on local drug matters, and in fact the whole affair can only be understood in the context of an impending contest for the state's US Senate seat. Like their Philadelphia counterparts, local political leaders made a national impact following sensational congressional hearings. This was also the pattern of the CAT scare of 1993, when the nationalization of Michigan's localized drug problem owed much to the activism of just one legislator.

In many of these cases, perhaps all, such legislators believed sincerely in the dangers over which they were raising an alarm: for many years, for instance, Congressman Charles Rangel has consistently pursued his anti-drug agenda, in which he clearly believes with all passion. At the same time, we must not overlook matters of political self-interest. Members of any political organization charged with investigating social problems of any sort will attempt to attract as much publicity as possible by presenting themselves as concerned, active and well-informed guardians of the public good, and there are few better opportunities to do this than by recognizing a problem at an early stage to prevent it from reaching crisis proportions. In Hawaii, Pennsylvania and Michigan, local issues offered legislators the chance to investigate and combat a drug problem in a proactive, far-sighted way and at no significant risk to themselves. If an ice epidemic or a CAT epidemic were actually to occur, the congressional committee in question would earn credit for having prophesied it and urging preemptive action; if it faded away, the committee could claim that its forethought had prevented a drug crisis. Conversely, much was to be lost by cautious or skeptical reactions to an incipient crisis. If the forecast menace materialized, an agency or administration stood to attract most of the blame for ensuing problems.

In fact, the drug panics of the last decade or so can all be correlated quite closely to the electoral cycle, the inexorable sequence of major national and state elections every two years, which sets American politics apart from those of most other advanced nations and which goes far toward explaining the constant generation of novel problems and panics in American society. In the Hawaiian case, the drug debate was urgent because of an approaching vote for the US Senate seat scheduled for 1990, while the politics of CAT were conditioned by the Democratic need to show activism on drugs in the run-up to the 1994 Congressional elections. In 1995 and 1996, the same need to be tough on crime ensured that the administration would exploit the discovery of a national methamphetamine menace, which was considered most alarming in politically vital states of the West and Southwest. Once the given anti-drug crusade was under way, the rhetoric was almost predetermined as yet again we were primed to hear the familiar stories of monsters and zombies, of the jungle intruding into the heartland and the violation of cherished boundaries. And in each case, the objective basis for such claims was far less significant than the political, social, ethnic and bureaucratic pressures that led groups or individuals to present them.

The scholarly neglect of synthetic drugs means that we often lose a crucial sense of historical perspective on both drug subcultures and anti-drug movements. This is especially true of the crack epidemic, which attracted so much public attention in the mid-1980s and which can scarcely be understood without knowing the recent synthetic panics upon which the new anti-drug campaign was drawing. Chapters 2 through 4 describe three major drug scares of the seventies and early eighties, each of which contributed substantially to the revised and much more severe attitude to drug use that became apparent around 1985–86. Though the substances at issue were quite different, the combined offensives against speed, PCP and the fentanyl analogues did much to create the conditions and rhetoric for the drug war. These substances allowed the revival of an idea that had been all but discredited during the 1970s—namely that illegal drugs were not merely a harmless private indulgence, but a genuine social menace demanding urgent government intervention.

Though rarely remarked on as extensively as heroin or cocaine, different members of the amphetamine family have enjoyed enormous popularity since the 1940s, often in illegal circumstances, and the concept of the violent and uncontrollable speed freak has had a potent influence on later stereotypes, including that of the crack user. The changing image of the amphetamine user is traced in chapter 2, which further shows how in the late 1970s, methamphetamine reappeared as a significant social problem. However, the focus of concern now shifted from users and individual speed freaks to the gangsters and organized criminals said to dominate the trade: this idea contributed much to the image of the drug kingpin, which became pivotal to law-enforcement strategies during the drug war of the eighties.

Chapter 3 addresses an event now largely forgotten. Though the drug PCP is rarely noted in the recent literature on drugs, it attracted enormous public fear between 1975 and 1985, and helped establish the vocabulary for the extremely successful movement against crack. As with crack in later years, the assault on PCP constantly reiterated themes of instant addiction, preternatural strength, uncontrolled violence and self-destruction, symbolized by the appalling image of users tearing out their own eyes. Horror stories about angel dust reached alarming heights between 1978 and 1980 and were very much in the news as the Reagan administration took office, making it easier to erect the walls of zero tolerance against all narcotics.

In the increasingly conservative political environment of the early 1980s, drugs became a primary symbol of the hedonism so widely blamed for moral decay, and a new intolerance for chemically induced experimentation was powerfully evident in the movement against the newly christened designer drugs, a term that mainly referred to fentanyl analogues, the so-called synthetic heroins. The events of the mid-1980s form the subject of chapter 4. Though some of the "new heroins" really did pose a direct threat to life and health, the designer-drug stigma soon extended to much less lethal substances, notably Ecstasy, an amphetamine derivative that had attracted wide interest for its possible therapeutic qualities. In the new environment, the very name Ecstasy epitomized everything that political leaders and law-enforcement agencies found most blameworthy. The movement against it reflected a distrust of pleasure, or of the loss of self-control, the approach which Peter Kramer has termed "pharmacological Calvinism."[29]

The crack wars fundamentally changed the political landscape of the drug issue to the extent that alarmist anti-drug claims achieved a degree of general acceptance unparalleled since the Eisenhower years. After the mid-eighties, society became far more vulnerable to claims about emerging drug menaces, claims that proved on closer examination to be poorly substantiated. The new wave of post-crack panics will be analyzed in chapters 5 through 8.

The first of these new synthetic threats grew out of local political conflicts in Hawaii, which created the perception that the nation was about to be overwhelmed by smokable methamphetamine (ice). These events are described in chapter 5. The ice phenomenon occurred just as the rhetoric over crack was still fresh in the public mind and the drug war was reaching its crescendo, and the issue might not have arisen at all if public expectations had not been conditioned by these recent precedents. The ice affair was closely paralleled a couple of years later by a similar panic over methcathinone (CAT), which forms the subject of chapter 6. Both stories followed broadly similar patterns: both ice and CAT were said to be becoming enormously popular, and both combined extremely addictive qualities with the advantages of cheapness, easy access and domestic manufacture. However, in neither case was concern sustained after the first year or so, and the issues soon either ceased to exist or became dormant. The twin incidents thus offer an unusual opportunity to trace the creation of drug panics from inception to eclipse.

Far more substantial and enduring was the growing concern over methamphetamine discussed in chapter 7. During 1995 and 1996, speed became the subject of official alarm to a degree not seen with any drug since the worst of the crack years, though, as we will see, quantitative claims about the supposed growth of usage were built on very weak foundations. The speed problem was better substantiated than either ice or CAT, as this drug genuinely was attracting a broad clientele, but even here, statistics cited about the harm allegedly inflicted by the drug were grossly misleading. The drug achieved its star status because it epitomized magnificently the racial dangers suggested by other substances, often veiled in terms of the threat to the heartland.

Problems evolve in response to changes in the wider society, which provides the necessary audience for claims: in this sense, the importance attached to the methamphetamine issue can partly be seen as testimony to the growing political significance of western and southern states. Demographic and social changes account too for the second wave of panic over designer drugs during the mid-nineties, which focused on party or rave drugs like Ecstasy, ketamine ("Special K"), and GHB. As is described in chapter 8, all were depicted as far more lethal than the drugs popular during the youth of the current generation of parents, such as marijuana. This change in rhetoric is a concession to the presumed make-up of the media audience, which includes millions of baby-boomers unlikely to be convinced by horror stories about the drugs they recall from their adolescence. Equally, the greater social and political status of women in recent years ensured that female concerns were reflected in these recent panics. Virtually all news reports covering the methamphetamine issue of the nineties presented the addiction problem through case studies of young women whose lives and families were destroyed by speed. In the case of the party drugs, the latest synthetic scare, it is charged, rightly or wrongly, that these chemicals are dangerous weapons encouraging rape and date rape.

Recent anti-drug movements have tended to stress very similar rhetorical themes. With these in mind, we should be able to apply a far more critical reading to future claims of the sort that will assuredly arise about other synthetics. Chapter 9 describes the scripts commonly deployed when a new drug menace appears and suggests how these charges can be evaluated and challenged. It also suggests that synthetic drug fads will continue to be presented as potential crises, threatening to ravage the entire country. The pressing need is for us to recognize the political and cultural factors that generate such misleading expectations.

In writing this book, I have three major goals. Firstly, I want to show that any comprehensive, reliable account of American drug policy, past or present, must take account of the synthetic drugs, which so rarely receive the attention they deserve. This is all the more necessary at a time when various synthetics have moved to center stage in the ongoing drug war. Apart from their intrinsic importance, the synthetic or designer drugs have over the years done much to form popular images of the drug user and the illegal drug market, images that have subsequently been transferred to more familiar substances like heroin and cocaine. Without a historical perspective, moreover, we will continually be surprised by what seem to be "new" synthetic drug problems, though in reality these situations usually have deep local roots.

Secondly, in addition to noting the long-standing neglect of the synthetics, we need to explain the reasons for their relative invisibility, a fact that relates to issues of race and region. In a society in which race has always played so prominent a role, it is not surprising that racial assumptions guide our approaches to social problems in the United States. Understanding the successive synthetic panics tells us a great deal about the shifting nature of racial attitudes over the last half-century, including how some drugs have been condemned because they apparently threaten to infect the white population with the dangerous tendencies of other races. We also see how profoundly racial assumptions are embedded in all of the statistical measures used to assess the American drug situation, even when no racial agenda is overtly stated. This observation applies to the most basic and seemingly self-evident remarks: when we speak of drugs as an urban problem, an inner-city problem, we have already unwittingly declared that we are going to devote our attention to black issues and subcultures, not white. In large measure, the story of the modern American encounter with illegal drugs must be read in racial terms.

Finally, studying drug panics tells us a great deal about the dynamics of other social problems, including why issues rise and fall over time and how they gain or lose public attention. I have repeatedly used the word "construction" to describe how problems are understood, though I stress again that construction does not imply fabrication or falsification, or any suggestion that problems are built around imaginary or harmless phenomena, that they are not "real." Still, the seriousness attached to a given problem rarely reflects an objective assessment of the social threat posed by the issue in question. A situation can last for many years without being viewed as a problem, and the fact that it is suddenly seen as a crisis or an epidemic does not necessarily mean that it has become dramatically worse. The drugs viewed as the most dangerous in any given era are not necessarily the most dangerous or prevalent of those currently in use, nor are they always more harmful than many legal products. An existing issue often becomes a problem when it is perceived in a new way or when new means are used to measure it, but in either case, the change is in the eye of the beholder, in the minds of the potential audience: to be is to be perceived. When we study the construction of a problem, our primary emphasis should be on that audience and how it interprets dangers to society under the influence of factors such as racial and demographic tensions, changing gender roles or political and bureaucratic activism. These forces determine the social meaning attached to any given substance or drug, and they decide whether that substance becomes the focus of a problem or panic.

Speed Kills

In America, the cars run on high-octane gas, the computers run on nanosecond circuits, and the people run on pills. Speed is essential.

—Gail Sheehy, 1971[1]

Synthetic or designer drugs were by no means an innovation of the 1960s, but it was in these years that current media stereotypes of the substances and their users were first articulated. These ideas would also shape the political discourse concerning other drugs. Over the last forty years, amphetamines in various forms have been at the heart of perhaps half a dozen separate drug scares, from the concern over teenagers misusing pep-pills in the early 1960s through the national methamphetamine epidemic of the mid-nineties. More frequently than we would gather from the standard histories of drug use in this country, speed in its various forms has been one of the most frequently consumed and abused stimulants. It has repeatedly provided a major incentive for anti-drug legislation and for the expansion of law-enforcement bureaucracies.

At the end of the 1960s, methamphetamine already had the distinction of being one of the very few drugs stigmatized within a drug culture of seemingly limitless tolerance: even enthusiastic drug users often viewed use of the drug as an acute medical and cultural problem. This drug developed a powerful, damaging association with extreme aggression and violence, through its ability to turn users into amoral speed freaks, but also through the later connection with organized crime and drug trafficking. Just as the speed-freak stereotype laid the foundation for later concepts of the drug user as marauding monster, so the link with such familiar villains as the Mafia and outlaw motorcycle gangs popularized notions of the sinister drug kingpin who urgently needed to be combated by federal law enforcement. Crucially, these ideas won credence among baby-boomers themselves, who derided similar charges about LSD or marijuana as absurd propaganda. The hyperbolic campaigns against amphetamines in the 1960s and 1970s constituted a preview of the national drug war that would have such an impact on American society in the Reagan years and afterwards.

In the beginning was the amphetamine. The amphetamine drugs are a chemical family initially synthesized in the late nineteenth century in order to mimic the effects of natural and herbal substances like ephedrine: they are archetypal designer drugs. Benzedrine (racemic or dextro-levo-amphetamine) was first synthesized in 1887, but its uses were not widely recognized until the 1920s, when its "right-handed" isomer, dextro-amphetamine or Dexedrine, also came into use. Also synthesized at about this time was d-phenyl-isopropyl-methylamine hydrochloride, better known as methamphetamine, which was marketed under the brand names Methedrine and Desoxyn. By 1970, over thirty amphetamine preparations were being distributed by fifteen pharmaceutical companies. The reason these drugs are so powerful has only become apparent with the investigation of the brain's neurotransmitters in recent decades. Amphetamines, we now know, have a close chemical relationship to naturally occurring catecholamines like dopamine, epinephrine and norepinephrine, which help regulate cardiovascular functions and the central nervous system. As sympathomimetic drugs, the amphetamines mimic naturally occurring neurotransmitters and help trigger the release of additional natural chemicals. Amphetamines thus cause the nervous system to become intensely aroused, mimicking the effects of extreme external stimuli.[2]

From 1932, amphetamines were widely used in the legal form of Benzedrine inhalers, marketed by the Smith Kline French corporation, and from 1936 tablets became available, ostensibly to treat the rare condition of narcolepsy. Through the mid-twentieth century, the amphetamine group was so widely prescribed for a variety of physical and emotional conditions as to make it seem an authentic wonder drug; coincidentally or not, 1932 was also the year in which Huxley described his fictional Soma. Amphetamines were associated with endurance, wakefulness, and the capacity to undertake long and demanding tasks of manual labor. As such, they were particularly favored by truck drivers.[3] The stimulant was a godsend for workers in heavy industrial plants operating under the shift system, which paid so little regard to normal biorhythms. The drug had military applications as well: during the Second World War and afterwards, the United States and other nations issued amphetamine products (mainly Benzedrine) to soldiers and sailors facing long periods without sleep. Illicit supplies were available to almost anyone living in proximity to a military base, an industrial plant or a major trucking center.

The appeal of amphetamine was many-sided. Women were likely to encounter amphetamine in its role as appetite suppressant. In middle-class circles, the drug found its main users among college and high school students studying desperately for exams. According to Harvey Cohen, "[a]mphetamine is very much an over-achiever's type of chemical," and as such it had a following among business people and executives. It also had a large surreptitious market in college and professional sports, as speed promoted desirable qualities of aggression and toughness; the habit was probably introduced by servicemen returning after the Second World War. In schools, amphetamine analogues such as Ritalin (methylphenidate) were prescribed for schoolchildren diagnosed, rightly or wrongly, as hyperactive. The amphetamine business became a vast and profitable economic enterprise: by 1958, some eight billion pills and tablets were produced legally each year in the United States, in addition to the sizable illegal market and clandestine imports from Mexico; by 1971 legal production had risen to twelve billion pills. Just the amount produced within the law had the potential "to provide a month's supply to every man, woman and child in the country."[4]

The potential for abuse was substantial, as amphetamines were readily available nationwide without medical supervision. The first reports of improper self-medication followed within a year or so of the introduction of pills in 1936, and the possibility of addiction was first raised by 1938; by the mid-1950s, the phenomenon of amphetamine psychosis was being reported in the medical literature. At least from the early 1940s, the press regularly reported that the cheap and ubiquitous Benzedrine inhalers were being abused by students, truck drivers and others. Less obvious at the time was the problem of abuse by women in middle-class, domestic settings, an issue that only gained recognition through later reminiscences and confessions. Only in 1990, for instance, did Kitty Dukakis, the wife of the presidential candidate, discuss her quarter-century-long addiction to amphetamine diet pills. According to the commissioner of the FDA, by 1970, perhaps half of the *legally* produced pills were being diverted into unauthorized channels—an amazing four or five billion pills each year.[5]

Amphetamines were at least as widely abused as better-known drugs. In the mid-1970s, an extensive survey of American men born between 1944 and 1954 suggested that some 27 percent had used an amphetamine stimulant at some point in their lives, and about a third of that group had used such a drug in the previous twelve months. Usage was significantly higher among men from Mountain and Pacific states and city-dwellers: men born in the period 1950–53, at the height of the baby boom, were more likely to have used amphetamines at some point in their lives than those born earlier or later. Almost 10 percent of the sample claimed familiarity with Methedrine, probably the riskiest of the various types. Unfortunately, the same study did not interview young women, whom we know from other sources to have been likely to use the same stimulants.[6]

The extent of illegal amphetamine use also emerges from the surveys taken occasionally by federal agencies, which ask various populations about their drug consumption. One of the most closely watched of these surveys concerns high school seniors, as drug experts believe that observing younger consumers provides a means of *Monitoring the Future*, as the program is called. Of course this survey is not perfect: it ignores youngsters who have already dropped out of school, it requires much allowance for the possible falsity of answers in such a sensitive area, and its questions and definitions change somewhat over time. On balance, though, the survey figures do appear to indicate long-term trends with some reliability. Table 2.1 shows changes in usage for some major drugs.[7]

Table 2.1 Use of Illicit Drugs by High School Seniors, 1975–95

Percentage Reporting Use in Last Twelve Months

	1975	1979	1983	1987	1991	1995
			Class of			
Marijuana	40.0	50.8	42.3	36.3	23.9	34.7
Cocaine	5.6	12.0	11.4	10.3	3.5	4.0
Stimulants*	16.2	18.3	17.9	12.2	8.2	9.3
LSD	7.2	6.6	5.4	5.2	5.2	8.4
PCP	NA	7.0	2.6	1.3	1.4	1.8

Percentage Reporting Use in Last Thirty Days

	1975	1979	1983	1987	1991	1995
			Class of			
Marijuana	27.1	36.5	27.0	21.0	13.8	21.2
Cocaine	1.9	5.7	4.9	4.3	1.4	1.8
Stimulants*	8.5	9.9	8.9	5.2	3.2	4.0
LSD	2.3	2.4	1.9	1.8	1.9	4.0
PCP	NA	2.4	1.3	0.6	0.5	0.6

*Not under doctor's orders or supervision

Stimulants have long been popular; they always outranked cocaine over this twenty-year period, usually by a large margin. This is not surprising, as amphetamine pills would be much more accessible to high school students, who have less disposable income than their elders. Through the 1980s, around two-thirds of seniors questioned believed that amphetamines would be very easy or fairly easy to get if desired, compared to an average of 85 percent for marijuana, 50 percent for cocaine and 33 percent for LSD.

While we would like to know more about the particular kinds of stimulants being used, the seniors were not asked this question. Not until 1982 was the survey phrased to distinguish between illicit and over-the-counter amphetamines. We may presume that the stimulants most often used were Dexedrine or Benzedrine tablets, but some at least would have been injected methamphetamine; a separate question about crystal methamphetamine use was not asked until 1990. And this usage picture grows cloudier when we note that even truthful respondents did not necessarily know what drugs they were actually using: by the late 1970s, many of the so-called amphetamine pills on the market were in fact look-alikes using caffeine or ephedrine, synthetic variants of the original synthetic product sold in the shapes and colors of the authentic drugs. One 1977 study suggested that only a quarter of the pills sold as amphetamines contained any amount of the drug whatever.[8] But what we can assume with confidence is that virtually all of the respondents thought, rightly or wrongly, that they were using one or more of the amphetamine drugs.

The vagueness of the survey questions about stimulant use is significant in its own right, indicating that the authorities sponsoring the surveys were much less interested in synthetic drugs than they were in the "real" problems of heroin, cocaine and marijuana. In fact, the data from Monitoring the Future's survey is often reproduced in textbooks with tables showing the figures for only those three drugs. Whatever the exact meaning of the term "stimulant," by 1991, 14.2 million Americans were estimated to have used illicit stimulants at some point in their lives, and 700,000 had taken them in the previous month. Compare those figures with an estimated 67.7 million who had ever used marijuana, 23.7 million who had used cocaine and 16.7 million who had used hallucinogens. Though stimulants were not the most commonly used drugs, they enjoyed an enormous market.[9] Fourteen million users scarcely represented a fringe subculture.

With such widespread amphetamine use, the tinder was always present for sporadic panics over the evils of "thrill-pills"; this term originated with an anti-barbiturate campaign of the 1940s, but was now commonly and confusingly applied to both uppers and downers. During the 1950s and 1960s, media concern focused on teenagers who used amphetamines, pep-pills, in combination with barbiturates, or goofballs, and sometimes (perilously) with alcohol. The favored form of amphetamine was Benzedrine, the ubiquitous bennie or peach, but other well-known pills included Dexedrine (dexies, oranges or purple hearts) and Biphetamine (black beauties). Youth counterculture was fueled by pills long before marijuana had made substantial inroads. Hunter S. Thompson describes the pill culture among the biker gangs of the mid-1960s: "Bennies ('cartwheels' or 'whites') are basic to the outlaw diet—like weed, beer and wine—but when they talk about getting wasted, the action moves onto another level. The next step up the ladder is Seconal ('reds' or 'red devils'), a barbiturate normally used as a sedative, or tranquilizer. . . . they prefer the reds—which they take along with beer and bennies 'to keep from getting sleepy.' The combination brews up some hellish effects."[10] The boom in amphetamine pills during those years was an international phenomenon, affecting teenagers in Western Europe and the Far East, and references to the drugs were commonplace in the songs of British Invasion music groups like the Who and the Small Faces. In Japan, amphetamines have represented the largest single drug problem since the Second World War.

Illicit amphetamine use in the United States became dramatically obvious in the early 1960s, when the quantities of drugs seized grew sharply. The Los Angeles police seized more illicit amphetamines in 1961 than it had in the years 1955 through 1959 combined, while barbiturate-related arrests in Florida increased tenfold between 1956 and 1964; it was about 1960 when the term pill-head entered the police vocabulary. Just how commonplace illicit amphetamines had become is indicated by a remarkable study undertaken by Dr. John Griffith in the mainstream midwestern community of Oklahoma City during 1963–64. At that point, police records listed 1,200 individuals in the city who had been arrested for possession of amphetamines or barbiturates, but interviews with dealers placed the number of regular users at up to five thousand in a community with a population of only 300,000. The city had six important peddlers, though no dealers of the very highest level. (These major dealers, known only by repute in Oklahoma City, were defined as those regularly trading pills in quantities of hundreds of thousands.) Each peddler supplied at least three to five hundred individuals a year. Self-described pill-heads or fiends bought amphetamines and barbiturates in roughly equal quantities at a rate of about three dollars per dozen pills. In addition, some users favored inhalers, and at least a few were injecting their drugs.[11]

Because this is an isolated study, we cannot be sure how typical Oklahoma City was at this time. It was an important center for the trucking industry, standing as it did at the junction of Route 66 and Route 77, the main road to Dallas and north Texas, but there is no intrinsic reason that the scale of amphetamine trafficking here should have been much greater than it was in other hub cities, such as Omaha or Little Rock. Yet Oklahoma City was a site with wider connections; in 1964, Dr. Griffith found that local speed peddlers belonged to a loose network operating across Texas and Oklahoma in a pattern that sounds quite similar to the modern organization of the methamphetamine trade: since the late 1980s, most of the illicit laboratories supplying Dallas have been based in Oklahoma.

Before 1960, neither amphetamines nor barbiturates attracted much media attention as a cause of substance abuse problems, and they were rarely featured in broad surveys of the American drug situation. This was largely because the substances were of little concern to the bureaucratic apparatus headed by Harry J. Anslinger of the FBN, which focused on the illicit use of heroin, cocaine and marijuana. As legal substances manufactured by large corporations, amphetamines and barbiturates were drugs rather than narcotics and thus fell under the jurisdiction of the Food and Drug Administration (FDA). This distinction was scientifically puzzling: cocaine is a stimulant rather than a narcotic, a term that indicates sleep-promoting properties, and it has far more in common with the amphetamines than with marijuana. The division was a matter of historical accident dating to the Progressive Era, when legal chemicals were regulated under the Pure Food and Drug Act of 1906, while other substances were proscribed under the Harrison Narcotic Act of 1914. The dichotomy would, however, have important legal and bureaucratic ramifications. By mid-century, the so-called narcotics were the realm of the FBN, a hard-nosed criminal justice agency that modeled itself on Hoover's Federal Bureau of Investigation (FBI), while the FDA was a civil regulatory agency with more limited enforcement powers. For instance, its unarmed agents normally lacked the power to arrest suspects or seize goods.

The drug/narcotic distinction shaped media perceptions of substance abuse, as the FBN had a long and successful track record of feeding the media a steady diet of atrocity stories concerning the substances that came under its jurisdiction, but not those that fell to the FDA. Nor did Anslinger wish to tread on the toes of politically powerful pharmaceutical firms like Parke-Davis and Smith Kline French, with which he had a congenial relationship. Individual states also varied enormously in the restrictions placed on non-narcotic drugs, with at least ten not regulating amphetamines at all.[12]

Matters began to change in the early 1960s. In 1962, President Kennedy identified synthetic "thrill-pills" as a potential menace, and the issue was addressed by a White House–sponsored national conference on narcotic and drug abuse, which was attended by four hundred law-enforcement and public-health officials. This gathering did much to integrate the synthetics into discussions of the national drug situation and ultimately to erode the legalistic distinction between drugs and narcotics.[13]

The problem of rampant pill abuse among teenagers and young adults was quickly taken up by law and order crusaders, and between 1963 and 1965, the U.S. Congress considered several measures to reform the federal regulation of amphetamines and barbiturates. The most visible activist and a key moral entrepreneur was the very conservative U.S. senator Thomas J. Dodd of Connecticut, who used his position on the Senate's Juvenile Delinquency Subcommittee as the basis of his campaign against amphetamines. Dodd alleged that perhaps a hundred thousand Americans were "seriously addicted pill-heads" and that several million more took the drug indiscriminately and without medical supervision: for the senator, amphetamines were "an unsuspected incendiary bomb ready to go off in every community in America." Amphetamine pills were depicted as succeeding marijuana as "the stepping stone to hard narcotics addiction," while anti-speed activists cited the drug's role in extreme instances of random violence and crime sprees. Among the "many" such cases cited in the mid-1960s was the following: "in Houston, one ex-convict, after swallowing several amphetamine tablets, shot and killed a schoolteacher, assaulted a fourteen-year-old farm girl, and committed two robberies. In Illinois, a normally mild-mannered truck driver suddenly went berserk near the end of a New Orleans to Chicago run, during which he had taken several amphetamine pills to keep himself awake. He deliberately smashed into parked cars, chased pedestrians down the street with his huge truck, and finally was subdued at gunpoint by police."[14] The laxity of official regulation was demonstrated by an investigative documentary shown on CBS's *McMullen Report,* which revealed how a bogus front company was able to obtain half a million dollars' worth of amphetamines and barbiturates through the mail, with no questions asked.

The amphetamine scare led inevitably to strict legislation and a significant expansion of federal criminal-justice powers. Under the Drug Abuse Control Act of 1965, which was bitterly opposed by the pharmaceutical industry, federal food and drug laws were amended so that some amphetamine products were removed from the open market, doctors reduced their prescriptions of the remaining drugs, and record-keeping procedures were dramatically tightened. Methedrine was largely withdrawn from legal use. Again foreshadowing the later drug war, these policies were to be enforced by a new enforcement agency under the FDA, the Bureau of Drug Abuse Control (BDAC). Its armed agents made it look more like the FBI and FBN than the FDA.[15]

The anti-pill movement faded away in the mid-1960s, not necessarily because the problem had been in any sense solved, but because more pressing issues had come to the fore. Between about 1965 and 1973, drug experimentation occurred on a massive and unprecedented scale in the Unites States, and by the mid-1970s these patterns were spreading beyond the youth counterculture to upper- and middle-class circles and thus to quite mainstream white society. Initially, marijuana was both the most commonly used illegal substance and the one most frequently denounced in the mainstream media, but LSD was another prime target, and heroin use was booming in urban areas. Yet even with so many competitors for public attention, amphetamine drugs continued to attract concern, especially in the form of injectable Methedrine. By the late 1960s, the practice of mainlining speed was regularly depicted as one of the most perilous aspects of the burgeoning drug culture.

Injecting speed (splash) was a potent fad that enormously enhanced both the pleasures and the dangers associated with amphetamines. The practice originated with ex-servicemen and was further spread by doctors who prescribed Methedrine as a treatment for heroin dependency and alcoholism. Mainlining also appealed to users of other narcotics, and some users mixed speed with heroin. Already by the late 1950s, splash-houses offered injectable drugs to users in several midwestern cities. A classic autobiographical novel on the underground New York methamphetamine culture of the early 1960s is *Speed* by William S. Burroughs, Jr., son of the author of *Naked*

Lunch. The younger Burroughs became severely addicted in his early teens through intravenous Methedrine use, and he notes that "demented crystal freaks" like himself were already regarded with suspicion and some hostility by the more responsible and traditionally minded portions of the drug underworld. From about 1962, law-enforcement agencies launched a crackdown on Methedrine, and a vigorous media campaign followed. By 1966–67, features in mass-circulation magazines such as *Time, Newsweek, Life, Look* and *Reader's Digest* popularized slogans like "Speed Kills" and "Unsafe at Any Speed."[16]

Major drug corporations reacted to the abuse problem by limiting supplies of Methedrine, but even as legal restrictions grew, the drug's popularity ensured that users would find illicit supplies. It was apparently a group of ex-servicemen who led the move to create an illicit manufacturing industry, and clandestine speed labs appeared in the San Francisco Bay Area around 1962. Though these labs have been claimed to be the first in the country, perhaps the Bay Area just happened to have an unusually large number of observers interested in recording the phenomenon.

Despite problems of addiction and bizarre behavior, methamphetamine continued to be popular because of its powerful reputation for destroying inhibitions and enhancing sensation: it was, and remains, "high-octane human rocket fuel."[17] It is above all a magnificent erotic drug. Perhaps for fear of undesirable advertising or else through naivete, the official literature on illegal drugs has rarely recognized over the years that the appeal of a given substance is often linked to its powerful reputation as an erotic stimulant. It is this element that has successively elevated the reputations of Methedrine, PCP, cocaine and Quaaludes among users. In contrast to the official silence, meth users themselves are frank about the drug's sexual powers. One recent journalistic account includes the following anecdotes: "Recently, Pam screwed a guy all night, a friend for twenty years, hallucinating so badly she couldn't remember who he was while doing him. . . . Pam bruised her legs and got her hair so twisted up into a 'fuck knot' that it had to be cut. . . . Meth 'turned me into a nymphomaniac,' says Ella. 'Sometimes one person wasn't enough: Two, three hours with one; two, three hours with another.'"[18]

The drug's orgasmic potential was well recognized in the 1960s. As Harvey Cohen writes,

> Methedrine rolls back the stone from the mouth of the cave. . . . on Methedrine you are capable of any form of erotic behavior. . . . Meth orgasms are like winding a spring for hours, building tension. Meth gives you convulsive total orgasms, it's like a grand mal seizure. Over-amped, balling for hours, detachment from textural flesh sensations, mad, possessed, mindless. Methedrine enforces a concept of sex as conquest and achievement, of endurance and power.
>
> Telepathy comes out strong on amphetamine. By the third day of being awake, the world changes. After that, everything is a miracle of telepathy, of wishes come true, of miraculous coincidence and of visions made clear. On the dark side also a world of paranoia.

This description is typical in its near-messianic tone. It is echoed by the portrait of the crystal Methedrine scene in 1960s San Francisco in Frankie Hucklenbroich's *Crystal Diary*:

> the rush is better than sex better than love you squares have never had anything so good there's no way at all for you to know. And now I am Alice flying upward toward the ceiling, my hands and arms reaching into the corners of the room and I rock with pleasure and while all this is happening my brain opens suddenly like a wide dark flower and the rush is so fine so fine so much better than poems music sky sunsets family friends oh! much better than anything that ever was or ever could be amen amen amen.

The reaction of the typical first-time user is, "Where has this been all my life?"[19]

With such powerful testimonials, it is not surprising that speed gained new adherents in the drug culture of the 1960s. But the drug acquired a very mixed reputation: increasingly, it was identified and attacked as an outlaw drug, even at a time when virtually all other stimulants seemed beyond reproach or stigma. Drug experimentation in these years was wide-ranging, enthusiastic, and almost—but not quite—indiscriminate. A few substances still remained beyond the pale, and amphetamine-related highs came to be condemned just as heavily in the alternative media as in mainstream publications and official statements.

But speed's ostracism from the drug culture was a gradual process; the amphetamines were popular in the early days of 1960s hippiedom, with the market for the synthetics overlapping considerably with that for the hallucinogens. This speed use spread alongside that of LSD and marijuana and may actually have grown as an unintended consequence of police crackdowns on these better-known drugs. The same network of underground laboratories produced both speed and other synthetics like LSD. Phantom chemists and neuromancers were also experimenting with other derivatives of the ever-versatile amphetamines, some of which would gain popularity under brand names like MDA and STP. The prototype of the emerging generation of chemical innovators was Augustus Owsley Stanley III, an underground legend until his arrest in 1967 and an inspiration to all subsequent clandestine drug-makers: "Owsley" became the most sought-after brand name for LSD. The Bay Area developed a tradition of synthetic drug labs that survives to the present day, although the type of drugs produced has changed frequently over time.[20]

But the relative harmony within the drug underworld could not last forever. By 1969, the alternative culture associated with drugs was disintegrating, as were idealistic visions of a society based on love and peace. Some sections of the youth movement became intensely politicized, while others drifted towards a more purely profit-oriented criminal subculture based on drug trafficking, or even towards bizarre and exploitative cult behavior. In 1969 and 1970, the most radical of the anti–Vietnam War activists launched an urban bombing campaign. The legendary peace-and-love event of Woodstock in August 1969 was followed within a few months by the violent fiasco of the Rolling Stones concert at Altamont and the arrest of the Charles Manson gang for the murder of Sharon Tate and her companions. Whether the demon figures were identified as Hell's Angels, cultists or Weatherman guerrillas, the youth subculture had taken a gruesomely wrong turn, and the upsurge of violent behavior was often blamed on the effects of drugs like methamphetamine. Some journalists used speed as a symbol of the cult violence they associated with biker and hippie groups, citing cases like the Manson family. According to journalist Michael Newton, "Outlaw motorcycle gangs—many of them linked to Satanic cults from the 1960s to the present day—monopolize production and sale of methamphetamines." Weather Underground activists extolled speed as a drug of working-class youth, and they used it as a means of declaring solidarity with that group.[21]

Most negative images of the speed freak had little to do with conduct as extreme or notorious as that of bombers or devil-worshipers, but rather arose from the unprovoked violence and exploitative behavior said to characterize the type. In New York, for instance, methamphetamine users became notorious for peddling deadly "poisoned speed" to unsuspecting buyers. In 1969, Gail Sheehy described the decline of civil order and respect for life she witnessed in New York's East Village, where speed, whether in pills or in intravenous form, had become the leading illegal drug: "Last month, nineteen people trussed up a boy in the apartment across the street and set him on fire. Thrill-killing is becoming fashionable here. Though more commonly, the neighborhood showmen—the motorcycle gangs—stick to raping girls and light stabbing of strangers. Bonfires are also popular." Soon after this was written, some young New York radicals began making bombs. Young people were turning into savages, no better than the most violent authority figures, the pigs themselves. "Cops have Mace; kids have speed." To the naive question "Where have all the flowers gone? Whatever happened to hippies, Yippies and the marshmallow-eyed mystics?" there was a simple answer: "It is not the military-industrial complex. . . . It is a change of drug." Even the vaunted sexual effects of speed, the so-called Magic Vitamin, had gone badly wrong, producing not just superior orgasms but also "elaborate sexual fantasies, striking changes in females who were frigid, sudden marked increase in sexual deviations, and extreme masochism."[22]

Speed became the scapegoat for the collapse of the peace-and-love ethos, "the drug that snuffed out the summer of love."[23] In San Francisco's Haight-Ashbury district, that had gained world fame as the glamorous capital of the Summer of Love, speed use and trafficking was largely blamed for an upsurge of murders and assaults during 1969. Yet it remains unclear how much these outbreaks resulted from intrinsic qualities of the drug and how much they stemmed from the unregulated nature of the marketplace and the lack of an established criminal subculture like that long associated with heroin. An abundance of reliable reports associates heavy amphetamine use with violent behavior, a connection that owes much to the paranoia induced by the drug, especially its injected form.[24] At the same time, to use the language of social science, at least some of the violence observed may have been systemic (reflecting the character of the illicit market) rather than psychopharmacological (arising directly from qualities of the drug itself). To use a historical analogy, during the era of alcohol Prohibition in the 1920s, hundreds of people died in conflicts relating to illicit booze, most notoriously during the St. Valentine's Day Massacre of 1929. While these deaths were in a sense connected to illicit substances, they were caused not by alcohol itself, but by the social and legal circumstances arising from the fact of prohibition. At least some of the speed-related violence in San Francisco and elsewhere might well have fallen into a parallel category.

Thus the reputation of speed plummeted in the drug underground, where already by 1966 traditionally minded drug users had adopted the slogan "Meth is death." The following year, the *Village Voice* described amphetamine heads as "a distinct group, semi-quarantined and often regarded with apprehension by fellow hippies. . . . The drugs seem to occupy opposite poles in the underground [amphetamines versus LSD or marijuana], in almost a Blakeian perspective of heaven and hell." Though the magazine *Life* was scarcely a reliable guide for trends in youth culture, it was not too far off the mark when it described Methedrine in 1967 as one of the "drugs that even scare hippies." The movement to stigmatize and outlaw amphetamines reached its height between about 1969 and 1971, as the message about their evils was being continually reinforced from within the underground culture. Timothy Leary regarded amphetamines as "much more dangerous" than cocaine. And beat icon Allen Ginsberg issued his "general declaration to all the underground community, contra speedamos ex cathedra. Speed is anti-social, paranoid-making, it's a drag, bad for your body, bad for your mind, generally speaking, in the long run uncreative and it's a plague in the whole dope industry. All the nice gentle dope fiends are getting screwed up by the real horror monster Frankenstein speed freaks who are going around stealing and bad mouthing everybody."[25] He had probably been influenced by having repeatedly rescued Billy Burroughs from his amphetamine addiction problems. At the height of the anti-speed reaction, in 1970, Burroughs published his nightmarish record of that time, *Speed*, in which he records the parlous effects of coming down after a meth high that might have lasted for weeks: "the participant's frame of mind can steer it anywhere from mere exhaustion to suicidal desperation, with hundreds of nefarious variations in between." Philip K. Dick drew heavily on the indictment of methamphetamine when describing the imaginary ultimate drug, Substance D, in his novel *Scanner Darkly* (1977): like speed, "D," or "Death," inflicted paranoid psychosis to the point of creating distinct multiple personalities.

Speed culture was accused, too, of promoting self-destructive values and practices. To quote a later methamphetamine manufacturer, "Back in the '60s, meth got a bad name because fools were shooting the stuff up constantly, starving themselves to death or getting hepatitis." Excessive use, he warned, could lead to "difficulty in thinking clearly, paranoid behavior and excessive weight loss, leading finally to amphetamine psychosis." Still worse problems could arise for anyone using the shoddily made and contaminated versions so readily available on the streets: these were "sticky, off-colored, and should be labeled with a skull and crossbones."[26] Just as lethal was the practice of simultaneously mainlining speed and barbiturates, an upper-downer mix that recalls the heroin-cocaine speedball.

The drug was also powerfully addictive: as Burroughs recorded in *Kentucky Ham*, "I wasn't using speed, it rather seemed that my entire metabolism had developed a speed deficiency." To quote Frankie Hucklenbroich, "I know people who've been doing crystal for years. I never yet met anybody who quit." In *Amphetamine Manifesto*, Harvey Cohen remarks, "If you take amphetamine, it destroys every relationship, everything crumbles, you can't hold a job or keep an appointment, everything else is completely irrelevant and irreverent—your only desire is to get a shot. In some ways, amphetamine is a worse insulator than horse [heroin]. . . . After ten years of speed the body turns into a carburetor, you age thirty years, you feel like an old man before your time, your brain gets looser than vegetable soup." Gail Sheehy argued, "Speed is not a clean bomb. Speed maims. . . . *Psycho-*

logically, amphetamines are the most dangerous of all the ill-used drugs—including heroin."[27]

These charges were actually no more horrific than those made at the same time against virtually all illegal drugs, including LSD. The difference was that the allegations against Methedrine gained wide credence among young drug users themselves. The evils of the drug were widely reported in a literature that conceded the existence of an amphetamine abuse problem, in an alternative culture reluctant to apply this term to more favored drugs. Frightening as these evils may sound, the anti-speed campaign must be understood in terms of the complex symbolic meanings of the drug. By the late 1960s, it was particularly associated with working-class youth whose behavior and aspirations often clashed with the more middle-class hippies. Speed's cultural connotations were the diametric opposite of those of marijuana or the hallucinogens, which were associated with leisure, contemplation and mystical exploration: in contrast, amphetamines were actively promoted by the military, drug corporations and school authorities to fuel an efficient and hard-working society. Amphetamine pills were issued to servicemen on long patrols in Vietnam in quantities far exceeding those of the Second World War, and it was no surprise to anyone familiar with the drug when it tended to make soldiers aggressive and paranoid: it certainly contributed to some of the notorious massacres and morale breakdowns among United States forces in the field in the late sixties. It was also in these years that a rising feminist movement was challenging the sexual hedonism of the hippie era, for which the macho aggression promoted by speed provided an apt metaphor. These political divides may explain why young, middle-class drug users were prepared to accept the negative stereotype of the speed freak while rejecting as official propaganda similarly grim associations attributed to other more popular drugs.[28]

Whatever the reasons, speed was now demonized among the middle-class young, and the slogan "speed kills" was widely used in the alternative press and even featured in rock songs. This opposition had rhetorical value in permitting advocates of illicit drugs to declare limits they were not prepared to cross, thus allowing them to present an image of responsibility rather than one of unbounded self-indulgence. In the cult film *Easy Rider* (1969), which is largely a paean to the drug culture, the song accompanying the opening titles proclaims total opposition to any substance "that my spirit couldn't kill" and to the pushers who trade in them. The line can equally be taken to indicate heroin or Methedrine, which shared a comparably evil reputation by this time. Paradoxically, then, attacking speed assisted in the defense of other drugs: if in fact amphetamines were so much more dangerous than substances like marijuana or cocaine, why was speed not penalized much more severely? Why had the Nixon administration not launched its war against Methedrine rather than heroin? The answers seemed to be that amphetamines were protected because of their corporate and establishment connotations, and that society needed to reevaluate its drug policies based on a rational assessment of dangerousness.[29]

By about 1970, criticism of amphetamines also stemmed from mainstream politicians and law-enforcement officials, as well as from popular magazines like *Reader's Digest* and *Parents*. The issue of addiction to amphetamine pills was popularized in studies of "normal," middle-class people, especially women, as in the 1971 TV movie *Believe in Me*. Between 1969 and 1971, a series of Congressional hearings examined the problems associated with amphetamine abuse and the massive over-prescribing of the drug by doctors, especially to women. As the House Select Committee on Crime asked in the title of its 1969 hearings, Why Eight Billion Amphetamines? In addition, from the early 1970s, law enforcement began drawing attention to the growing issue of illicit methamphetamine manufacture, which motorcycle gangs were now carving out as one of their chief activities. The drug acquired ever-grimmer associations of crime, violence and dependency, and this condemnation extended from the injected versions of the drug to the more benevolent-seeming pep-pills.[30]

These associations were continually reinforced by new scandals in the sports world. Not until 1971 did the National Football League (NFL) officially ban amphetamine use by players, and illegal use continued long afterwards. In 1973, the U.S. Senate held hearings on the "proper and improper use of drugs by athletes" in which amphetamines were identified as the chief villain; over the following two years, speed-related scandals struck repeatedly in the NFL. Abuses in professional football were described by Dr. Arnold Mandell, who found it "amazing the way Americans buy good tickets to watch speed freaks try to kill each other!" The issue reached an even wider audience when the cartoon series *Doonesbury* used a story line about drug aficionado Uncle Duke becoming the manager/speed pusher to a professional football team. (Duke, a character heavily based on Hunter Thompson, is *Doonesbury's* vehicle for commentary upon the drug culture). Professionals in other sports, including baseball, used these stimulants just as enthusiastically.[31] Even in a society grown tolerant of mellowing drugs like marijuana, amphetamine was depicted as a violent intruder.

Though heroin always attracted the largest share of attention, the speed-freak panic contributed to the major reorganization of anti-drug efforts in the Nixon years. In 1970, American drug policy was systematized by the Comprehensive Drug Abuse Prevention and Control Act of 1970, and one portion of this measure, the Controlled Substances Act (CSA), established regulatory principles that remain in force today. The CSA created five escalating categories into which drugs might be placed, depending on both their usefulness and the likelihood of abuse. Heroin, for example, was a Schedule I drug, prohibited even for medical use beyond limited research because its medical benefits did not outweigh the substantial dangers of abuse and addiction. Substances with more benefits and fewer obvious dangers were placed in progressively less stringent schedules, so that minor tranquilizers like Valium, for instance, were placed in Schedule IV, and anti-tussives in Schedule V. The system of balancing advantages and dangers was sensible in itself, and the law massively reduced penalties for marijuana possession, but classifications were not always sensible; marijuana, for example, was placed in Schedule I, out of bounds for medical use.

In a pattern that would often emerge in subsequent drug controversies, the stigma attached to a given substance depended less on an objective assessment of its harms and benefits than on the political and economic power of its advocates. Over the coming decades, media-generated panics caused an ever-increasing number of chemicals to be classified as dangerous drugs in Schedules I or II because they were being developed and used unofficially, outside the approved corporate channels. Conversely, other drugs that were potentially just as dangerous were scheduled at lower levels because they had the support of the pharmaceutical industry. A ferocious battle surrounded the scheduling of amphetamines, which Senator Dodd wished to see severely regulated despite desperate lobbying by the drug companies and the American Pharmaceutical Association. The amphetamines were initially kept in the more benevolent Schedule III, permitting controlled medical use with refillable prescriptions. Only injectable liquid methamphetamine was listed in Schedule II. Though methamphetamine pills could easily be liquefied and injected, they were still placed in Schedule III. Only after some years of further campaigning was Methedrine moved into Schedule I and most other amphetamines into Schedule II.[32]

Also in the early 1970s, the Nixon administration created a centralized federal drug enforcement bureaucracy by combining previously disparate and competing agencies. A previous merger had already consolidated the BDAC, founded in 1966, with the older FBN, agencies whose responsibilities overlapped but which were divided by the eccentric distinction between drugs and narcotics. In 1968, the two agencies were merged into a new Bureau of Narcotics and Dangerous Drugs (BNDD) under the aegis of the Justice Department. In 1973, under Nixon, BNDD was joined with still other units into the DEA: among other things, this agency was given the power to classify substances under the CSA. Since that date, the DEA has been the chief protagonist in successive anti-drug campaigns, the leading force in the drug war. Throughout its history, the agency has striven successfully to ensure that drugs continue to be seen as a matter for law enforcement, not for medical or social intervention and still less for any form of decriminalization. Incidentally, this unification measure also marked the end of the old drug/narcotic dichotomy, so that henceforward amphetamines and other synthetics would definitively be considered part of an overarching drug problem.

The anti-speed reaction had complex results, including some quite unforeseen by reform advocates. Initially, speed suffered a serious if temporary eclipse in popularity: in 1971, Hunter Thompson suggested that the drug culture had shifted decisively to downers, to the extent that young people "never even bothered to try speed. Uppers are no longer stylish. Methedrine is almost as rare on the 1971 market as pure acid or DMT." And legal use of amphetamine drugs declined precipitously after the 1970 CSA: between 1971 and 1986, the number of new prescriptions for Dexedrine fell by over 60 percent and for Biphetamine by 95 percent, while Benzedrine ceased to be prescribed altogether. The barbiturates suffered an even sharper decline in prescriptions. However, the near-elimination of legal supplies did not eradicate the taste for amphetamines. By late 1977, amphetamines still accounted for 1.6 percent of drug-related emergency-room visits monitored by the DAWN network, compared to around 2.8 percent for marijuana and hashish, 2 percent for PCP and 1 percent for cocaine.[33] Moreover, those figures certainly underestimate the prevalence of amphetamines, as DAWN statistics focus on urban conditions, ignoring rural and suburban usage.

The loss of access to pills may actually have increased the taste for more potent forms of the drug, especially methamphetamine. Neither police vigilance nor anti-speed publicity could eradicate methamphetamine, which retains pockets of usage up to the present day, especially in California and Arizona. In 1972, the number of arrestees testing positive for Methedrine in the Washington, D.C., jail system briefly hit 15 percent of the total sample, and the drug gained an ever-stronger foothold as the decade progressed: between 1975 and 1979, seizures of methamphetamine labs nationwide rose from 11 to 137 and represented the largest single category in 1979. By 1988, the number of meth labs raided had risen to 629. As the speed industry grew, its organization changed, shifting official attention away from the drug's users to its makers.[34]

Methamphetamine would again be at the heart of a perceived social problem in 1980, just as it had been in 1970. But the issues at stake in the respective periods were very different, so much so that it is difficult to credit either response to any inherent qualities of the substance itself. While the emphasis in the earlier period was on the individual speed freak, concern in the late 1970s shifted entirely to the makers and dealers—in short, to gangsters. In its role as an organized crime problem, the drug earned its greatest fictional celebrity in the 1985 film *Witness*, in which the Philadelphia detective played by Harrison Ford confronts a drug-dealing ring entirely composed of fellow officers. The drug in question is methamphetamine, naturally enough, since—as the Ford character declares—"Philadelphia supplies all the major cities in the country with speed." However, not once does the film portray the use or effects of the drug, and the speed-freak image is never mentioned. The emphasis is entirely on trafficking in the vital precursor chemical P2P (phenyl-2-propanone) and the official corruption required to maintain the trade.

This fictional view had its echoes in the real world. Just at this time, in 1985 and 1986, the President's Commission on Organized Crime (the Kaufman Commission) was using conditions in the speed capital of Philadelphia as Exhibit A to support the controversial belief that traditional organized crime (that is, the Mafia) dominated drug trafficking.[35] This would be a crucial lesson for the sweeping federal legislation that followed over the next year or two, which provided Draconian penalties for major dealers and real or supposed drug kingpins. At the same time, far-reaching new provisions permitted the seizure of any money or assets associated with such criminal enterprises. This new construction of the methamphetamine problem was controversial: though organized crime certainly had developed a foothold in the drug's manufacture and trafficking, it is by no means clear that this domination was as absolute as law-enforcement sources were suggesting. Nor was Philadelphia necessarily the speed metropolis of legend. As we so often find in the history of illicit drugs, both ideas were highly political in their origins, owing much to the rhetorical work of moral entrepreneurs and bureaucratic activists.

Methamphetamine had many attractions for would-be drug manufacturers and traffickers, including traditional Mafia figures and biker gangs. As the drug was American-made, it did not initially require the sophisticated importation networks required for heroin or cocaine. Most of its chemicals were easily accessible; the chief difficulty was procuring the essential precursor chemical P2P, commonly called oil or prope, a bulk chemical normally sold in 55-gallon drums. It was originally obtained through legitimate chemical concerns, which sold it for the use of exterminators. But in 1980, P2P was added to Schedule II of the CSA, which meant that supplies would have to be either synthesized in illegal labs or imported from Europe, where the drug was cheap and legal. As with cocaine or heroin, there would henceforward be a high premium on successful smuggling.

Organized-crime groups did play some role in the methamphetamine trade. In the 1970s, several outlaw motorcycle gangs were heavily involved in the business; they were said to control perhaps a half of all manufacture nationwide and a major part of distribution. Depending on the region, this might have meant the Hell's Angels in California, the Confederate Angels in Virginia and the South or the Pagans and Warlocks on the East Coast. Biker groups worked closely with established organized-crime networks with footholds in illegal labor and union enterprises. In Philadelphia, the supposed speed capital itself, the methamphetamine business was inextricably linked to labor racketeering and to the long-standing syndicates that provided illicit goods and services among sections of the blue-collar workforce. Union links provided the market for stimulant drugs as well as a distribution system. Trafficking in methamphetamine and its precursors provided a common bond between Philadelphia's white criminal groups, whether Italian, Jewish, Irish or Greek, in alliance with corrupt police officers, union leaders and political officeholders. This was a subculture in which drums of P2P regularly acted as currency, gifts, rewards and incentives, and control of the Philadelphia speed trade provided the crucial backdrop for the prolonged gang war that decimated the local Mafia family between about 1980 and 1983. Despite occasional disasters, many of the individuals identified as speed cooks and pushers in the late 1970s have remained major manufacturers in the region right up to the present day, still producing multimillion-dollar quantities of the drug.[36]

But this gangster context does not of itself explain the peculiar and near-total emphasis of the official reaction to the methamphetamine trade in the early 1980s on the organized-crime influence. In reality, the speed capital concept is doubly misleading, as it both exaggerates the hierarchy and organization supposed to characterize the trade and distorts its geographical emphasis. Speed manufacture was a highly decentralized concern with lots of room for independent entrepreneurs, while labs were at least as prevalent in the western United States as in southeastern Pennsylvania; was it really plausible that Phoenix, Dallas and San Francisco obtained their drugs from Pennsylvania, not their own long-established local factories? It was by no means obvious that any city would deservedly acquire the reputation that earned Philadelphia global notoriety with *Witness*. We know about Philadelphia activities in such intricate detail because the city was subjected to such intense scrutiny; equally sharp investigation might well have turned up similar enterprises in other regions in these same years. Belief in the notion of a speed capital encouraged agencies to investigate and prosecute methamphetamine-related offenses in the area, which in turn created statistics that confirmed views of the scale of the threat: both the media and politicians are notoriously prone to seeing arrests and raids as an accurate index of criminal activity.

The idea of a speed capital was rooted in regional politics, and above all in racial fears. This newsworthy tag originated during special hearings of the House Select Committee on Narcotics Abuse and Control during July 1980. The main advocates for intervention against speed included two important Republican congressmen from Pennsylvania, one of whom was U.S. Representative Robert S. Walker (R) from the conservative Sixteenth District in Lancaster County, a region that has long feared the spillover of urban ills from Philadelphia; these fears of crime and urban blight developed potent racial overtones. Walker was reacting to the recent trend of illicit drug laboratories being established well outside the metropolitan region, in Chester and Lancaster Counties and the Poconos. Walker's worries were shared by Lawrence Coughlin (R), who represented a wealthy district in suburban Montgomery County. Both stood to make political capital from exploiting local fears of urban problems, and Coughlin was in an excellent position to do this as a member of the House Committee on Narcotics Control.

Largely at the behest of Walker and Coughlin, the select committee was persuaded to hold special hearings in Philadelphia on the theme of illicit methamphetamine laboratories in the Pennsylvania/New Jersey/Delaware area. The investigation concentrated on the Pagans' role in speed production and the drug's importance for the Mafia. Local politicians and agencies made every effort to make the problem seem as large and organized as possible and thus an issue deserving national concern: the DEA "considers organized crime to be a dominant, if not the dominant factor in clandestine methamphetamine laboratories in the Philadelphia area." These were the opinions reiterated during the Kaufman Commission hearings some years later, and in both cases, claims of Mafia hegemony were grossly exaggerated, as the speed trade produced abundant evidence of independent entrepreneurs only loosely affiliated with larger syndicates and of other criminal groups far removed from traditional Italian-American operations.[37] But at the time, the Philadelphia lesson seemed obvious: drugs could not be controlled without defeating the kingpins who manufactured and trafficked in them. This lesson was freely applied to all other illicit chemicals.

In neither official documents nor the mass media do methamphetamine users even seem to exist in the late seventies or early eighties, though presumably somebody was buying the quantities produced in Pennsylvania and elsewhere, providing an ever-expanding market for the proliferating laboratories. In part, this change in the conceptualization of the methamphetamine problem reflected the immediate political needs and concerns of the political figures presenting the evidence, but racial concerns and prejudices also played a role. We can see this by comparing the treatment of the other "bad drug" of the late 1970s, namely PCP or angel dust, which had urban and minority associations, to the approach to methamphetamine, which connoted white consumers. Speed users by this point were almost viewed as victims of the gangsters who exploited them; in contrast, angel dust was discussed almost entirely in terms of its users, the suggestion being that its consumers were desperate or gullible individuals who let themselves fall prey to this terrible drug. Methamphetamine was thus viewed as an organized-crime problem, while angel dust was seen as a symptom of social dislocation and personal irresponsibility. While methamphetamine provided the material for gangster stories, PCP inspired works about the ruined lives of users.

THREE

Monsters

The PCP Crisis, 1975–85

It's a real terror of a drug. Everything people used to say about
marijuana is true about angel dust.

—Robert Du Pont, director of National Institute on
Drug Abuse (NIDA), 1977[1]

The synthetic scares surrounding methamphetamine and PCP shared
a similar chronology, reaching a climax in the late 1970s and early
1980s. For all their differences of content and rhetoric, the two movements had a similarly far-reaching political significance, reviving public
hatred and fear of narcotics and demolishing the broad tolerance that
had emerged during the hedonistic 1970s. Just as the anti-speed campaign of the 1960s prepared the way for the subsequent war on dealers
and drug kingpins, so PCP established later expectations about the
devastating impact of crack cocaine on users and communities.

Growing concern about synthetics reflected changing usage patterns,
as criteria such as laboratory seizures and emergency-room incidents
show that PCP and methamphetamine really did come into heavier
use in the late 1970s. Still, the intense focus on these drugs had agendas beyond a simple reaction to changing circumstances. These years
were critical in changing American attitudes towards drug abuse,
which was widely tolerated through the 1970s and much more harshly
stigmatized in the Reagan years. The focus on synthetics was politi-

cally useful for drug-enforcement authorities and anti-drug politicians, in focusing attention on those illicit substances against which a solid popular consensus could be formed. Libertarians could not find easy defenses for such widely condemned public menaces as PCP and speed, so measures of suppression were easily justified. In contrast, such general agreement could not be reached when other, more familiar drugs were involved, such as marijuana, cocaine and LSD; all of these drugs had acquired a substantial middle-class following.

The movement against synthetics must be seen in the broader context of a remarkable tolerance accorded to illegal substances: Americans were far from ready for a full-scale drug war. Marijuana use was still common among the young, including a large high school and college market. (As we saw in the previous chapter, surveys of high school seniors showed very high usage of illegal drugs, peaking between about 1978 and 1982.) From about 1974, cocaine gained recognition as what the *New York Times* called "the champagne of drugs." Ironically, it owed some of its popularity to the earlier anti-speed clamor, which had driven users in search of a safer stimulant: when one door closes in the drug culture, another always opens. Between about 1977 and 1982, cocaine enjoyed a huge vogue among urban and suburban middle classes, and by 1985, some twenty-two million Americans reported having used the drug at least once. Cocaine received wonderful if unintentional publicity from magazines such as *Newsweek,* which noted the drug's use in high society alongside "Dom Perignon and caviar" and mentioned the use of fourteen-karat-gold coke spoons. Heavy cocaine use demanded a related vogue in the synthetic drug Quaalude, a depressant that regular cocaine users needed to bring their metabolic systems back down to appropriate levels of operation. Throughout the decade, cocaine, amphetamines and Quaaludes were integral to the drug-saturated disco culture, which originated in the metropolitan gay club scene and is so lyrically depicted in Andrew Holleran's novel *Dancer from the Dance*.[2] As has so often occurred in recent decades, a drug trend that originated in the gay clubs soon spilled over into the wider national culture. The disco fad of the mid-1970s, too, helped popularize its associated drugs. Also at about this time, some wealthier users took to reducing cocaine to its crystalline form, or freebasing, an expensive habit similar to the later means of preparing crack. For a few years, cocaine became an inescapable part of popular culture, particularly in media aimed at teens and young adults. In 1977, rock artists Eric Clapton and Jackson Browne separately recorded songs entitled *Cocaine,* and the drug was the subject of countless performances by standup comedians, as well as of knowing jokes on network television comedies like *Taxi, WKRP in Cincinnati* and (most consistently) *Saturday Night Live.* Drug use was depicted sympathetically, even humorously, in many films between about 1977 and 1983, including *Looking for Mr. Goodbar, Where the Buffalo Roam, Jekyll and Hyde—Together Again* and *Fast Times at Ridgemont High,* and in several comedy features by Cheech and Chong. Cocaine-related themes appeared in the comedy film *Annie Hall,* while the 1980 film *Airplane* included broad jokes about cocaine, amphetamines and glue-sniffing.[3]

In the face of this respectable drug boom, strict enforcement of drug laws seemed benighted and futile. Even under the Republican Ford administration in 1975, a presidential task force admitted the impossibility of wholly suppressing drug abuse and urged that the emphasis of official action be shifted from law enforcement to treatment and prevention. In 1977 and 1978, Congress heard testimony from several federal agencies urging that the possession of small amounts of marijuana no longer be a criminal offense, a position supported by President Carter.[4] Eleven states and several cities followed this policy of decriminalization, and seventeen more significantly reduced their penalties. Few advocated open tolerance for cocaine, but a remarkable number of respectable experts went on record as denying that even this drug caused any significant harm or dependence.

But the new tolerance had limits. The height of the decriminalization movement in 1977–78 coincided with a growing conservative reaction against what was seen as the decadent legacy of the radical 1960s—in matters of sexuality and personal behavior as much as in drug abuse. While feminists and conservative religious groups allied against pornography, parents' groups organized to combat illegal drugs, and during 1977, morality campaigners won significant victories by focusing on aspects of the new permissiveness to mobilize mass constituencies. A movement against child pornography was the first strategy in several decades that succeeded in reversing public tolerance of sexually explicit materials. Closely related to the child pornography issue was an official campaign to suppress pedophilia and child molestation, a theme used indirectly to stigmatize homosexuals and gay rights laws. A new politics of morality became apparent in efforts to defeat gay rights referenda in Florida, California and other jurisdictions. This conservative mood provided the context for the official severity towards methamphetamine and the even harsher attitude towards PCP.[5]

Though public tolerance towards drug abuse did not end suddenly in the late 1970s, the emphasis on synthetics did succeed in creating a plausible anti-drug rhetoric with wide social appeal. Like child pornography, PCP and methamphetamine seemed literally indefensible. The best-known leader of the anti-child-porn crusade was Judianne Densen-Gerber, who also campaigned against angel dust use among young people. During congressional hearings about PCP in 1978, one witness aptly observed that in drug matters, "right now, it seems to me that the pendulum has swung back to support law enforcement."[6] While I am not suggesting that conservative or anti-drug forces deliberately focused on these alternative drugs as a surreptitious means of attacking more mainstream substances, their earlier campaigns did set the rhetorical stage for the full-scale drug war of the 1980s, establishing the symbolic vocabulary of later agitation. These early phases might be described as the phony drug war, or even as the stealth war on drugs.

In the late 1970s, by far the most intense publicity concerning the damage done by illicit drugs focused on PCP, or phencyclidine. This drug raised the issue of how one's humanity could apparently be destroyed by drugs, leaving a savage and primitive monster, and racial rhetoric implied that such atavistic reversion was especially likely for African Americans. One widely read autobiographical account of drug and gang activities in the Los Angeles of the 1980s would be called simply *Monster.*[7] Throughout, the paramount danger was that savage "jungle" habits would be transmitted to the young white middle class.

Like heroin and the amphetamines, PCP originated as a legal product of experimentation by mainstream drug companies before launching its outlaw career. PCP was originally developed by Parke-Davis in

1956 as a powerful anesthetic under the brand name Sernyl, but legal use on human subjects was discontinued in 1965 because of evidence of side-effects such as dissociative psychosis; in modified form, the drug continued to be used for veterinary purposes. In the late 1960s, it attracted interest in the northern California drug underground, though the details of this story are open to some controversy: as so often occurs, our knowledge of the history of any illegal drug is distorted by the limits of the official mechanisms by which usage can be tracked.

The two histories of PCP, official and otherwise, deserve careful comparison. The often-retold official version claims that the drug originally appealed to Bay Area hippies, who took the abbreviation PCP to stand for "*PeaCe Pill.*" Use soon spread to New York, but the drug soon lost popularity on both coasts due to its fearsome side effects, and it suffered a period of near-total eclipse before reemerging in about 1974. However, this account may be a bureaucratic folklore shaped retroactively by the drug's vicious reputation in the late 1970s, when it seemed incredible that anyone could have continued to experiment with PCP once they had some knowledge of its effects, even in a community presumed to be as suicidal and self-destructive as the nation's baby-boom drug users. In fact, we have virtually no reliable usage data for PCP before the mid-1970s. Most of the major official measures of drug abuse before this time did not report the drug because they were not looking for it, or if they did come across it, they lumped it together with the hallucinogens. The annual survey of high school seniors did not ask a distinct question about PCP until 1979, at which point it was beginning to decline in popularity. Furthermore, the emphasis on San Francisco and New York may just mean that these particular metropolitan areas had the largest concentrations of medical experts and law-enforcement people interested in following drug trends.

An alternative history of PCP, one based on ethnographic research, suggests a quite different picture. It shows that the drug was in constant use in several cities from about 1967, though without the alleged period of hostile reaction: it retained its audience for over a decade in cities as diverse as Philadelphia, Miami, Chicago and Seattle.[8] Though approached gingerly due to its unpredictability, PCP was seen as a drug that, when taken in a supportive setting, could be used responsibly. Flirting with the drug's bad effects added an extra element of risk and excitement and separated experienced users from casual amateurs, who deserved whatever misfortunes came their way. Despite reservations among users, then, PCP was a known and appreciated element of the illicit pharmacopoeia.

Whatever the origins of the habit, by the mid-1970s, PCP enjoyed a growing vogue in many different regions, largely replacing barbiturates, or goofballs, which became ever more difficult to obtain after the passage of the CSA. According to one account, "By 1972, people never much interested in psychedelics were getting into PCP, and indeed accepting it as the drug of choice. The government was cracking down on reds (Seconals) but people who wanted to achieve that truly helpless, irresponsible, wall-banging euphoria—people who wanted to get *all* fucked up—could take a couple of tokes on a KJ [Kristal Joint, i.e., PCP.]"[9] The "zombified" movements of a person under the influence of PCP were colloquially known as moonwalking, a phrase commemorated in the title of Michael Jackson's best-selling music album (though Jackson may not have understood the drug connotations). Angel dust was even seen as a safe alternative to some other substances, as it did not hold the same terrors as an injected substance like Methedrine or heroin and had the reputation of being less dangerous or uncontrollable than LSD.

PCP was accessible and familiar to a generation thoroughly accustomed to marijuana: though the new drug could be snorted, it was commonly sprayed on parsley leaves, which were then smoked in a cigarette resembling a marijuana joint. In fact, PCP was viewed as, at most, a mild escalation from pot, and the substance appeared as an adulterant in much of the marijuana sold in this period. The association between the two drugs was a valuable weapon for contemporary anti-drug campaigners, who argued that seemingly benevolent pot might often conceal this far more dangerous ingredient. The confusion with marijuana was all the greater because PCP was marketed under misleading nicknames: it was variously sold as supergrass, cannabinol or THC ("tic" or "titch"), and THC is the vital active chemical in marijuana. PCP was also sold under the nickname crystal, which caused officials and the media to confuse it with

methamphetamine. In California, the drug was nicknamed angel, supposedly after the Hell's Angels who made and sold the drug.[10]

Often combined with other illicit chemicals, PCP became a popular
party drug for poor and working-class youth, who could not afford to
share the cocaine fad of the more affluent. The drug generally appealed
to younger adolescents (ages fourteen to seventeen), though the actual
cultures to which it appealed varied greatly from place to place. It certainly found a niche in the gay dance world. It was commonly used to
make sexual conquests easier: as one Washington user reported, "I
mainly smoked angel dust with women. It makes them defenseless,
makes them easy to get along with. I would talk a little bit more. My
rap was stronger." At least in male eyes, this was "a drug women love.
In varying degrees of sophistication, the men interviewed felt PCP increased the likelihood of intercourse with women." Other accounts
suggest a less subtle sexual element: as one San Jose woman reported,
"Men . . . would give young girls KJ and encourage them to smoke
great amounts until their senses shattered and their brains burst, and
then the men would have them, one after the other, all night long, and
the next day the girl would wake up, and the long bad night would
come back to her only in vague shadows."[11] PCP was a precursor to
the rape drugs of which so much has been heard in recent years.

PCP use grew impressively in the mid-1970s, with the annual rate
of increase reaching perhaps fifty to a hundred percent between 1976
and 1978. By 1977, the number of Americans who had ever tried the
drug was estimated at seven million, 80 percent of whom were twelve
to twenty-five years old: users were equally divided between male and
female. The following year, 13 percent of high school students said
they had used PCP at least once. Additional clues to the drug's prevalence come from the Drug Abuse Warning Network (DAWN), which
tracks drug-related emergency-room visits in selected hospitals nationwide, chiefly in metropolitan centers: in the last quarter of 1977, PCP
accounted for 2 percent of such visits, compared to 4.9 percent for
heroin and 1 percent for cocaine.[12]

At different times, the drug had very different racial connotations.
In the early 1970s, black users were said to dislike PCP, as they dis-
trusted hallucinogens and were repelled by connotations of PCP's use
as an animal drug by veterinarians. However, the drug developed a

Table 3.1 PCP Lifetime Use (1993):
Percentage of Population Admitting to PCP
Use at Some Point during Lifetime

ever used	4.1
Sex	
male	5.5
female	2.7
Race/ethnicity	
white	4.5
black	1.9
Hispanic	3.2
Region	
Northeast	4.0
North Central	3.2
South	3.6
West	5.9

strong and enduring niche in some African-American urban communities, and by the 1980s it was often seen as a black drug rather like crack: indeed, the habit of smoking PCP may well have prepared the way for the growth of the smokable cocaine habit in the mid-eighties. Among the PCP-related deaths reported in Los Angeles in 1976–77, 53 percent were African American, 40 percent Hispanic or white. As a British newspaper commented, PCP "seems to have an appeal for the dispossessed, minorities, the racially oppressed, or those with a deep grudge against established society."[13] Table 3.1 suggests that blacks certainly used the drug, though they were outnumbered by whites. Unfortunately, the racial and ethnic classifications employed here make it difficult to discern the relative numbers of Anglo white and Hispanic users.[14]

On the East Coast, the drug was most popular in and around Washington, D.C., notably in the black, southeastern sections of the city. The drug attracted official attention here in about 1973, when it was blamed for an upsurge of psychiatric commitments; this chronology contradicts once more the "official story" about the drug's disappearance in the early 1970s. In the greater Washington area, PCP was second only to marijuana among illegal drugs, and in 1978, a regional Clandestine Laboratory Task Force was created to combat the drug.

For a few years, PCP was the most common substance found in people arrested in Washington for non-drug felonies, who were routinely subjected to urinalysis: in 1984, 30 percent of arrestees tested positive for the drug, compared to 15 percent for cocaine and 20 percent for heroin. Of course these figures are limited in their usefulness, as some drugs linger longer in the system and are thus more easily picked up by testing long after use, and PCP happens to be such a lingering drug. Nor should the figures be extrapolated to the city as a whole. But they do indicate heavy PCP usage in (black) Anacostia, if not in white Georgetown. By 1987, the PCP figure had risen to 40 percent, though by this point around 60 percent were testing positive for cocaine. PCP had a smaller but not negligible presence in other cities, and arrests and emergency-room incidents suggest pockets of usage in Detroit and New York City. In 1984, around 12 percent of New York City arrestees were showing traces of the drug, compared to 42 percent for cocaine.

The drug's popularity in California ensured that the PCP scare would receive full media attention nationwide. It also meant that the drug would be much in the minds of the California politicians and bureaucrats who dominated the Justice Department after the Reagan administration came to office in 1981. Angel dust was much used in northern California communities such as Berkeley and Oakland, and the East Bay community of Hayward was commonly known as "the PCP Capital of the World"—though media reports would also award a similar title to San Jose, Los Angeles and Washington, D.C. Though PCP crossed racial lines in the West, it was most prevalent among Hispanic users. The drug was a pressing law-enforcement concern in southern California, where phencyclidine developed a market among youth gangs and came to be associated with urban crime and violence.[15]

By the early 1980s, all the indices for PCP use in southern California were soaring, and the drug accounted for almost 40 percent of all felony narcotics complaints in the L.A. metropolitan region. In 1974, the Los Angeles Police Department (LAPD) arrested 130 people for PCP-related violations, compared to 2,538 in 1977. Seizures of the drug grew dramatically in the region during the same years, rising from 253,000 units in 1974 to five million in 1977 and 16.5 million by 1979. The number of PCP laboratories raided in Los Angeles County grew from three in 1975 to five hundred in 1977. It is open to debate whether these statistics reflect an actual upsurge of manufacturing and consumption or just a more proactive official approach to the problem. The LAPD tended to give drug issues a much higher priority than some other urban areas, especially after 1978, when the new police chief, Darryl F. Gates, demonstrated his crusading mission to fight drug abuse. Having identified PCP as a major criminal menace the LAPD organized an active task force in 1980 that made many arrests and seized even larger quantities of the drug.[16]

In both East and West, the drug's popularity declined sharply from about 1985 with rising competition from crack: high school seniors reporting PCP use in the previous twelve months fell sharply from 2.9 percent in 1985 to 1.3 percent in 1987, and the figure never again rose to the levels of the early eighties. Still, as with speed, angel dust never went away entirely: by 1991, 7.3 million Americans were recording that they had used it at some point in their lives, and an estimated four-hundred thousand within the past month, a figure only a little less than that for crack. As recently as 1997, a Los Angeles street gang was accused of running a PCP operation worth some thirty million dollars.[17]

The mass media discovered PCP as a national problem in about 1976, and news coverage ballooned from mid-1977 onwards: one study of news stories in the national press found only 33 articles between 1970 and 1977, compared to 247 in 1978 alone. The anti-PCP crusade recalled the most extreme charges made against narcotics in previous decades—marijuana in the 1930s and heroin and the hard drugs during the 1950s. In congressional hearings during 1978, PCP was called "a deadly, mind-crippling, mind-altering drug, with the ability to induce psychotic and schizophrenic behavior . . . the King Cobra of all hallucinogens . . . [it] should be better known as hellfire." It was said then that "PCP is dynamite. It can do to the brain what TNT can do to a building." PCP was "one of the most dangerous and insidious drugs known to mankind"; "a threat to national security . . . children were playing with death on the installment plan." In short, this was "the most devastating drug of modern times."[18] Resemblances to older anti-drug charges were so close as to cause embarrassment among a generation of doctors and journalists that had come to deride media claims about devil drugs as cheap demagoguery.

In mid-1977, a series of media reports almost presented PCP in terms of demonic possession, as a real-life counterpart of Robin Cook's fictional Ultra. Among the press headlines from this period were "Schizophrenia Epidemic Here Linked to Youths' Use of PCP" (*Washington Post*), "Angel Dust: The Devil Drug That Threatens Youth" (*Woman's Day*), "Angel Death" (*New Times*) and "PCP: A Terror of a Drug" (*Time*). As the *Detroit Free Press* headlined, "A little bit of this angel dust can bring on a whole lot of hell." This was "the most insidiously dangerous of the underground mindwares." A typical text aimed at parents and community groups included subheadings about the drug's greatest dangers to life and limb, namely latent psychosis and seizures, drownings, tragedies and "flashbacks (psychotic episodes)." PCP was said to remove all sexual inhibitions, and anecdotes told of users being driven to assault and rape bystanders; an alleged nude syndrome was said to drive users to strip in public places. Far more seriously, it was believed to threaten mental health and stability. Allegedly, over a three-year period, over a thousand young people from southeastern Washington alone had been driven to seek psychiatric treatment for schizophrenic symptoms induced by PCP, which drove users to extreme paranoia.[19] During 1973 and 1974, PCP use was reported to be the leading cause of admissions to St. Elizabeth's, the city's mental hospital.

The most deadly accusation against the drug was that it drove users to acts of irrational violence against themselves or others. The first press reports of a user tearing out his own eyes surfaced in Baltimore in 1971, though the man himself insisted that the drug involved was not PCP but another substance altogether (para-chlorphenylalanine); nevertheless, the story was reported in the context of PCP and publicized as such in Hunter Thompson's *Fear and Loathing in Las Vegas.* Thereafter, the tale circulated freely, becoming almost an urban legend. Atrocity stories accumulated during the growing panic atmosphere of 1977, when the *Washington Post* declared that "[PCP] can knock out an elephant, but it can turn a person into a raging semblance of a cornered wild animal." One newspaper report from this time told of Washington-area cases in which "one man 'attacked everyone in sight,' another was found 'singing naked in a supermarket,' and a third was 'choking a boy in an apartment corridor.'" There were other tales of self-mutilation: one Los Angeles man was reported to have been under the influence of PCP when he cut off his penis, and a handful of documented cases told of users blinding themselves. Some users perished from behavioral toxicity: in other words, as *Rolling Stone* reported, "people fall from great heights, burn to death, drive their cars into large stationary objects or drown in a few inches of water because they don't recognize the danger, or simply because they were too fried to do anything about it, even move."[20]

Whenever a sensational crime of violence occurred, the media were swift to stress any evidence that the perpetrator was a PCP user. Among the most-told horror stories was that of drifter Charles Peters, who was supposedly under the influence of PCP when he walked into a house selected at random in San Mateo, California. There he proceeded to kill a baby and stab a pregnant woman in the stomach: "Police arrested Peters in the street, where he had taken off his clothes and, smeared with blood, was shouting 'Glory Hallelujah.'" The Los Angeles media speculated at length on whether the Hillside Strangler serial murder case of 1977–78 might be the work of a demented PCP user, a view reinforced when one suspect held briefly for questioning admitted using the drug. Public panic about angel-dust-inspired violence in southern California reached "near hysteria" following the random robbery-murder of journalist Sarai Ribicoff in Venice in 1980. Under the influence of PCP, it was suggested, criminals "don't just rip someone off, they destroy the home or threaten to kill someone."[21] In contrast to the accusations leveled at heroin, violence and death were believed to result not from PCP's legal or social status, but from evil qualities inherent to the chemical itself.

Initially, coverage was concentrated in the regions in which PCP had developed a niche, chiefly Washington, D.C., and California, but the threat was soon taken up by the national media. An early television report, and one of the most shockingly memorable, was broadcast on the CBS newsmagazine *60 Minutes* in October 1977, in a segment that offered a preview of literally hundreds of drug-related news items over the next two decades. The story was told from the standpoint of one city with unusually high PCP usage—San Jose, that "hotbed of laboratories and abuse."[22] The problem was presented through the experience of police, emergency medical workers, drug prevention authorities and so on, all of whom agreed that conditions arising from the drug had almost created a state of siege in the community. This barrage of images about out-of-control PCP use could not fail to suggest to the viewer that these were somehow normal urban conditions and that San Jose was a model for the bleak future. Pessimistic themes ran through the interviews offered: "Labs, the DEA told us, are springing up faster than narcotics agents can shut them down. . . . It's in a growth phase." Future growth was considered all the more likely because current users were so young, often only fourteen or fifteen, and presumably had many years of abuse ahead.

Naturally, the *60 Minutes* report focused on the most extreme manifestations of the drug's ill effects, and two case studies told of men who had carried out murders while under the drug's influence: one was Charles Peters, who was interviewed for the piece, while another alleged user named Barry Braeske had shot his parents. This report climaxed with perhaps the most disturbing story of all: "There was a man that the police had picked up down on [San Jose's] First Street. And he was acting very crazy: he was very hostile, very angry, was breaking windows. So they took him to a cell. . . . When they returned back, the man—it's the assumption that he had been seeing something horrible—took out both of his eyes with his hands. He just tore them out."

Shortly afterwards, both *Time* and NBC's *Today* program ran strikingly similar stories, both recounting this tale and the Peters case. One claimed, "Without question, it is the most dangerous drug available . . . more dangerous than heroin or barbiturates."[23] PCP had become an urgent national problem: as the *Today* report concluded, "So it is something for everyone, no matter where they live, to be aware of." This judgment was repeated in other television programs and national periodicals, including *Rolling Stone,* which generally took an easygoing attitude to most illegal drugs—not surprisingly, given its own counterculture origins. On PCP, however, the magazine quoted exactly the same horror stories and expert opinions as the more mainstream media.[24]

Curiously, media coverage during these first few months said little about what would soon become perhaps the most powerful element of the anti-PCP indictment, namely that the drug endowed users with superhuman strength. This theme emerged spottily in some of the 1977 stories, originally with the statement that the drug gave users *delusions* of great strength. But soon, the strength was said to be all too real. From early 1978, this mythology came to dominate news stories: police claimed users broke through steel handcuffs, and alleged incidents of this kind in Pasadena in 1978 were recounted uncritically for years afterwards. An exposé of these years offered case after case of what had been portrayed as characteristic incidents of suicidal or maniacal behavior, effects that made the substance "unique among street drugs." Here is one typical outcome in such accounts: "[The PCP user] then tried to reach for the guard's revolver. The guard retreated, fired one warning shot into the air, and then fired another, while the man laughed and repeated that he was stronger than God. The man lunged at the guard. The guard fired and struck the man's chest. The man got up after being shot in the chest and attacked the guard, who then shot and killed him."[25]

Horror stories proliferated. In one of the most publicized incidents, a 35-year-old biochemist named Ronald Burkholder was said to be

> nude and climbing a street sign when the [police] sergeant saw him. Burkholder, in an exhibition of superhuman strength, took the sergeant's baton twice and then lunged at him. [The officer], as a last resort, found it necessary to use deadly force by fatally shooting [him]. . . . There have been numerous situations in Los Angeles and other cities throughout the country where phencyclidine (PCP) users have gone berserk and have barricaded themselves in buildings while using weapons to ward off the police. . . . It is not unusual for insane individuals and those under the influence of PCP to be absolutely immune to the effects of tear gas.

According to conservative congressman Robert Dornan, "the police are becoming frightened in the field of encountering PCP criminals, referring to them as 'Hulks.' They claim PCP will enhance some criminals' strength six or seven or even eight times. I don't understand the physiology involved here."[26] The "Hulk" reference came from the contemporary television show *The Incredible Hulk,* in which radiation transformed a normal man into a monster of incredible strength.

This notion that a drug could reduce its users to an animalistic state had a long prehistory, notably in the charges levied against cocaine in the Progressive Era. Cocaine supposedly made blacks immune to pain and impervious to small-caliber weapons that would disable or kill a lesser man: this belief explains why American police forces in the early twentieth century tended to favor larger-caliber firearms, moving from .32s to .38s.[27]

The vision of the junkie as juggernaut would recur in the marijuana panic of the mid-1930s, when one of the most frequently retold episodes of reefer madness involved a killer who tore out the eyes of his victims. Another direct antecedent of the PCP mythology was the speed-freak rhetoric of the sixties. As with speed, it is quite possible that PCP induced bizarre or self-destructive behavior in some users, but these incidents were wrongly portrayed as typical.

The potential effects of PCP were again in the headlines in the early 1990s, following the notorious beating of Rodney King by Los Angeles police. Police charged that such violence had been required to control him because he was under the influence of PCP, making him what officers termed a "PCP-crazed giant." Police describing the incident as it occurred compared the scene to the film *Gorillas in the Mist,* suggesting that the drug caused the black user to revert to apelike savagery. The PCP-related allegations against King surfaced in the trial of the officers accused in the beating, and the predominantly white jury that heard the case during the officers' first trial were sufficiently convinced to acquit, causing public outrage that led directly to the 1992 Los Angeles riots. An otherwise inexplicable acquittal must be understood in light of the potent mythology surrounding angel dust: incidentally, there was no medical evidence that King had been using the drug at or near the time of the attack.[28]

The role of PCP in the King case suggests a fundamental problem with accepting any such account at face value. Stories of bizarre drug-induced behavior normally stem from police or security guards who have found themselves in violent confrontations with citizens and have to justify their violent or even lethal actions, so that they have a vested interest in making the other party seem as fierce or deranged as possible. The reports appear before juries or internal inquiries, situations where the officer's career depends on portraying a confrontation with an uncontrollable maniac who thinks himself stronger than God. Once PCP-related violence had become such a widely credited notion, it was no doubt tempting to use this as a blanket excuse for any confrontation in which police had used excessive force, and such instances were all too common in the Los Angeles of the 1970s and 1980s. When suspects died when subjected to police chokeholds, LAPD's Chief Gates countered that the fatalities resulted not from police misconduct, but from the suspect's abuse of cocaine or PCP. Moreover, once police officers expect that a given offender is extremely dangerous, a lethal Hulk, they are all the more likely to resort to violence themselves and to interpret the suspect's actions in the most threatening way. Unfortunately, alert citizens in the 1970s were not equipped with video cameras when police allegedly had such encounters. Conversely, if the Rodney King encounter had not been filmed, anti-drug textbooks might well be citing it today as an example of the disastrous effects of PCP on its users and praising the police for their cautious and disciplined response. In reality, the evidence for a linkage between PCP and uncontrolled violence is at best tenuous. Several studies in the mid-1980s concluded that the savagery widely attributed to PCP users was at best rare, while arrestees who tested positive for the drug were no more likely to be accused of violent crimes than users of other stimulants.[29]

Substantiating other charges against the drug is equally difficult. If users had flashbacks or psychotic episodes, was this attributable to PCP, or to the other substances that most of them had experienced earlier, or even to causes unrelated to drugs? Most had graduated from LSD and had long histories of multi-drug use, creating the potential for any number of barely understood drug interactions. The complex role of drugs in causing violence is apparent when we read a case presented as a characteristic example of the typical effects of PCP. Noting a case in which two children were killed and mutilated, Representative Dornan reported, "This burglar turned psycho-murderer had worked the Los Angeles coastline area for many years, he was a multiple offender, had served time and had added PCP to his twisted mental condition before this particular burglary turned into a nightmarish and ghoulish type murder." Based on this account, it is difficult to see that PCP made much difference to a preexisting aberrant mental condition. When *60 Minutes* interviewed a PCP user who had murdered his parents, the program neglected to mention that the crime was a financially motivated conspiracy in which he and a partner hoped to gain from an inheritance. Nor did they remark that the offender had excellent legal motives for depicting his crime as the result of drug-induced insanity, a claim rejected by the trial jury.[30]

A related problem occurs when we examine PCP-related deaths, the number of which in 1977 was estimated at around a hundred nationwide. As we will see in the context of other drugs like methamphetamine, the interpretation of drug-related deaths would long prove a knotty question (see chapter 7). Much depends on the subjective attitudes of individual medical examiners and on their willingness to determine that the presence of a given drug in the victim of a suicide or sudden death was directly connected with the fatality, which is often open to debate. If PCP was so common in some regions and some subcultures, it was inevitably going to be present in a sizable proportion of criminals, suicides and participants in personal violence, whether or not it actually contributed to a given incident. Though overdose deaths related to the drug were reported in large numbers by the mid-seventies, more careful analysis suggests that most were wrongly diagnosed and that death rarely results from pharmacological overdose: the upsurge of death reports reflects instead the enhanced sensitivity of police and doctors to what was suddenly perceived as a lethal drug.[31]

Paradoxically, the very popularity of PCP supports the idea that its effects were being grossly exaggerated. Though millions of young Americans used PCP at least sporadically, only a minuscule proportion of users manifested the bizarre behavior said to characterize the drug's effects. Seven million Americans had not turned into instant schizophrenics, nor were they drowning in pools, tearing out their eyes, stabbing babies, murdering their parents or charging naked into police gunfire. By 1978, less than six thousand out of perhaps twenty million individual PCP trips resulted in visits to an emergency room, suggesting a rate of problems and adverse reactions rather better than that for many legal prescription drugs.[32] Though chronic PCP use might indeed have horrible consequences, there was no justification for the idea that a single or occasional experience transformed an individual into a raging monster.

By early 1978, PCP use had been identified as a fully fledged national crisis, and pressure mounted to upgrade the drug from its existing Schedule II status (controlled medical uses) to Schedule I (prohibited). Significantly for later developments concerning designer drugs, this was the first anti-drug movement in which authorities tried to suppress the manufacture of a synthetic by denying access to crucial precursor chemicals like piperidine rather than by merely regulating the finished product. These issues were addressed that summer by two well-publicized congressional hearings, respectively before the Juvenile Delinquency Subcommittee of the Senate Committee on the Judiciary and the House's Select Committee on Narcotics Abuse and Control: both aired the most extreme charges against the drug, and in so doing provided a new impetus for sensational media coverage. Incidentally, the hearings did much to counterbalance the relaxed attitudes toward illegal drug use that had characterized the previous year's discussions of the possible legalization of marijuana.[33]

PCP horror stories were much in evidence in the hearings. In the words of Representative Norman Mineta of San Jose, "One man murdered his parents, another stabbed a tiny baby to death, another ripped out his eyes with his own hands." Another user, it was said, had tried to expiate his sins by eating a large portion of the glass pane from a shower door. That the situation had "reached epidemic proportions" was confirmed by expansive, and misleading, use of the available statistics. Evidence of soaring PCP use was overwhelmingly based on figures for seizures and lab raids in a couple of major centers, particularly Los Angeles, with the false implication that these conditions were typical. One House member further implied that the seven million who reported ever having tried the drug were in fact "an estimated seven million of our nation's youth [who] are *daily* using this deadly drug." One-time use was portrayed as if it represented regular practice, and as so often occurs in such cases, congressional investigators drew no distinction between mere use of PCP and chronic dependency: "a PCP *user* will eventually be reported to a hospital emergency room as a DOA [on] a one-way ticket to immediate self-destruction."[34]

The 1978 hearings initiated a period of several years in which PCP-related horror stories became a staple of media reporting, while angel dust became a central target in anti-drug literature aimed at parents and teenagers. A 1980 book on the subject described the drug as the *Number One Teen Killer,* and the following year brought a study of the Devil's Dust: PCP was *The Dangerous Angel.* The furor continued well into the mid-eighties, and as late as 1984, *U.S. News and World Report* published a special report titled "The Deadly Path of Today's PCP Epidemic."[35]

Numerous TV treatments aimed to warn teenagers about angel dust. In 1977, actor Robert Blake starred in a commercial that warned, "PCP is a rattlesnake. It'll turn around and it'll kill you." By 1979, PCP-related horror stories were featured in shows such as *Quincy, CHIPS* and *Police Story.* In the space of a single week late in 1979, network viewers could have seen the documentary *Angel Death* and a TV movie entitled *Angel Dust: The Wack Attack.* Narrated by Paul Newman, *Angel Death* focused on use among white suburbanites, depicting the drug as their refuge from personal and family crises. Meanwhile, newspaper advertising for *The Wack Attack* depicted a genial young black man in disco clothing, with this text: "This man is really a monster with superhuman strength. It's true. And it's not funny. He may seem to be a nice young talented musician. And he really is. Until he turns to Angel Dust. Then he becomes a madman. Tonight KABC-TV's dramatic presentation will open your eyes to the horrors of PCP, the deadly drug. Now you will understand those stories about people who jump to their deaths, run in front of automobiles and attack armed policemen barehanded."[36] The movie was later retitled, starkly, *Death Drug.*

Productions like this and the later *Angel Dusted* (1981) were noteworthy not because of any great qualities of the films themselves, but because they represented a revival of a genre most had thought long extinct, the depiction of the devastating effects of an addictive drug. These moralizing efforts had once been commonplace, but they had been quite discredited by sensationalist items such as *Cocaine Fiends, Reefer Madness* and their successors. By the 1960s, these earlier films were regarded as camp comedy numbers, but at a time when marijuana and cocaine were regarded as harmless vices, angel dust was regarded as sufficiently serious to merit a public warning. In contrast, cocaine attracted nothing near as dark a treatment for some time afterwards: the first TV movie on the harmful effects of that drug did not appear until 1983, and the barrage of fictional screen treatments only arrived after 1987.

Other films of the late seventies and early eighties used PCP to present prohibitionist anti-drug messages that could not have been applied to other drugs at this time. In the 1981 comedy *Trading Places,* Dan Aykroyd plays a successful lawyer who falls victim to a conspiracy intended to ruin his life. He is framed for possession of angel dust, to the horror of a police officer, who angrily asks, "Have you ever seen what this stuff does to kids?" The film is an accurate reflection of its time to the extent that no other drug would have had such dreadful connotations—not cocaine or marijuana and probably not even heroin. Also in 1981, the urban police drama *Fort Apache, The Bronx* used an angel-dust user to represent mindless animal savagery. The film opens when black prostitute Charlotte (played by Pam Grier) carries out a random shooting attack on two police officers: she is "wacked" from smoking angel dust, because "that shit'll make you crazy." Charlotte wages a personal war against men, luring them into situations in which she appears to be offering them sex, then slashes their throats or faces with a razor blade held between her teeth. In a menacing scene, she portrays herself as a seductive but deadly snake, with the razor blade as her lethal bite.

Scarcely less monstrous than the homicidal snake-woman was the image in the 1984 Arnold Schwarzenegger film *The Terminator,* which provides a fascinating counterpoint to the gangster story presented in *Witness* shortly afterwards. The terminator of the title is a virtually unstoppable android from the future, sent by a machine race dedicated to the extermination of humanity. The terminator robot has been sent to track down and kill a woman from our time, and his pursuit of her involves incredible feats of strength and endurance that would have resulted in the death of any human being. When the woman claims that this could be no normal man, the (Los Angeles) police officers assure her that he is undoubtedly high on angel dust, which prevents him from feeling pain. Though the film was pure fantasy, this scene does accurately convey the thinking of many police departments about the drug in the early 1980s, to say nothing of the attitudes of news media and politicians.

One curious feature of the anti-PCP campaign was its racial content. In the spate of books and television programs, the assumption was that the drug posed a problem for white youngsters and that the middle classes were particularly vulnerable. As one medical expert told the Senate committee in 1978, with PCP, "you generally find the rich, young and bored users, and as the more frequent users, young white males. Wealth is no protectorate [*sic*], not with this crowd."[37] This assertion is flatly contradicted by much other evidence, in which PCP users emerge as much more ethnically diverse, with strong minority contingents in centers like Los Angeles and San Jose and strongholds in African-American centers like Washington, Detroit and Oakland. Nor does this image take account of the drug's popularity among women. Nevertheless, the image of the PCP user as white, suburban, teenage boy acquired a firm hold: the drug was wreaking havoc among "good" (white) teenagers, who had been seduced into the habits of the ghetto or barrio.

Themes of racial and social crossover are evident throughout Todd Strasser's popular 1979 novel *Angel Dust Blues,* which was aimed at a young adult market. It tells the story of Alex, a high school senior in a wealthy Long Island community whose growing involvement in using and dealing drugs leads to an arrest that blights his chances for college and social advancement. Influenced by his friend Michael, Alex begins traveling into Brooklyn to buy drugs from West Indians in order to begin dealing on a commercial scale: "You kids took a little bit of the South Bronx and put it in Deepbrook." Angel dust is seen as the most destructive of their commodities: it reduces Michael to a neurotic and paranoid state, eventually causing him to be committed to a mental hospital. Upon release, Michael engages in acts of random and irrational violence until eventually he dies of an overdose. Though Alex survives, he has transgressed racial and social boundaries so thoroughly that his life is already ruined: "he had crossed the line for good."[38]

With so much media attention, few could doubt that an urban epidemic of phencyclidine was in full swing, or that the drug was causing insanity, mutilation and violent death among America's young to a degree unparallelled since the marijuana panic of the late 1930s.[39] For a few years, PCP represented what crack would become in the late 1980s, namely the death drug, the maker of monsters, and that "monstrosity" was expressed above all in racial metaphors. Yet, this indictment was built upon shaky foundations: though PCP might have had bad effects in individual cases, a few atypical incidents were projected as if they represented a normal experience. Equally questionable were the assumptions about the drug's usage patterns: by the time the drug was discovered as an impending crisis, it was already passing the peak of its popularity, while statements about the racial profile of users usually owed more to the rhetoric of racial panic than to any serious observation.

Given the evidence available in the early 1980s, it was by no means obvious that speed rather than PCP would attract the epidemic label and be seen as such a calamitous threat. By any available index, both the manufacture and the use of methamphetamine were expanding rapidly in these years, and had observers cared to do so, they could have made just as convincing a case for a methamphetamine epidemic in the early 1980s as they did for a PCP crisis: certainly speed labs were coming to light in impressive numbers. The fact that PCP nevertheless continued to attract so much of the attention is dramatic testimony to the concentration of the drug war in the cities and among racial minorities.

By 1985, a burgeoning anti-drug movement was already focusing attention on the PCP epidemic, as well as on the threat of organized crime and corruption raised by methamphetamine. At this point, growing fears about the expanding illicit pharmacopoeia found an additional focus with a panic over designer drugs, a phrase that now entered the lexicon of media and law enforcement. The new label proved potent in incorporating existing fears about synthetics and intensifying the most alarming rhetoric about all laboratory-made narcotics. Building on existing fears, the designer-drug issue opened the way for yet another escalation of the emerging drug war.

| F O U R |

Suppressing Ecstasy
The Designer Drug Crisis

My God, this is a drug of the suburbs!
—Dr. Gary Henderson, 1984.[1]

The designer-drug concept gained notoriety following a series of media exposés and official investigations during 1985. In an atmosphere of growing anti-drug panic, discussions of designer chemicals misleadingly bracketed together many recently developed synthetics as if they were part of one wave of sinister laboratory concoctions, all posing a like danger to life and sanity. Some of the new synthetics certainly were dangerous, at least in the way they were used on the streets, but others really did not deserve their new notoriety. The blanket condemnation of so-called designer drugs contributed to an ever-growing restriction on pharmaceutical experimentation, or at least on any undertakings pursued outside the labs of the giant corporations. Appropriately enough, the prohibition movement chose as a primary target the popular euphoric nicknamed Ecstasy, which was condemned in just the years when the corporate product Prozac was achieving its global triumphs. In more senses than one, this was part of a wider war against unapproved ecstasies, a systematic revenge against the hedonism of the 1960s and 1970s.

The concept of designer drugs entered the public consciousness quite suddenly. In 1984, the print media offered just four stories using this phrase, compared to almost four hundred for the years 1985–86.[2]

Table 4.1 Designer and Synthetic Drugs in
the Mass Media, 1984–95: Number of News
Stories Containing These Keywords

Year	Designer Drugs	MDMA
1984	4	0
1985	179	73
1986	206	40
1987	126	23
1988	113	25
1989	176	46
1990	161	15
1991	175	16
1992	254	75
1993	225	33
1994	378	83
1995	357	187

The sudden interest reflected several wholly distinct trends in actual usage, though they were presented as a single problem. Since the LSD boom of the 1960s, many drug users had used their chemical skills to synthesize hallucinogens and other illegal substances, and the 1970s were a great age of experimentation and enterprise. Once the chemical composition of a particular drug was known, it was possible that a minor alteration in molecular structure would produce another and equally interesting drug, which might find a profitable mass market.

One promising avenue of research sought drugs comparable to heroin, which was of course difficult to import in any quantities, so that a cheap, laboratory-made substitute would be a valuable commodity. Two existing anesthetics were seen as likely sources for synthetic heroin: the more popular was fentanyl, marketed under the name Sublimaze, but drug designers also experimented with meperidine (Demerol or MPPP), which had itself been synthesized in the 1930s as a substitute for morphine. In 1979, a fentanyl analogue called alpha-methyl-fentanyl (AMF) was sold in California as China White, a name that suggested the legendary, pure-white heroin from Southeast Asia. The new drug swiftly gained a following, but its extreme potency had disastrous results, reportedly causing eighteen overdose deaths in the next two years. Several new fentanyl analogues appeared over the next few years amid remarkable claims abut their potency. By the mid-1980s, the latest variant was 3-methyl fentanyl(3MF), which "in its purest form . . . is 70,000 times more potent than morphine and 1,000 to 3,000 times more potent than heroin." Sold as Persian White, the drug was associated with several deaths in the San Francisco Bay Area. Between 1979 and 1983, the total number of fentanyl-related deaths was reported as twenty-eight, with forty-nine more in 1984 alone.[3]

Fentanyl seemed on the verge of becoming a significant problem. By 1985, it was estimated that a fifth of California's heroin users might in reality be using fentanyl-derived synthetics, and the new drug family gained a market in the upscale communities north of San Francisco, such as Marin County.[4] Incidentally, the chronology of the new synthetics boom explains the origin of the name designer drugs, as designer jeans were so much a presence in popular culture between about 1979 and 1982. This was the height of advertisements for the Sergio Valente brand name, and applying the phrase to drugs reinforced an image of hedonistic consumerism. The year 1984 marked the popularization of the term "yuppie," with all it implied about mindless faddishness.

Some of the new analogue drugs were far more dangerous than their established counterparts, not so much because of any intrinsically lethal or toxic qualities, but because of their immensely greater power. Most heroin users in the 1970s were using severely diluted versions of the drug, often only 5 percent purity or less, and compensating for the weakness by injecting the drug intravenously. When purer forms of heroin became available from new suppliers, purity would improve more or less overnight to 80 percent or better, with the result of hundreds of overdose cases and some fatalities. Similar results followed the creation of an analogue drug vastly more potent than the old commodities. Some skepticism is needed when considering the actual potency of the new drugs: in the expert testimony about 3-methyl fentanyl before the U.S. Senate, its strength relative to morphine was reported in wildly contradictory terms.[5] Nevertheless, the dangers were real. Taken in the appropriate microscopic quantities, the analogue would neither harm nor kill, but the overdose danger was all too great. Few users could adjust to the microgram amounts required for the new substances, and there are plausible stories of victims dying before they had the chance to remove the hypodermics stuck in their arms.

Moreover, a few of the new drugs were actively toxic. The best-known horror story of these years concerned the substance MPTP, which came to light through what became known as the case of the frozen addict. This case concerned a drug user who, in 1982, was found unable to move or communicate and who demonstrated all of the classic symptoms of advanced Parkinson's Disease. This condition had been caused by an unsuccessful attempt to synthesize a form of meperidine that had instead produced MPTP, a substance highly destructive to the human brain. Toxic MPTP had been sold on the streets as "new heroin," and some four hundred related cases were identified. Though the victims themselves were beyond help, the story was of great scientific value for what it suggested about the workings of the human brain, particularly about the nature of Parkinson's Disease. As such, the scientific puzzle attracted interest in the popular media and was reported in the magazine *California* in February 1985. The incident reached national attention through a PBS NOVA documentary, "The Case of the Frozen Addict," which was broadcast the following year and often repeated thereafter. For the general public, this frightening story provided the context for understanding the new phenomenon of designer drugs.[6] The image of a personality imprisoned within a nonresponding body was all the more convincing because it meshed so well with recent accounts of how PCP drove users to commit monstrous acts when they had lost control of their bodies.

The new synthetics existed in a legal limbo. While the proscription of drugs like cocaine or heroin was well defined, underground chemists were moving far ahead of legislators in creating new substances that had not officially been outlawed. This created painful anomalies. Though using a harmless drug like marijuana could theoretically lead to a severe prison sentence, making or manufacturing a dangerous substance like MPTP or China White was not clearly illegal until the DEA specifically scheduled it as a controlled substance. This issue initially surfaced during the PCP panic of 1977–78, as laboratories had experimented with twenty or so chemical variants of phencyclidine, none of which could be suppressed by police because they had not been explicitly proscribed. Based on difficulties of regulation alone, synthetics were even then identified as the "problem of the future." China White was legal from its invention in 1979 until its prohibition in 1981, and sellers only ran a risk if they sold it under the guise of heroin. Designer drugs were legal but lethal, and the range of future combinations was apparently limitless: there were said to be two or three thousand possible variants of the amphetamines and hundreds for fentanyl, and some at least could be quite as devastating as 3MF. In 1984, the federal Comprehensive Crime Control Act gave the attorney general emergency power to schedule substances in order to avoid imminent hazard to the public safety.[7]

Concern about designer drugs reached a new intensity in the spring of 1985. Major stories or investigative reports appeared in all major newspapers and newsmagazines. Between March and May, such items appeared in the *Wall Street Journal,* the *New York Times, Time,* the *Chicago Tribune,* the *Sacramento Bee,* the *Dallas Morning News,* the *Detroit News* and the *Christian Science Monitor. Discover* warned of "The Looming Menace of Designer Drugs" and *Time* examined "Death by Design," while *U.S. News and World Report* featured an alarming report called "Designer Drugs—Murder by Molecule." The more extreme reports argued that a new synthetic-drug revolution was imminent in which "[h]eroin, cocaine and marijuana are as obsolete as the horse and buggy. The drugs of the future have arrived, and they are made in test tubes." Television news programs demonstrated their lamentable tendency to present new drugs in near-advertisements: NBC's *Nightly News* featured a drug user praising synthetic heroin as better than the real thing, "definitely better as far as the rush and the high is concerned."[8] Designer drugs were a natural theme for the talk shows, which were at this point evolving in a far more sensationalist direction, including material that would once have been condemned as tabloid. It was during 1986 that Fox's program *A Current Affair* opened the floodgates on the new television tabloid journalism, and all the networks shortly followed suit. A few months later, the *Phil Donahue Show* made designer drugs the subject of a special exposé.

These media treatments were fairly homogeneous in tone. All recounted basically the same set of disaster tales, from the discovery of

China White in late 1979 through the frozen addict case and into the upsurge of new synthetics in California in the early 1980s. Virtually all concentrated on the two most damning aspects of the problem, the danger of overdose from fentanyl analogues (universally dubbed synthetic heroin) and the threat of brain damage from MPTP or its counterparts. In addition, all relied on a narrow base of sources, with two individuals quoted in virtually all of the accounts—Robert J. Robertson, director of California's Division of Drug Problems, and Dr. Gary Henderson of the University of California, Davis. Henderson was then one of the very few professionals with any expertise in the fentanyl issue, and he was credited with coining the phrase "designer drug." He freely shared his alarm about the new issue, and in so doing offered the media a range of excellent quotes. He suggested that the new drugs were likely to grow enormously in popularity because they were cheap to make and faced none of the difficulties of importation, while the infinite variety of possible new substances made them a legal nightmare: "This is the wave of the future. . . . You haven't seen anything yet. My perspective is that synthetic drugs are the drugs of the future. It does not make sense to import a drug halfway around the world when you can make it in your home or backyard for a few hundred dollars." Lacking the stigma of street drugs, the new analogues would appeal to new social categories, to suburbanites and the middle classes. Henderson warned of the massive gap that had emerged between the drug-makers and the law-enforcement response: "It seems we are still watching reruns of *The French Connection* while there is someone out there using a computer to search the chemical literature looking for new drugs to synthesize."[9] His account was disturbingly plausible.

In March 1985, the synthetic menace attracted the attention of two of the politicians most associated with drug issues, namely Senator Lawton Chiles of Florida and Representative Charles Rangel of New York. Together they introduced legislation that would call on the administration to confront the emerging problem, and in July, designer drugs were the theme of two separate congressional hearings. The hearings before Chiles's own Budget Committee represent the hyperbolic tone of the era. In his keynote statement, Chiles claimed that although designer drugs were presently limited in popularity, they threatened to "revolutionize the way drugs are used and sold in this country. The drugs are thousands of times more potent than the illegal narcotics presently flooding the country, and over a hundred deaths have been identified with designer drug use so far." The recent precedent of the speed capital was very much in mind as Chiles claimed that "the potential exists for organized crime, which controls the heroin and cocaine markets, to enter into the designer drugs area." The synthetic industry was said to be in the hands of "aggressive lonewolf chemists, motorcycle gangs, and segments of the Philadelphia mob."[10]

Chiles's declaration set the tone for the whole hearing, and the warnings of imminent doom were repeatedly emphasized in the printed report by the tabloid-style, editorializing subheadings scattered through the document:

- Designer Drugs Are Extremely Dangerous
- Chemical More Lethal Than Heroin
- Designer Drugs: Menace of a Decade
- Drug's Chilling Terror
- Synthetic Drugs Are Drugs of Future
- Byproduct Is Deadly Poison
- Prisoner in Own Body
- Resources Not Adequate
- Inherent Dangers of Designer Drugs
- Many Not Aware of Designer Drug Problem
- We See Only the Tip of the Iceberg
- Young People Being Turned into Zombies
- The Intellectual's Heroin

This rhetoric was applied indiscriminately to a wide variety of synthetics as if all designer drugs were equally likely to kill or cause crippling brain damage, and Senator Chiles even treated amphetamines as part of this single problem.[11]

Designer drugs were said to represent the worst hazards of uncontrolled scientific experiment on innocent human victims, and the hearings were pervaded by images of perverted science transforming subjects into monsters or zombies. As Chiles claimed repeatedly, "It is something that will give you Parkinson's Disease or kill you. We need to understand, users and parents need to understand, what kind of thing we are flirting with, what kind of Frankenstein's Monster is being created as a result of playing with these drugs." "These phantom chemists," he said, "are experimenting with human beings and playing with forces that are thousands of time more potent than heroin, and horrible. . . . They can blow minds and bodies apart by what they are putting out on the street." Chiles's analysis was echoed by the expert voice of Dr. J. William Langston of California's Santa Clara Valley Medical Center, who had originally investigated the frozen addict case: "It would not be an overstatement to say they are turning young people into zombies and it is permanent." "With these new synthetic narcotics," he claimed, "the first animals are street users. In other words, drug addicts become, in a way, human guinea pigs." This view was reinforced by the testimony of the mother of Barry Kidston, perhaps the first clandestine chemist to synthesize MPPP (around 1976): he developed Parkinson's symptoms, contributing to his early death. Evidence from an anguished mother gave a human face to an otherwise abstract problem.[12]

For all the potent imagery, Chiles's committee faced an uphill struggle in trying to make the new drug menace appear suitably threatening to a national audience. At this point, designer drugs were neither widely known nor widely used in the drug underground, so it required some imagination to portray them as fomenting a crisis. Chiles dealt with this ingeniously by the rhetorical trick of using the lack of official data as a sign of an official inability to confront the issue rather than as a reflection of its insignificance. Normally, the numbers of seizures of drugs or drug laboratories provide a valuable index of usage, with more seizures indicating the greater popularity of a given drug. By this standard, the designer drugs did not present a particularly threatening picture, as only four labs had been uncovered nationwide for the period 1984–85, in contrast to several hundred facilities making amphetamines. Nevertheless, Chiles presented the *lack* of recorded activity to show how woefully ignorant law enforcement was of the menace it would have to confront.[13]

Furthermore, the designer-drug problem as it existed in 1985 was a localized California affair. Of the four labs seized to date, two had been in North and West Hollywood, one in San Diego, and one in Texas. Most of the main witnesses in the hearings had come from California, the only region that had thus far faced the need to research the problem: the witness group included Drs. Langston and Henderson and Randy Rossi of the California Bureau of Narcotics Enforcement (BNE), an activist in the movement to prohibit all fentanyl analogues in that state. However, Senator Chiles cited the worrying precedent of the PCP epidemic, which according to his account had begun with limited use in Los Angeles before sweeping the nation (a view that contradicts all available literature on the topic). "These synthetically manufactured drugs," he said, "present some of the same issues that PCP presented in the early 1970s." Others cited the LSD experience in the 1960s: "As California goes, so goes the rest of the nation."[14]

With such dire warnings, the U.S. Congress required little prompting to pass the legislation requested by anti-drug advocates. The Senate approved a prohibition measure by voice vote, without debate. The Anti-Drug Abuse Act of 1986 contained a Controlled Substance Analogue Enforcement Act, commonly called the Designer Drug Act, which was intended to end the legal immunity of synthetic drugs closely related to some better-known chemical, such as any new variant of the fentanyl family. It did this by a sweeping prohibition of analogues "substantially similar" to existing substances, a dramatic curtailment of legal experimentation. Specifically, the law allowed the prosecution of anyone involved with a substance "(i) the chemical structure of which is substantially similar to the chemical structure of a controlled substance in Schedule I or II (ii) which has a stimulant, depressant or hallucinogenic effect on the central nervous system that is substantially similar to or greater than the stimulant, depressant or hallucinogenic effect on the central nervous system of a controlled substance in Schedule I or II."

Though not officially declared scheduled drugs, analogues were treated for legal purposes as if they had been officially scheduled. The principle of similarity was extended further by the 1988 Chemical Diversion and Trafficking Act (CDTA), which regulated the precursors and essential chemicals needed for synthesizing illegal drugs. The new range of listed chemicals made the federal register resemble a college textbook, with notations concerning "ephedrine, its salts, optical isomers and salts of optical isomers. . . . Any salt, optical isomer or salt of an optical isomer of the chemicals listed above in subparagraphs M through U of this paragraph." Within five years, the CDTA listed twenty-seven precursors and seven essential chemicals.[15] The measure seemed comprehensive and was far-reaching enough to cause difficulties for serious researchers, yet at the same time it could scarcely succeed, because chemists could evolve still newer psychedelics and stimulants from chemical families yet unknown to the legislators. These would in turn be added to the list of analogues in an ever-spreading net of prohibition.

Though most of the designer drugs identified problematic had little immediate impact on the real world, the furor over synthetics did create much greater hostility and suspicion about any new drug that gained popularity in the underground culture. One early casualty of this process was methaqualone, or Quaaludes, a drug used widely as a legal sedative and hypnotic in the early 1970s, when some four million prescriptions were written annually. As so often occurs, the drug gained popularity because it was viewed as a safe and accessible alternative to another stigmatized substance, namely barbiturates, which had become far harder to find after the passage of the CSA. But methaqualone also attracted official displeasure in its own right because of its high rate of abuse and potential for creating dependency. It became a Schedule II drug in 1973, making it more difficult to obtain, and a sizable illegal market developed over the next decade. The drug became a familiar part of the seventies disco scene, largely because of its reputation as an aphrodisiac: in fact, it was said to create intense sexual lust in women while placing men in a soporific slumber, and the drug was referred to freely in songs like David Bowie's 1973 "Time" (with its reference to "Quaaludes and red wine"). In 1981, the DEA seized enough illegal methaqualone to make two hundred million tablets. In 1982, the state of Florida moved the drug to Schedule I, meaning prohibited status, and the federal government followed suit in 1984.[16] This rapid evolution from legal prescription status to outright prohibition reflected a far more stringent attitude toward drugs of all kinds, but especially toward laboratory-made synthetics.

This new hostility occurred at a time when drug designers were experimenting with a broad range of new chemicals intended to expand the scope of human consciousness, which now found themselves tarred with the damaging label of designer drugs. Many of the new substances were derived from the pathbreaking work of Dr. Alexander Shulgin, who created a range of new psychedelics from the late 1960s onwards and who experimented with hundreds of phenethylamine compounds. These were publicized in his book *PIHKAL,* its title an acronym for "phenethylamines I have known and loved," which offers full manufacturing instructions accessible to anyone with a knowledge of college chemistry. Shulgin's work had an evangelistic flavor, as his new psychedelics were intended to promote something like an evolutionary leap forward for the human race: "The potential of the psychedelic drugs to provide access to the interior universe is, I believe, their most valuable property." *PIHKAL* offers recipes and consumer reports on drugs like 2C-B, a short-acting psychedelic that "heightens all the senses. You'll enjoy food, smells, colors and textures" as well as pleasurable erotic effects. And that is only one of 179 intriguing substances on offer, while another fifty-five from the tryptamine family are described in lavish detail in his later book, *TIHKAL.* As long as books like these are available, the official effort to suppress designer drugs is futile, and even if the book were withdrawn, the information is now easily accessible through the Internet.[17]

It was these drugs, intended for spiritual exploration, that anti-drug authorities now treated as indistinguishable from more perilous substances like China White. The most prominent casualty of the new furor was the substance nicknamed Ecstasy. This was targeted as a rising menace in 1985, at the height of the perceived crisis over synthetics, so that the media focus on Ecstasy coincided precisely with the publicity about frozen addicts, Parkinson's Disease, zombies and lethal synthetic heroin. Ecstasy was damned by the company it was believed to keep.

Ecstasy is more properly known as MDMA (3,4, Methylene-dioxymethamphetamine), and as its name suggests, it is yet another derivative of the amphetamine family. Its chemical relatives included DOM, which was marketed under the street name STP—Serenity, Tranquility, Peace—during the 1967 Summer of Love. Another immediate predecessor was MDA, which originally attracted attention as a love drug in the hippie culture of Haight Ashbury in the late sixties. As the drug created mellow feelings of warmth and safety, MDA was popularly known as Love, the Hug Drug, or the Businessman's LSD. The drug provided a legal alternative to proscribed substances like LSD, and it fit well with the hippie ethos of love, peace and inner exploration. MDA was supposedly developed as a U.S. military experiment designed to weaken the will of enemy forces, while American troops were to be chemically galvanized for violent action by better-known amphetamines: in this era at least, the concept of a drug war was no mere metaphor.[18]

MDMA, which shares many properties with MDA, was originally synthesized in 1912 by the Merck Corporation. It was rediscovered by Shulgin in 1965, when he remarked that "it was not a psychedelic in the visual or interpretive sense, but the lightness and warmth of the psychedelic was present and quite remarkable": in fact, the drug has some chemical relationship to mescaline and its derivatives. Open experimentation with human subjects was revived in the early 1970s, and from about 1976, largely under Shulgin's advocacy, the drug was used increasingly by therapists, who found it valuable in creating a psychologically safe environment in which patients could explore traumatic feelings or memories. In essence, it offered the advantages of the hallucinogens without the potential loss of control and the resulting catastrophe of a bad trip. To quote novelist Douglas Rushkoff, "You get the insight without the pain. You see how things are but, unlike with acid, the knowledge doesn't spin you into the drug's control. The only way to have a bad E trip is to be afraid to look. You can't shut down the process. Just look, love, laugh." Shulgin himself comments that "MDMA allows you to be totally in control, while getting a really good look at yourself . . . it does away with . . . the fear barrier, the fear people have of seeing what's going on inside them, who they are." It was "penicillin for the soul, and you don't give up penicillin, once you've seen what it can do."[19]

MDMA now played a central role in what was termed the neuroconsciousness movement, in a close approximation of the use of LSD by radical therapists during the early 1960s. One psychologist "spent his time training people, mostly therapists, in the use of MDMA. He's introduced several thousands of them across the country to this drug, teaching them how to use it properly, for themselves and their patients." Under the nickname ADAM, the drug gained an enthusiastic following among spiritual seekers and New Agers, who explored analogies between these chemically induced states and the mystical conditions described by the traditional religions.[20] MDMA thus had a respectable following, and its use in controlled and discreet settings meant that it was unlikely to attract attention from law-enforcement agencies. Through such means, perhaps half a million doses of the drug were distributed in a decade.

Matters changed fundamentally during the early 1980s as the drug acquired a politically damaging reputation for giving pleasure. Entrepreneurial drug-makers in Texas marketed the chemical as a party drug, choosing the brand name Ecstasy, or XTC. It found its way into the upscale party and dance-club scenes of Dallas and Austin, where it was sold openly over bar counters as a yuppie psychedelic, and it was a smash success in the gay clubs of New York and Chicago. The media reported that the drug was gaining popularity at an alarming rate and portrayed it as the new drug of choice for the young and affluent. Of course, the more sensational the press reports, the better the advertising for the drug, as would-be yuppies across the nation asked themselves what pleasures they were missing. Many users were apparently attracted to MDMA as a safe alternative to cocaine, which was then attracting such awful publicity following tales of severe addiction and celebrity deaths. At this time, MDMA was not subject to the increasingly severe criminal penalties prescribed for cocaine and Quaaludes.

In the atmosphere of the burgeoning drug war, Ecstasy was condemned as much by its name as by its cultural connotations. As a therapeutic aid, MDMA had most of the positive features and few of the drawbacks of other commonly used drugs of the 1970s and 1980s, but the name Ecstasy suggested a link with the discredited cultures of the 1970s: we might ask whether it would have aroused official outrage if it had been given its first intended name, Empathy, or even retained the nickname ADAM. The drug was also attacked on the basis of studies purporting to show that it caused brain damage, and the media presented a familiar series of scares about the drug threatening to ravage the entire nation. The DEA undertook an emergency reclassification of the drug, placing it in the prohibitive Schedule I, on par with heroin and thus in an even more restrictive category than cocaine or morphine. The scheduling decision was immediately attacked, and contentious administrative law hearings followed in early 1985. The federal judge who initially reviewed the evidence recommended placing the drug in the permissive Schedule III, permitting use through medical prescription, and many medical experts and therapists were prepared to testify about the drug's positive properties. The times were wrong, however, for such an enlightened approach, and the emergency scheduling decision was confirmed in July.[21] The suppression of Ecstasy epitomizes the anti-drug movement at its worst, when it resorts to panic over-reaction to combat a questionable menace at the cost of potential gains in medical research.

In early 1985, then, Ecstasy became the subject of a drug panic in its own right, as well as a focal point for broader concerns over synthetics and designer drugs. The yuppie context alone ensured that the drug would be newsworthy: not recorded once in the media in 1984, Ecstasy received 73 references in 1985 alone. Media reports appeared in mainstream publications like *Newsweek, Time, Omni,* and *New York,* as well as in professional journals. Typical of the new wave of damaging Ecstasy exposés was the article in *Harper's Bazaar,* which issued a "Hug Drug Alert: The Agony of Ecstasy." *Doonesbury* cartoonist Gary Trudeau depicted drug-loving Uncle Duke expressing his horror at the prohibition, which would have dire effects on chemical research: "Sure, there are risks, but that's a small price to pay for progress." Duke then ruins his point by repeating the same phrase exactly, confirming charges that the drug damaged the brain, particularly the memory. The same criticisms of the drug's effects were made repeatedly in other outlets, though in a more serious context. *Psychology Today* warned that the drug really offered "Madness, Not Ecstasy."[22]

Images of insanity and brain damage were reinforced through the decade as stories continued to repeat claims about the drug's harmful effects, though the actual evidence remained controversial. It was rarely more convincing than the periodic scare stories that erupt on a regular basis about virtually every legal foodstuff and chemical used by Americans and that have done so much to generate public incredulity about these sporadic health warnings. More convincing were cases of

MDMA-related deaths in the Dallas area in the mid-1980s, incidents that perhaps reflected the drug's effects on patients with underlying cardiac disease.[23] Ecstasy was condemned on such slight evidence because it was labeled a designer drug. The parallels between Ecstasy, fentanyl and MPTP were slim indeed; all they really had in common was that all were laboratory products used to produce some kind of chemical high. But in the fevered atmosphere of mid-1980s anti-drug politics, all were equally blameworthy. "PCP, Ecstasy and fentanyl" were indiscriminately bracketed together in discussions of the new menace. In May 1985, the *Dallas Morning News* warned of a wave of new substances, including both synthetic heroin and Ecstasy; the *Sacramento Bee* was referring to Ecstasy in 1985 when it headlined "Legal Designer Drug Is Following in Cocaine's Tracks." When the book *Designer Drugs* appeared in 1986, the cover listed the names of the chief substances that together constituted "the number one problem we face," and below Crack were the names Dust, Ecstasy, MPTP, Crystal and China White. In 1989, a book for young adults about designer drugs addressed four major substances—fentanyl, Ecstasy, PCP and methamphetamine.[24] The same year, publicity material for the educational film *Designer Drugs and Human Physiology* described PCP, Ecstasy and fentanyl as "concentrated synthetics that are illegally formulated in clandestine laboratories for enormous profit. [The film] shows the devastating effects of these drugs on the human cardiovascular and neurological systems."

That the boundary between licit and illicit drugs depends upon their symbolic associations was indicated yet again in exactly the years that Ecstasy was under such devastating assault. At just this time, another designer drug with somewhat similar effects was beginning a brilliantly successful career as a universal panacea and consequently as a commercial triumph. In 1987, following the approved range of official trials, the Lilly Corporation marketed its antidepressant Prozac, which, like Ecstasy, alters mood by manipulating levels of neurotransmitter chemicals in the brain. Both drugs inhibit the reuptake of serotonin, thereby raising its levels in the brain: this has the effect of making users calmer and more confident. Prozac offered much the same range of wonder-drug accomplishments as had recently been claimed for MDMA. And like Ecstasy, Prozac's effects on some lives were so profound as to lead users to describe it as the foundation of a new spirituality. By the mid-nineties, Prozac was being prescribed to an estimated twenty million users worldwide, with five million regular consumers in the U.S. alone, and annual sales were projected to hit $4 billion by 2000. The drug's usage swelled through a kind of bracket creep as the conditions it was intended to treat expanded steadily, from depression and obsessive-compulsive disorder to panic disorders, premenstrual tension, chronic back pain and, in short, any personal malaise.[25]

As with Ecstasy, or indeed any effective medication, Prozac has its down side. Users might experience nausea, diarrhea or sexual dysfunction, and must take great care to avoid a potentially fatal combination with some other drugs, such as MAO-Inhibitors. And controversial claims were made from the drug's earliest days about its possible links with violent behavior, charges of a sort that, incidentally, were never made against MDMA. Lilly came under pressure in the early 1990s to warn users of possible outbreaks of suicidal behavior, and the company was sued by individuals who claimed that their violent acts were Prozac-inspired. Particularly bad publicity followed incidents in which mass killers were found to have used Prozac shortly before committing their crimes: in one such case in 1989, a Louisville man who had used the drug killed eight people in a murder rampage, and in 1998, a teenage Prozac user carried out a high school shooting spree in Oregon. Partly because of the feared side effects, some European countries have shied away from Prozac, preferring instead herbal remedies such as St. John's Wort. In response, defenders of Prozac note that excessive claims about side effects are inevitable in a society as litigious as the contemporary United States, and the drug's precise effects remain open to debate: the Prozac Defense has consistently failed in American courts. On the other hand, if effects of this sort were alleged against an illicit drug, with however weak a foundation, we can be certain that they would be trumpeted widely and uncritically and used to justify ferocious measures of suppression. And analogies to illicit drugs can be extended further: Prozac's defenders argue, fairly, that just because an individual has been using a particular drug does not necessarily imply that it directly caused a given act of violence—a position that could equally well be extended to users of illegal drugs like methamphetamine or PCP.[26]

The accumulation of charges against Prozac, justified or not, raises intriguing issues about the legal environment of approved pharmaceuticals. The FDA was notoriously slow about approving new drugs until the industry agreed in 1992 to pay large (six-figure) user fees to expedite the process. By 1997, the FDA had received over $320 million in fee income, mainly from the largest drug companies, enabling the agency to take on six hundred new employees to review applications. However, not a penny of this money can be used to track adverse reactions to the drugs once they have received the FDA stamp of approval. In contrast to the streamlined approval process, the observation of adverse drug reactions is relegated to a far less efficient and proactive system: once a pharmaceutical is approved, the work of exposing harmful effects is chiefly a matter for private activist groups and attorneys. Matters are unlikely to change as long as the pharmaceutical industry wields such enormous political power, not least through substantial campaign contributions to both major parties.[27]

While not doubting that Prozac is a worthwhile pharmaceutical breakthrough that has caused much good in many lives, one can't help but wonder why this drug went on to glory, while Ecstasy found itself in the company of chemical outlaws like fentanyl and MPTP. The main reason was that one drug arose through approved corporate channels, while the other did not. We can only imagine how Prozac would be regarded if the drug had been popularized through unofficial networks of therapists and had developed a reputation among nonspecialists for its pleasurable effects. Still worse, what if it had attracted a playful nickname like Feelgood? It would assuredly have been classified alongside Ecstasy and the other prohibited designer drugs.

Contrary to the predictions of the mid-eighties, the vast majority of the newly identified designer drugs failed to gain a significant market, and a "wave about to sweep the nation" receded to virtually nothing after 1986. Certainly there would be other deaths and lesser mishaps associated with synthetics, and fentanyl continued to enjoy a horrible reputation: through the early 1990s, there were sporadic reports of multiple deaths linked to "heroin's savage clone," this "serial killer" of the drug world. In early 1991, the appearance of fentanyl in heroin samples in the New York City region led to a dozen deaths and over a hundred known overdose cases, and 126 fentanyl-related deaths were officially recorded across the East Coast over the following two years. A major investigation led to the discovery of the nation's largest and most efficient fentanyl laboratory in Wichita, Kansas, which was raided in early 1993, stemming the drug's availability. Still, while designer drugs attracted continuing attention over the next decade through popular exposés and professional texts, the imagined wave of thousands of new analogues never emerged, or at least only a handful of the substances gained any following.[28]

If the warnings at the height of the 1985–86 crisis proved so false, we must then ask whether the expert analysis was wholly wrong, or if a genuine threat was forestalled by effective early intervention. Clearly, drug enforcement authorities would prefer to claim the latter, as a rare example in which an anti-drug campaign succeeded in eliminating its target. Undeniably, deterrence had some impact: drug users watch television and read the news like anybody else, and some at least became wary of anything that could turn them into frozen addicts. At the same time, Ecstasy flourished, even though as a Schedule I drug its users were subject to severe mandatory penalties even for first-time convictions, and this and other designer chemicals boomed as party drugs in the early nineties (see chapter 8). Deterrence worked in some cases, but not others.

The primary reason that designer drugs faded so rapidly was economic, a matter of changes in production and marketing. In a very short time, it became so much easier to obtain better-known substances with a stronger brand-name reputation, especially heroin, than to venture into the murky and speculative world of the fentanyl derivatives, the popularity of which had represented a strategy of desperation. Synthetic heroin was scarcely necessary when large and dependable new supplies of the real thing came on line in the late 1980s, with a dramatic increase in product purity, which reached close to 80 percent. When the drug could be consumed by snorting or smoking, the terrors associated with hypodermic needles were removed, above all the threat of AIDS, but also the danger of unknown contaminants. The new conditions made heroin available to a middle-

and even upper-class clientele. By the mid-nineties, heroin enjoyed a revived presence in popular culture through depictions in films like *Pulp Fiction, Killing Zoe* and *Trainspotting*, while numerous stories of overdose and death confirmed the drug's influence in rock music and anti-drug critics attacked the heroin chic of the fashion world. In 1997, President Clinton even claimed that "we now see in college campuses, in neighborhoods, heroin becoming increasingly the drug of choice."[29]

Meanwhile, a shift in manufacturing techniques permitted a revolutionary shift in the making of that old staple of the drug world, methamphetamine, which could now be produced from easily available precursors. Even at the height of the designer-drug vogue, between 1981 and 1984, half of synthetic-drug labs seized were still producing methamphetamine, and by 1988, the figure would exceed 80 percent.[30] Finally, the designer drug panic occurred in precisely the months when both the media and the urban drug culture were discovering the new method of marketing cocaine in its crack form, which for a while offered cheapness and accessibility beyond the dreams of the most enthusiastic advocates of the synthetics. Who needed a poor man's cocaine like PCP when the real thing was available for five or ten dollars a vial? The designer-drug crisis faded not because those chemicals ceased to exist, which they did not, but because drug users themselves shifted to other substances. And the media turned away from designer drugs when they found such rich copy in one of those newly popular substances above all—crack cocaine.

| FIVE |

The Menace That Went Away

The Ice Age, 1989–90

The narcotics nemesis of the nineties.
—Rep. Charles Rangel, 1989[1]

In retrospect, the synthetics scares of the early eighties look like a first draft for the real drug war, which started when crack hit the scene. The turning point was 1986, when the media discovered crack as perhaps the most fearsome problem in the long American encounter with illegal chemicals. The synthetics rapidly faded in significance, so that official concern about even PCP and Ecstasy went underground for several years. But synthetic drugs were still being used, and it was only a matter of time before concern reignited. By the end of the decade, their rediscovery by politicians and journalists would be mistaken for a reemergence of the substances themselves, and methamphetamine would again be the center of a drug panic, a nightmarish vision all the more exaggerated because of the precedent of crack: this long-established drug was now relabeled the new crack cocaine, the next drug epidemic. Ice, or smokable crystal methamphetamine, was believed to be the rising threat: during 1989 and early 1990, it was supposedly booming in popularity and was said to have the potential to overwhelm the nation in a few months or years.

Of course ice never became the drug of the nineties, and the prophecies of those months now look so exaggerated as to be ludicrous. This panic was a strictly regional event, largely confined to

Hawaii, and the language of epidemic and explosion arose from partisan and bureaucratic rivalries within that state. The transformation of this local concern into a national crisis was made possible by the existence of specialized agencies and investigative bodies focusing on drug issues and by the intensification of public expectations and fears following the crack scare. Public willingness to believe in an imminent ice age reflected the successful packaging of the new menace, with its symbolic associations with several contemporary nightmares: crack of course, but also other, subtler fears, including the threat of alien (particularly Asian) incursions into white, Anglo culture.

The ice panic grew directly out of the Reagan-era drug war, when drugs came to serve as a centerpiece for American domestic policy. Hostility to drug abuse became much more intense following the election of 1980, as the incoming conservative regime placed the anti-drug agenda in the forefront of its social priorities. A new prohibitionism was reflected in slogans such as "zero tolerance" and "Just say no," the latter being Nancy Reagan's personal contribution to the policy debate. Savage new criminal penalties went far in deterring white, casual drug users, a trend reinforced by new publicity concerning the grave effects of cocaine, which had for years been touted as harmful and nonaddictive. Indeed, earlier statements minimizing the harmful effects of the drug were now quoted to show the dangers of naive tolerance of any new substance. Bad publicity about drugs now surfaced regularly, most spectacularly from the deaths of celebrities. In 1982, entertainer John Belushi perished from a heroin-cocaine cocktail. In June 1986, the death of young basketball star Len Bias seemed to confirm allegations about the potentially lethal effects of cocaine: apparently, he used cocaine in a powdered form, though the ensuing publicity was employed to justify severe measures against crack. From about 1982, drug use nationwide began a steep and general decline among all age categories, reaching its trough in about 1992. The proportion of high school seniors who admitted having tried illegal drugs fell precipitously: in 1981, 12.4 percent of seniors reported having used cocaine in the previous twelve months, compared with only 3.1 percent by 1992 (see table 2.1 above). For all the rhetoric claiming an epidemic, Americans were in fact entering a comparatively clean and sober era.

Declining white and middle-class usage permitted the drug problem to be framed as a distinctively urban and minority phenomenon, especially as a black issue. This change in rhetoric was made easier by an authentic shift in usage patterns, as the growing popularity of crack cocaine from about 1984 displaced more established drugs and created the image of a crack epidemic, which was blamed for the appalling problems facing inner cities. In 1986, *Time* declared the crack problem the issue of the year, and *Newsweek* proclaimed it the biggest story since Vietnam and Watergate. NBC's *Nightly News* remarked how crack was "flooding America" as "America's drug of choice." Much-quoted estimates claimed that crack was enslaving three thousand new users each day, a million every year. These fears made it easier for the federal government to demonize all illicit drugs and resort to stringent law-enforcement solutions, abandoning any consideration of therapeutic alternatives or social intervention.[2]

The new approach emphasized strict repression of drug use, with extensive use of paramilitary tactics against a drug underworld seen as an evil empire within America's own frontiers. In early 1985, the news media published their first reports of fortified crack houses, which were scenes of open drug-taking and sexual excess, and shortly afterwards the LAPD used armored vehicles and battering rams to smash into such premises. These tactics were in keeping with the ideas of LAPD chief Darryl Gates, who in the 1970s had sponsored the city's pioneering SWAT team. Partly because of Gates's own family problems with substance abuse (his son was repeatedly arrested for drug-related offenses), he was fanatically opposed to any softening of public attitudes toward the drug crisis. His department initiated the Drug Abuse Resistance Education Program (DARE), which carried the message of the absolute evil of all illegal drugs to schools across the country. In 1990, Gates told the Senate Judiciary Committee that, quite simply, "The casual drug user ought to be taken out and shot."[3] By this point, his views sounded neither extreme nor eccentric, as the Gates/LAPD approach to drugs had become national orthodoxy.

The drug war was in full spate. In 1986, a sweeping federal law permitted the military to gather intelligence in the war on drugs and massively increased criminal penalties for users, dealers and traffickers. Mandatory life sentences were provided, and harsh minimum sentences enforced. Charges that rivals were soft on drugs flew freely during the congressional election campaigns of that year, as conservatives realized they had acquired a potent ideological weapon. As Reagan's press secretary declared during the 1988 elections, "everybody wants to out-drug each other in terms of political rhetoric."[4] That same year, William Bennett was appointed federal drug czar—head of the White House Office of National Drug Control Policy—with the charge of coordinating drug-control strategies.

Reactions to the crack epidemic reached a climax at the end of the decade, when President George Bush made combating it a key component of his domestic agenda and drugs conditioned U.S. foreign and defense policy. In 1989, American activism against international traffickers provoked a near-civil war in the nation of Colombia and led to an actual invasion of Panama that December. Drug fears led to an official redefinition of national security as the concept of narco-terrorism was born. The incessant diet of alarming stories had its impact: the proportion of Americans citing drug abuse as the nation's most important problem soared from 3 percent in 1986 to 64 percent in 1989. In September 1989, the president made a nationally televised address on drug-control strategy in which he stated, "All of us agree that the gravest domestic threat facing our nation today is drugs . . . our most serious problem today is cocaine, and in particular, crack." The president asserted that the drug was "as innocent-looking as candy, but it is turning our cities into battle zones, and it is murdering our children. Let there be no mistake, this stuff is poison."[5]

The drug war had far-reaching social consequences, not least in vastly expanding the resources available to criminal justice agencies to fight narcotics: the DEA fielded 1,900 special agents in 1980, 2,900 in 1989, and 3,400 by 1998, while in 1997, the agency boasted its first billion-dollar budget. The amount of federal money spent on drug-control efforts grew from $3 billion in 1986 to $8 billion in 1990, and from almost $12 billion by 1992 to $15 billion by 1997. By

1998, the federal government was spending $1.7 billion annually just on drug-control activities along the U.S.-Mexican border, where a force of 7,700 special agents was mobilized. And those figures do not include the massive anti-drug spending by state and city agencies, such as California's BNE: many states acquired their own bureaucratic hierarchies of narcotics enforcement, including local drug czars. Drugs also had an untold impact on the correctional system. Prison populations swelled dramatically from the mid-1980s, mainly due to the incarceration of nonviolent drug offenders. Between 1985 and 1997, the American incarceration rate more than doubled, from 313 to 645 per hundred thousand population: in New York State, about a quarter of the prisoners entering the jails and prisons in the mid-1990s were drug-only offenders, with no record for other types of crime.[6] As a major employer and a significant component of the economy in most states, the penal-industrial complex became yet another force supporting strict anti-drug policies.

The ever-expanding scope of criminal forfeiture came close to making the drug war self-financing. Under a 1970 law, authorities were permitted to seize any goods or property intended to be used in connection with drug manufacture or trafficking, a concept soon extended to cover monies: the Omnibus Crime Control law of 1984 allowed agencies to seize any property allegedly used in connection with the narcotics trade. Cumulatively, the new legal apparatus meant that goods could be confiscated even if the actual owners of the property were unaware of the illegal conduct for which it had been used and by means of a process in which the accused possessed few rights. In a 1996 decision that partly concerned the prosecution of two alleged methamphetamine dealers, the U.S. Supreme Court ruled that authorities could seize assets through a civil procedure in addition to prosecuting offenders criminally, even though this was a prima facie violation of the constitutional guard against double jeopardy. As confiscated goods could then be used to fund further anti-drug efforts, state, city and local agencies had a vast incentive to seek out drug trafficking, and many certainly cut legal corners in the process: who was prepared to defend the rights of alleged drug dealers? In 1993 alone, the U.S. Justice Department seized property valued at over $600 million, to say nothing of seizures by other bodies.[7]

There was in short an enormous vested interest in adopting the harshest possible view of illicit drugs, while the mass media showed absolute credulity in reporting claims from the drug-enforcement bureaucracy. The range of acceptable opinions about drug policy narrowed frighteningly in these years. Advocates of decriminalization had long been shut out from the debate, but now it became impossible for any but the most courageous politicians or professionals to advocate the kind of tolerance freely discussed in the Carter era. By the late 1980s, a similar taboo extended to suggestions that drug treatment might replace warlike criminal justice responses. The televised stereotype of drug control involved groups of heavily armed and armored paramilitary police units storming supposed crack houses, scenes that provided the staple of the true-crime and real-life-policing shows that proliferated in these years. Though agencies justified this Rambo approach in terms of the heavy weapons that dealers were presumed to possess, the effect of such nightly images was to suggest that American cities had become literal war zones, under siege from the drugs, though it is open to question whether the violence stemmed from the substances themselves or from the repression they inspired.[8]

The drug-war era promised rich political dividends for any group or individual who could successfully draw attention to a plausible new drug menace and create a clamor over substance abuse in the public marketplace of social problems. Moreover, the precedent of crack gave anti-drug advocates an ideal prefabricated script that could be used to spread their message. Declaring a drug the next crack cocaine, or as addictive as crack, created an instant public resonance.

The first of the new post-crack scares involved methamphetamine, which was of course anything but a new drug. As we have seen, it had been manufactured illegally at least since 1962, and by the late 1970s, methamphetamine had become the main product of the nation's clandestine laboratories, which shifted away from other synthetics like PCP and LSD. This trend may have reflected an increasingly tough police line against PCP, as well as years of horrendous publicity concerning the effects of that drug. The rate of meth lab seizures boomed in the mid-1980s, though this alone should not necessarily be taken as a sign of increased speed production, as the legislation allowing police agencies to confiscate drug-related property gave them an incentive to intervene more proactively. A better index of usage comes from the emergency rooms contributing statistics to the DAWN system, which did indeed show a steady growth of methamphetamine-related events from 1985 to 1987.

The major reason for the growing popularity of methamphetamine was technological change. During the speed capital years of the early 1980s, speed cooks relied on imported supplies of P2P, but an alternative ephedrine/red phosphorus method removed the need for a controlled precursor chemical. Would-be chemists could now make methamphetamine entirely from domestic legal materials. Laboratories required no elaborate facilities or natural resources, and distribution demanded little more than convenient access to the interstate highway network. Speed manufacture was attractive because the process required little expertise, and detailed instructions could be found in cheap, hands-on manuals like the comprehensive *Secrets of Methamphetamine Manufacture* by the pseudonymous Uncle Fester, who claims to have been involved in the business since the late 1970s.[9] As the old economic law holds, supply creates its own demand, and increasing supplies of speed may well have generated new markets.

The drug could also be very profitable, as a laboratory could make five to ten pounds of methamphetamine in a week, and the pure substance would usually be cut repeatedly for street sale. A lab's annual production could theoretically be worth several million dollars, though few labs operated so consistently over long periods. In 1989, a Dallas police officer remarked, "We think the profit is much greater when we look at methamphetamine production, as compared to heroin or cocaine. We know that an investment of $3,000 to $4,000 in chemicals, in glassware, can turn a profit of $25,000 to $30,000."[10] This was a much more realistic evaluation of the scale of production for an average lab than the multimillion-dollar profits implied by other police accounts in these years. Both the use and manufacture of methamphetamine tended to be strongly regionalized. Philadelphia may or may not have been the speed capital of the world in 1980, but there certainly were many labs in the area, and other regions played a similar role in later years. Later in the decade, the focus of media attention shifted decisively to the western United States, though it is open to question whether this reflected an authentic change in production patterns. In the mid-1980s, the city of Eugene, Oregon, was a major manufacturing center, while some observers stressed the importance of both San Diego and the San Francisco Bay Area. In 1987 and 1988, over three hundred methamphetamine laboratories were seized in the San Diego area alone, and the city's police chief Bob Burgreen complained in 1989 that his city "is to crystal what Bogota is to cocaine." In 1986, a member of the California BNE complained, "We are the leading state in production of methamphetamines and the problem is growing worse all the time. These labs are everywhere. Our Sacramento field office can't seize them fast enough to keep up." The western concentration of labs and usage is confirmed by drug tests performed on arrestees in selected cities under the Drug Use Forecasting (DUF) system. By 1990, the proportion of individuals testing positive for methamphetamine was 25 percent in San Diego, and a little over 10 percent in San Jose, Phoenix and Portland, Oregon, with some use recorded in Denver, Dallas, Los Angeles and Seattle.[11]

Within particular areas, the drug appealed to subcultures that were quite distinct from the stereotypical crack user: most significantly, they tended to be white rather than black. Nationally, in the late 1980s, "the typical methamphetamine user is a white male 22 to 26 years of age, who is employed in a blue-collar job. The most frequently cited occupations are in the construction trades and the trucking industry." In the San Diego region, "abusing populations are predominantly white, lower middle income, high school educated, young adults ranging in age from 18-35 years." And a Texas police officer stated, "The persons who we most often encounter in Dallas, the users we most often encounter are primarily Caucasian, primarily lower income. . . . This group of methamphetamine users is mainly comprised of bikers, topless dancers, prostitutes, and those involved in auto theft rings."[12]

Ice users also differed from the underclass stereotypes familiar from crack. In Hawaii, ice was "popular in the workplace, particularly among blue collar workers, people who do mechanical tasks, and it has also spread into office workplaces as well . . . [it is] the drug of choice for on the job use in Honolulu. . . . It is generally in the blue collar community and the service community." Women were particularly vulnerable: "In Honolulu, most ice users range in age from the late teens to the early thirties. The drug is popular with young women, perhaps because users tend to lose weight."[13] Anecdotal evidence suggests that many women users were introduced to the drug by boyfriends and husbands, who wished to explore its effects in enhancing sexual pleasure.

Meth's appeal extended into the gay clubs and bars, where indeed the nickname "crystal" was popularized. The enduring gay vogue for crystal is not hard to explain, given the crucial importance of that community in San Francisco, where the long-established tradition of speed use had never entirely succumbed to later fads for drugs like cocaine. By the nineties, crystal meth had become a fixture of gay club life: the drug was advertised through variations on the code word "party," so that someone advertising in a contact magazine as a party boy was likely to be a crystal supplier as well as a sexual partner. In southern California, one estimate placed the number of regular crystal users in the gay section of West Hollywood by the mid-1990s at around ten thousand. The question "Why love crystal?" on the graffiti-covered "talking wall" in San Francisco's Castro District drew many answers, including these: "Sex fantasies become real," "Similar to coke but cheaper," "Being able to dance forever," and "The community is full of grief, and people just want to go out and party." The drug's aphrodisiac effects were blamed for undermining safe-sex campaigns, which had been successfully reducing the number of new AIDS infections. A British journalist observed in Los Angeles that "crystal has in recent years become a gay men's drug. It has a liberating as well as a stimulatory effect, and enables users to stay up for hours, often days, indulging in abandoned sex with multiple partners. Its disinhibitory effect means users temporarily forget about safe sex." By the mid-1990s, crystal was being cited as a factor in roughly half of all new AIDS cases in Los Angeles County.[14]

Regional patterns shaped the ways the drug was consumed. Methamphetamine can be injected, smoked, snorted or ingested orally, and local subcultures vary in their tastes and traditions. Intravenous use offers the most intense rush, but also features severe drawbacks. Unless they already belong to a subculture in which needle use is a commonly accepted practice, usually for injecting heroin, most novice or casual users tend to be repelled by this method. Injecting also poses a high risk of dependency. Smoking is a much more approachable method, though by the late 1980s this had unfortunate connotations from the crack scare, and smokable methamphetamine needed to be of very high purity. Even an aficionado like the drug-chemist Uncle Fester was "not going to endorse or encourage the foolhardy practice of smoking meth."[15] By far the most common method of consumption was snorting, a technique popularized during the glamorous boom years of powdered cocaine in the late 1970s. This offered the lowest risks of dependence, overdose and infection, and was most easily reconciled with maintaining a job and a regular life. Snorting was the means particularly favored by many white, working-class users, though a striking number did eventually graduate to the traditional speed-freak technique of injection.

The vogue for smokable ice developed in Hawaii and some western states, under the influence of the wider Pacific Rim region. Amphetamines had long been popular in Japan and other East Asian countries, where, though illegal, these drugs were stigmatized far less severely than opiates, cocaine or even marijuana. Some estimates place the number of regular amphetamine (*shabu*) users in Japan alone at over half a million in the 1980s. Smokable methamphetamine became fashionable among upwardly mobile urban dwellers in several Pacific Rim nations, including Taiwan, South Korea and the Philippines. Illicit markets were supplied by sizable narcotic networks with roots in organized crime, including the Chinese Triads and the Japanese Yakuza. The Yakuza manufactured methamphetamine in South Korea, from which they supplied much of East Asia, and Triad gangs were active in Hong Kong, while distributors might be nationals of any of a dozen Asian nations. It was not surprising, then, to find an ice habit developing in the state of Hawaii, which finds so many of its cultural and economic affinities in East Asia and where Japanese organized crime had developed a foothold. Yakuza-supplied amphetamines were identified in the state during the 1970s, and Korean-manufactured methamphetamine appeared in the following decade. From 1987 onwards, island authorities identified an ice problem, which was linked to Filipino youth gangs and Korean groups.[16] The drug was largely imported at this stage, as few American garage or backyard labs were capable of achieving the high purity required for the smokable form of the drug. The presence of the huge naval facility at San Diego helps explain the taste for an Asian fashion in that city.

In 1989, American officialdom discovered the ice problem. Police found evidence of manufacture and importation, first in Hawaii and subsequently in and around San Diego. Twenty southern California meth labs were raided by federal agencies during March 1989 alone, and concern about ice in Hawaii was given a new focus that same month by the uncovering of a substantial importation ring. There were few signs of any wider threat, and even in Hawaii, the problem was largely confined to Oahu proper, but a media campaign now emphasized the national dangers posed by the new drug habit.[17]

Familiar code words presaged the onset of a drug panic. The *Los Angeles Times* was one of many sources to warn that a "Potent Form of Speed Could be Drug of 90s," and the *Economist* noted that ice was a drug that could make crack seem almost benign. The theme of national danger was taken up by all the major regional newspapers and national newsmagazines, as well as by specialized publications serving the medical and pharmaceutical communities. Jeremiads about ice were most frequently heard between about September 1989 and February 1990, and this anti-ice movement can be closely associated with the two major congressional hearings on the topic. In October 1989, Charles Rangel's House Committee on Narcotics Abuse and Control addressed *The Re-Emergence of Methamphetamine,* while a follow-up session called the *Drug Crisis in Hawaii* was held in Honolulu the following January, amidst criticisms that hearings in such an enviable location were little more than a congressional junket.[18] These hearings offered the media a wealth of material about the supposed ice age, and between September and December 1989, major stories appeared in all of the main metropolitan newspapers. The *New York Times* gave an ice-related story pride of place on the front page of the paper's main section, and equal prominence was given to similar stories on the front pages of the *Los Angeles Times* and the *Chicago Tribune*: that October, the *L.A. Times* presented four stories on ice within a nine-day period.[19] As this outpouring of concern came only weeks after Bush's apocalyptic televised speech about the crack menace, the public was sensitized to drug nightmares to an unprecedented degree. Even as the crack war continued, the ice age was beginning.

Certain themes and ideas recurred with striking regularity in the congressional hearings: ice was new, potent and dangerous, and it had acquired high prestige as the new in drug, so it was assumed that usage was about to expand rapidly, creating a national menace comparable to crack cocaine. Every ice age story was buttressed by the opinions of prominent law-enforcement officials, police and prosecutors, together with academics and doctors. The potential epidemic thus appeared both plausible and threatening.

The central argument was that where Hawaii led today, the rest of the nation would soon follow. The record of "Ice in an Island Paradise" was alarming, as ice "has escalated in such leaps and bounds that we have not been able to keep pace." Supposedly, there were already signs of a wider spread. Honolulu police chief Douglas Gibb told how a New York City Korean gang had flown members to Honolulu to attack some local Samoans: "The whole purpose . . . was to come into town to establish a connection for ice, a line for ice to take back to New York." He continued: "It is probably only a matter of time until other parts of the country start to see crystal meth and its attendant problems . . . we fully expect the Ice Age to spread east from Hawaii." Committee member Stan Parris noted, "We have got ice in Virginia . . . it is for sure coming our way and we had better get ready for it," while Hawaii state representative Daniel Akaka claimed, "Reports are already filtering in of ice use in New York and Washington, D.C." The idea that ice was gradually penetrating areas of the mainland gave a local angle for media reporting of the drug in cities such as Atlanta, Boston and Philadelphia. *Rolling Stone* quoted law-enforcement views that the Hawaiian epidemic would soon reach the mainland, where the drug would surpass both heroin and cocaine, marking a new and still more deadly era in drug abuse.[20]

One paradox was that by its nature, ice negated some of the obvious advantages of methamphetamine: as it was still largely an imported drug, it faced all of the obstacles and expense involved in crossing national borders. Still, witnesses at the hearings repeatedly emphasized that domestic manufacturers would soon learn to reproduce Asian techniques so that ice would conquer the American market. As a

Dallas police officer declared, "We have cooks, we have numerous cooks scattered throughout the country, literally thousands of persons who are qualified to make methamphetamine. So, we have the processes in place to make ice. I think we also have a ready consumer market out there, individuals who want the drug. I have no doubt that ice will come to the United States."[21] The notion of an epidemic was evocative, with all the word's implications of plague, disease and uncontrollable spread. During the congressional hearings, Hawaii's U.S. Attorney Daniel Bent described Hawaiian ice usage as already being an epidemic. When a DEA spokesman denied that an ice epidemic was imminent, he was taken to task by the committee, as "epidemic" was a politically valuable concept that would not be lightly yielded: Representative Tom Lewis of Florida described the spokesman's opinion as "irresponsible" and "lackadaisical." Other potent terms included "deluge," "plague" and "crisis": Congressman Rangel remarked that Honolulu police were "deluged" by ice, sociologist Elliott Currie spoke of "this hidden methamphetamine plague," and the January hearings of the Narcotics Subcommittee were explicitly devoted to the "Drug Crisis in Hawaii." Speaking of an "emerging" crisis suggested that what had gone before was trivial compared to what was to come.[22]

The very term "ice" offered potential for journalists seeking attention-grabbing headlines: the phrase "ice age" implied that the drug could somehow so dominate American society that it could give its name to an era. This phrase was employed by both Police Chief Gibb and Daniel Akaka in the congressional hearings, and it was used for major investigative accounts in *Rolling Stone* in 1990 and in the *Washington Post* in 1991. "Ice" further suggested the concept of chilling: the *Atlanta Constitution* headlined "Police Chilled By New In-Drug: Ice," and the *Christian Science Monitor* warned, "Ice Chills U.S. Anti-Drug Officials."[23]

The ice panic would have been inconceivable without the immediate precedent of crack cocaine, and there were superficial parallels between the two drugs. The crack analogy made ice an attractive and easily comprehended menace, so parallels were repeatedly hammered home in the congressional hearings. Ice was accused of causing as much social damage as cocaine in terms of overdoses and emergency-room admissions. And Representative Akaka stated that in Hawaii, ice contributed to the problems that elsewhere were linked to crack: "ice-addicted babies, gang activities, turf battles and hospital emergency cases of overdoses. . . . this drug has the capacity to drag our country even deeper into the dark abyss created by crack." He continued, "It doesn't make any difference whether it is ice, crack, crank, cocaine. We are losing kids. We are corrupting our police departments. We are corrupting our political arena. We are breaking up families." Daniel Bent claimed that ice "is presenting the same problems to Hawaii as crack cocaine has in areas of the Continental United States in terms of its popularity, availability, addiction potential and destructiveness." The two drugs appeared all but indistinguishable, to the point that Akaka asked a witness, "Can you explain to me the differences between crack, crank, ice and croak?"[24]

Witnesses even claimed that Hawaii was seeing the birth of a generation of crystal meth babies. This concept was so potent because the dreadful imagery of crack babies had been so much in the news over the previous two or three years, with the implication that the drug left children permanently impaired, unable to engage in any normal human interaction. Around this time, the Department of Health and Human Services (DHHS) was projecting the birth of perhaps a hundred thousand such crack babies, at an annual cost to society running into many billions of dollars: indeed, drug czar William Bennett made the astonishing suggestion that perhaps one tenth of all babies born in the U.S. might be crack-impaired. In response, legislatures nationwide tried to penalize women who gave birth to such "addicted babies," or at least to force pregnant users into treatment programs: this was the age of what has been called the pregnancy police. More recently, the concept of mothers delivering drugs to unborn babies has even been extended to include drug-using mothers breastfeeding their infants, and at least one criminal conviction has been obtained in such a methamphetamine-related incident. Of course the whole crack baby theme was vastly exaggerated, as observers were assuming that birth defects suffered by the children of poor women in ill health were drug-related. The notion was nevertheless widely credited by a media that knew better than to challenge such a magnificently pathetic story, which helped reinforce the indictment of methamphetamine. Who could permit the birth of a generation of ice babies?[25]

In some ways, ice could be made to appear even more dangerous than crack. It cost less and offered a longer high, reported to be anywhere from four to fourteen hours, compared to a few minutes for crack. Ice also lacked the frightening features that might safeguard individuals from experimenting with other substances, as it did not require injection like heroin does. And while crack was associated with cultures of violence and extreme urban poverty, methamphetamine was linked to hard work and long study, and insofar as it had any racial overtones, these were white or Asian. Ice could appeal to white or Asian middle-class people, with teenagers being especially at risk. In the loaded words of a *Good Housekeeping* article, ice was a "New drug nice kids can get hooked on." The suggestion was that ice could wreak havoc in all sections of society, not merely in the inner cities. Representative Rangel was tapping into potent fears when he wrote that "we shudder to think of what would happen in this country if the devastation of the crack crisis were doubled or even tripled by adding on a whole new layer of illicit drug abuse."[26] Ice was an urgent danger to nice kids, to suburbanites, to white people.

Why was the ice menace created at the time it was, and why, given the slim foundations on which it rested, did it achieve such instant credibility? At first sight, we might be tempted to blame official bodies like the DEA or FBI, who have a decades-long record of using crime scares to generate support for increased resources, but such an interpretation would not apply on this occasion. Indeed, the DEA minimized the ice problem, in sharp contrast to the hysteria of the politicians. Instead of examining national agencies, we should consider instead the needs of the political interests within Hawaii that first identified an ice epidemic and that served as the source for most of the claims disseminated nationwide. The major claims-makers heard by the congressional committees included two leading figures in the state's law-enforcement bureaucracy, namely Honolulu police chief Gibb and U.S. Attorney Bent. The evidence offered by these two witnesses took up over a third of the total testimony presented during the

October hearings, and both stressed the overwhelming nature of the ice threat. As in the case of the DEA, an ice panic would undoubtedly enhance the reputation of local police agencies, as well as their access to resources. In addition, the powerful office of U.S. Attorney often provides the opportunity for any incumbent to win prestige and visibility that can subsequently be translated into a wider political career. Though both men were presenting their honestly held opinions concerning the ice problem, both also had a clear bureaucratic interest in formulating the issue in a particular way.

Local electoral politics also shaped official interpretations, though this would not have been obvious to the vast majority of observers, who were unacquainted with the details of Hawaiian factional squabbles. At the opening of the 1989 hearings, which put ice on the map of American social problems, Congressman Rangel stressed that the impetus for concern came chiefly from the Hawaiian congressional delegation of U.S. Representatives Daniel Akaka and Patricia Saiki. Both had a strong interest in appearing active in drug issues and in adopting hard-line, anti-drug stances; both stood to benefit from making ice look as perilous and threatening as possible; and both emerge as classic moral entrepreneurs. Their actions must be seen in the context of recent political developments in the state of Hawaii, traditionally one of the most loyally Democratic in the nation: throughout the 1980s, both of its Democratic U.S. senators could regularly count on receiving 70 to 80 percent of votes cast, and the governor's office remained in firm Democratic hands throughout these years. Republicans were poorly placed, winning offices chiefly when Democratic factions were split, as occurred when Saiki won the First Congressional District. By 1989, she had retained this in two elections, but with ever slimmer majorities. Meanwhile, Democrat Akaka had remained firmly in control of the Second District in every contest since 1976.[27]

Crime and drug matters—law and order—offered the only area of potential vulnerability for Democrats, and conversely a potential source of strength for Saiki's Republican Party. Throughout the decade, Democratic authorities were involved in multiple corruption scandals that exposed alleged links between organized crime and the labor unions, which play so crucial a role in state Democratic politics.

These incidents reached a climax in 1984 with the investigation by Honolulu's city/county prosecutor, Republican Charles F. Marsland, into a series of gangland murders; Marsland targeted a political ally of Democratic governor George Ariyoshi as the alleged godfather of organized crime in the state.[28] While the ensuing scandals and lawsuits did not destroy Democratic power—in fact, the next governor, elected in 1986, was a close associate of Ariyoshi—the incident did suggest one area in which Democrats could be attacked. Akaka himself, an Ariyoshi protégé, could potentially be associated with the ethnically Hawaiian "godfather" at the center of the scandals. In the following years, Saiki and Akaka clashed repeatedly on crime-related issues: for instance, Saiki voted for a federal measure to extend the death penalty to major drug dealers, which Akaka opposed.

The rivalry between the two grew all the more significant in 1989, as it became increasingly likely that both would soon be vying for a U.S. Senate seat. The junior senator's position was currently held by Spark Matsunaga, a popular figure first elected in 1972, but health problems meant that he was unlikely to run in 1990. Within a year, Saiki would be challenging Akaka for the hitherto solidly Democratic Senate seat, and the balance in this apparently unequal match could be tipped in a number of ways. One would be the ethnic factor: Akaka is a native Hawaiian, Saiki a Japanese American, so she would be likely to appeal to the Japanese Americans who comprised the strongest faction in the Democratic Party. In addition, Republicans were likely to portray the relatively liberal Akaka as soft on drugs and organized crime. But Akaka found an opportunity to rebut such anticipated charges through his membership in the House Subcommittee on Narcotic Abuse. Though both Hawaiian representatives needed media credentials as anti-drug crusaders, local ethnic and partisan alignments circumscribed the kinds of campaign rhetoric that would be appropriate. While organized crime was denounced enthusiastically, little of the ice rhetoric focused on the specifically Japanese component of drug manufacture and distribution or on the role of the Yakuza, so frequently described by other law-enforcement agencies and investigators. Perhaps the forthcoming electoral contests made candidates muffle such accusations for fear of perpetrating ethnic slurs against one of the most influential communities in the islands.

In fact, both Akaka and Saiki succeeded in gaining significant political capital out of the ice issue. Saiki earned credit for having brought the problem to national attention and for requesting increased anti-drug resources. But Akaka also benefited: it was Akaka who introduced the potent term "ice age" in the hearings and who drew some of the starkest analogies between ice and crack. Thus both rivals confirmed their roles as standard-bearers of their respective parties. When Senator Matsunaga died a few months afterwards, in April 1990, Akaka was the natural choice to fill the unexpired portion of his term, and both he and Saiki easily won the nominations of their parties for the November election. That contest should have been a Democratic walkover, but Saiki had so established her prestige that she made it a close race and lost only narrowly to Akaka, who became the first native Hawaiian in the U.S. Senate.[29]

Domestic politics made it likely that Hawaii's two state representatives would focus on a drug problem of local significance, but it was by no means obvious that these issues would come to wider attention, as Hawaiian conditions and controversies rarely impinge on the national media. That opportunity was provided by Akaka's service on the narcotics subcommittee, where he was aided by Pennsylvania representative Lawrence Coughlin, who had been so active in exposing Philadelphia as speed capital in 1980. Coughlin, now the ranking Republican on the subcommittee, was instrumental in bringing Akaka's views to the attention of Rangel, and Coughlin's advocacy was significant in showing that ice was causing concern far outside Hawaii and could legitimately be presented as a national issue. Coughlin was a long-standing protagonist of the notion of a speed menace, and it is not surprising to see the limited experience of Hawaii extrapolated to the entire nation in the 1989–90 hearings, just as had happened to Philadelphia conditions a decade previous. For Rangel, meanwhile, it was advantageous to focus attention on a drug issue that, unlike crack, did not chiefly afflict African Americans and other urban minorities. The ice affair showed that other ethnic groups shared these problems.

Ice, then, had the potential to cause havoc in geographical, social and ethnic settings as yet untouched by crack. Moreover, a plausible ice danger could easily have flourished on the strength of existing ethnic and xenophobic stereotypes, given the drug's Pacific Rim connotations. Yakuza drug dealers could well have attracted the stigma that decades earlier had adhered to gangsters from immigrant ethnic groups such as Jews and Italians. Moreover, the time seemed exactly right for a new form of Japan-bashing: the late 1980s were marked by growing anti-Japanese rhetoric in the United States, as many Americans feared that they were letting down their economic defenses in the face of an overwhelming Asian challenge. Some Japanese financial incursions proved traumatic, notably the takeovers of media giants like Columbia pictures in 1989 and MCA/Universal the following year. A spate of major books on these themes included Pat Choate's *Agents of Influence,* Burstein's *Japan's New Financial Empire and Its Threat to America,* and the fictional account in Michael Crichton's bestselling *Rising Sun.* One 1991 title even forecast *The Coming War with Japan.* Hawaii was a sensitive element in this overall picture, and a 1986 book on the Yakuza already called that state the forty-eighth prefecture, annexing it to the forty-seven administrative units of the Japanese home islands.[30] Both press and congressional reports in these years often stressed the Japanese origins of the ice habit and the ice imported into the western United States.

Yet of course the ice danger did not materialize as a national crisis, still less an international one; the prospective plague faded rapidly in early 1990. Media accounts became far less frequent from February onwards, and there were virtually none between August 1990 and the spring of 1991. Through the 1980s, the print media surveyed by LEXIS/NEXIS showed a dramatic rise in stories concerning crystal methamphetamine, reaching a high point in 1990, but the number of stories soon plummeted, as warnings of an epidemic had proved illusory. Indeed, evidence from the emergency rooms suggests that methamphetamine usage actually fell somewhat between 1988 and 1991.[31]

The sudden eclipse of the ice problem requires explanation. One difficulty facing anti-drug advocates was that claims about the drug were so blatantly overblown, so that, for example, early reports about large numbers of ice-related deaths were soon proved inflated. Early

Table 5.1 Crystal Methamphetamine in the
Mass Media, 1985–95

Year	Number of News Stories
1985	55
1986	122
1987	155
1988	115
1989	168
1990	401
1991	74
1992	48
1993	54
1994	106
1995	184

in the 1989 campaign, Honolulu police chief Gibb had stated that over the previous four years, "there have been 32 deaths in Honolulu attributed to ice," including eight homicides and seven suicides. But on closer examination, this meant rather that "32 people were confirmed to have crystal methamphetamine in their system at the time of deaths," which establishes no causal link between the drug and the fatality.[32] On further examination, the number of "ice-related deaths" in Hawaii in a given period plummeted from thirty-two or so to three, and the media eventually became chary about reporting related statistics.

Interestingly, the DEA itself was not enthusiastic about promoting the new threat. During the October hearings, one agency spokesman commented, "I can confirm there is a drug out there called ice, which is certainly bad news. But DEA agents are not looking for it yet. . . . It will take a while for ice to proliferate. When we get reports from police departments that ice has gotten to be at the epidemic state, such as crack did in 1985, then we will move in."[33] The reasons for DEA's caution are not difficult to find, since at this stage the agency simply did not need additional support in order to seek increased resources and powers. It was already doing wonderfully well from the crack clamor, and in late 1989, the president was arguing that the drug-control budget for the coming year should be raised by over a third from the 1989 figure, to eight billion dollars. Moreover, showing caution on the highly speculative ice issue enhanced the agency's credibility about other claims.

Confirmation of a national spread of the drug, the feared epidemic, failed to arrive. In January 1990, the head of the DEA's Honolulu office wrote that ice was still confined to Hawaii and "very limited West Coast areas," and that otherwise "we know of no ice samples [having] been analyzed elsewhere in the United States." Though amphetamine use was widespread in a few western cities like San Diego, the figures did not appear to be growing. Though many people surveyed knew the substance by reputation, overwhelmingly their knowledge had been acquired from the media rather than from information provided by friends or dealers, even in a center like San Diego. Nationwide, the proportion who admitted ever having used ice nowhere exceeded three percent (though no Hawaiian community was included in the survey). Other survey data presented a similar picture. For instance, ice had made only limited inroads among sex workers in San Francisco, even among those already using methamphetamine in other forms.[34] Based on such data, law-enforcement and DEA officials concluded that the danger of ice had been substantially overstated, and media rhetoric subsided within a few months of the congressional hearings.

Is this in fact one instance in which a burgeoning panic was derailed by a sober, objective assessment of the claims offered? If so, it would be in stark contrast to most such movements, in which repeated reality checks have little effect on quelling public fears. Two factors made this particular panic relatively easy to control. One was the authoritative nature of the sources expressing scepticism, particularly the DEA, which had acquired great public respect in previous years. If this agency saw no great problem, then perhaps the scare did indeed reflect media hype. Also critical was the timing. Even in the face of DEA caveats, the ice problem still retained a fair degree of momentum through the first half of 1990, right up until the month of August, when it died abruptly. This change can be directly attributed to the media's intense new concern with political affairs in the Middle East, following the Iraqi invasion of Kuwait that August and the growing likelihood of impending war: the threat from Saddam Hussein dominated the headlines from August through the following

March. The media found new and far more important things to become alarmed about, and public concern about drugs fell correspondingly. Even the crack issue no longer inspired such instant terror, while ice was dismissed as a fad: the ice age perished, scarcely mourned, barely even noticed.

The CAT Attack, 1993–94

The scenario seems right out of some science fiction nightmare. A dangerous addictive drug that is cheap and easy to manufacture appears out of nowhere, and creates a potential drug crisis. . . . Unfortunately, it isn't science fiction. It isn't fiction. It is Indiana's most recent drug threat—methcathinone.

—William J. Bailey, 1995[1]

With its recent experience of ice in mind, the media should have been doubly careful when presented with a comparable barrage of claims about another new substance, one said to be booming already in one small area and soon to become the nation's new drug of choice. They weren't. Barely three years after ice was forgotten, a new drug epidemic was supposedly sweeping the nation. This time around, it was the drug methcathinone, popularly known as CAT, yet another relative of the amphetamine family. CAT was often in the national headlines during 1993 and 1994, and in June 1993, the imminent onslaught was the subject of an alarming report on ABC's national nightly news broadcast. The program warned that, though methcathinone bore superficial resemblances to cocaine, "this new drug . . . makes coke seem tame," and a detective stated that the problem "has basically reached epidemic proportions." Michigan's state drug czar announced that "in the history of our nation, I don't think there's ever been a drug like this. . . . a drug of this potency that is this easy to make." In concluding, the ABC reporter noted that "authorities are afraid this drug could soon become a national threat." In congressional hearings in August 1994, CAT was listed alongside heroin and methamphetamine in a list of the major "new challenges facing the DEA."[2] About this time, both media and law-enforcement agencies were urging the nation to prepare itself for potential disaster.

The ice script was replayed quite faithfully, with equally flimsy foundations. Though methcathinone still continues to be produced and used clandestinely, it shows no signs of gaining significant popularity, and within a couple of years, the news media were acknowledging that CAT no longer posed a major threat, if indeed it ever had. Viewed together with ice, the CAT scare suggests an extreme degree of media gullibility when faced with claims about illicit drugs, even when these claims emanate from bureaucrats whose motives for making exaggerated statements are transparent. Furthermore, the experience of CAT illustrates how a social problem is nationalized by the media through adoption by national television networks and newspaper chains of stories emanating from local reports. This apparently bizarre example, in fact, offers an object lesson in the manufacture and distortion of American drug problems.

Methcathinone is chemically related to substances that have a long history as stimulants and have often been subject to abuse, especially in Middle Eastern cultures. The name originates with the shrub *catha edulis*, the leaves of which were chewed for the pleasurable effects produced by the psychoactive chemical cathinone, a naturally occurring amphetamine analogue. In this form, the drug is known as Khat or Qat and is still used, illegally, by some immigrant communities in North America.[3]

Methcathinone itself is a modern, laboratory-designed, synthetic drug that was originally invented and used quite legally. Pioneered in Germany in 1928, the chemical was used as an antidepressant in the Soviet Union and other European nations from the 1930s onwards. In the 1950s, the American corporation Parke-Davis experimented with the drug for its appetite-suppressant qualities but found that its potential uses were outweighed by serious drawbacks, including dependency. The drug can induce a feeling of energy, euphoria and even invulnerability, as well as intense and extended wakefulness, so that users can go four days or more without sleep. But as with other relatives of the amphetamines, overuse can cause paranoia, weight loss, rising blood pressure and rapid physical decline. Modern illicit manufacturers warn of other dangers—for example, that the discharge of chemical byproducts through the pores causes users to become "very stinky."[4]

As it was a legal drug, the manufacturing process required patenting, and it was duly registered in 1957 as Patent 2,802,865, which in years to come would be freely used by illegal chemists. In 1989, methcathinone came to the attention of a University of Michigan student interning at Parke-Davis. Manufactured and used by his associates, methcathinone enjoyed an underground vogue in the Ann Arbor area, where it entered the local drug culture under nicknames like ephedrone, Goob, Jeff and CAT; the drug was most commonly snorted, although some users took it orally, mixed with a soft drink.[5]

In the early nineties, illegal manufacture spread beyond Ann Arbor. As the process produced a powerful bad smell that could not fail to attract law-enforcement attention, city-based CAT labs were vulnerable, and the first raid occurred in Ann Arbor in June 1991. It soon became necessary to relocate manufacture to a non-urban setting, so the center of production shifted to Michigan's Upper Peninsula, especially around Marquette, where a local market developed. More raids followed in Michigan, and in 1992, the first seizure occurred in Wisconsin. Over the next two years, methcathinone became the subject of intense investigation, and the number of raids increased dramatically, as shown by table 6.1.[6] In May 1992, methcathinone was placed on Schedule I of the federal CSA on an emergency basis, and this classification was made permanent in November 1993.[7]

The spread of CAT in these years offers a classic case study of the difficulties of regulating synthetic drugs. Once CAT was known as a stimulant, its popularity was bound to spread through both word-of-mouth advertising and the Internet, as the actual manufacturing process was relatively simple. In Michigan in the early 1990s, "At first they were selling the recipe and then they were giving it away just like a cookie recipe."[8] The same sources, notably the electronic bulletin boards, distributed consumer reports from users, though these usually reported disappointment with the drug's effects. Users scorned the suggestion that this was a superior form of methamphetamine, as its effects were relatively dull in comparison to those of speed. Still, if

Table 6.1 Seizures of Clandestine
Methcathinone Laboratories

Seizures by Agency			
	State	*DEA*	*Total*
1991 (June–Dec.)	1	5	6
1992	13	6	19
1993	4	23	27
1994 (Jan.–June)	*	10	10+
TOTAL	18+	44	62+

Seizures by State	
Michigan	33
Indiana	13
Wisconsin	11
Ohio	1
Illinois	1
Washington	1
Colorado	1
Virginia	1
TOTAL	62

*Data not collected.

the media were hyping it so intensely, CAT must be worth experimenting with.

The case of CAT shows the dangers of media reporting in drug matters, as virtually any account of the drug gives clues to its manufacture that can be adopted by an able teenager with an aptitude for chemistry. One autobiographical account available on the Internet describes how a college student initially "heard about a new drug craze that had just been detected in Michigan by the local authorities," probably in mid-1993. Fascinated by media reports, the author resolved to make CAT, though initially armed only with the name and the knowledge that it was derived from the common decongestant ephedrine. Presumably, he concluded, CAT bore a relationship to cathine similar to that which methamphetamine bore to amphetamine: while methamphetamine is made by reducing ephedrine, oxidizing the same precursor produces methcathinone. From these two simple facts, the deduction was simple: "Combine this with the fact that ephedrine is none other than n-methyl cathine, and it becomes obvious: one simply needs to oxidize the hydroxyl group of ephedrine to a keytone *[sic]* to produce methcathinone."⁹ Frustrated with his experiments on ephedrine, the anonymous chemist turned to the related brand-name product Sudafed (pseudephedrine), and he successfully devised an idiosyncratic manufacturing process by which he may have produced the first methcathinone ever snorted in the state of California. Although his own experiences with the drug were ultimately disastrous, the chemist nevertheless posted detailed manufacturing instructions on the Net for the instruction of others.

Once one knew the fundamental chemistry, the actual process of manufacturing this "kitchen-improvised crank" is straightforward: the information is available gratis on several World Wide Web sites, one of which, "Methcathinone Synthesis," includes a comprehensive, five-thousand-word account of the process and its possible difficulties, "for informational purposes only." The role of the Web in disseminating such information intensified public fears about the chances of the new drug spreading rapidly.

It was exactly in 1994 that scare stories about the potential of the Internet were peaking, usually in the context of young people gaining access to pornographic materials on line or being seduced by cyber-stalkers. Though the new medium was poorly understood by most parents, it swiftly became familiar terrain to teenagers, who seemed to their elders to be roaming out of control in this Cyberian bandit country. When in 1997 a fifteen-year-old California girl used the Net to synthesize CAT in her home, a drug counselor expressed the fear of many parents when she asked, "Do you want your kid reading the diaries of drug addicts who make their weeklong highs sound like a fantasy vacation? Do you want your kid seeing 'advice pages' to help them correct a bad batch of dope? Or where to shop for the ingredients?"¹⁰

Just how simply CAT could be manufactured was demonstrated tellingly when a DEA official demonstrated the entire process to a congressional investigating committee. He produced a box containing all of the necessary equipment, an apparatus seized in northern Wisconsin: "The labs are entirely mobile . . . I call this process a shake and a bake because that is all it is. All I need is two mason jars and a source of heat and I can manufacture this drug, or I can take two glasses that you commonly drink water out of, and manufacture this drug." To produce the drug, ephedrine was ground up, then put in a mason jar with sulfuric acid and distilled water and shaken. The result was placed in another mason jar, where it was mixed with battery acid, sodium dichromate and red devil lye. This jar then contained liquid methcathinone and other chemicals; a solvent such as toluene was employed to separate the desired drug. Once the water was removed by Epsom salts, the liquid methcathinone could be converted to a solid form through a form of distillation employing muriatic acid. Through this simple process, four thousand ephedrine tablets could be converted into two ounces of methcathinone, so that for an investment of sixty dollars, the chemist would have manufactured a quantity of the drug that could sell for two thousand. In 1993, a manufacturing ring in northern Wisconsin was holding a methcathinone "cook" once or twice a week, each of which produced four or five ounces of the drug.[11]

Suppression of an illegal drug requires more than simple reactive policing, and control of a synthetic is generally achieved by restricting the supply of the required precursor chemicals, together with any specialized equipment. From this perspective, methcathinone posed serious difficulties, as CAT cooks employed familiar household ingredients with quite legitimate uses. As the chair of a congressional committee investigating the problem remarked, "[M]ost of the chemicals necessary to produce CAT can be found at your local hardware store." The main components included battery acid (sulfuric acid), paint thinner (toluene), drain cleaner (sodium hydroxide) and over-the-counter drugs, and even the more arcane-sounding substances could be purchased legally: sodium dichromate is used to refine petroleum, while muriatic acid is employed for sandblasting and to scrub dried mortar off the face of bricks. As to specialized equipment, the process required familiar kitchen staples like coffee filters and Epsom salts.[12]

The only substance that might conceivably pose a problem was ephedrine, which was needed in such huge quantities that purchasers inevitably drew attention to themselves: a single cooking operation required three or four thousand tablets. If police correctly estimated that the amount of CAT manufactured at just one Wisconsin site was four pounds, that would imply the use of over a hundred thousand ephedrine tablets over a period of several months (though prosecutors customarily exaggerate quantities manufactured to support more severe criminal charges). As the crisis developed, authorities concentrated on reducing the legal availability of ephedrine, causing great inconvenience to legitimate users, such as asthma sufferers.[13] In 1993, a federal Domestic Chemical Diversion Control Act tightened the restrictions on precursor chemicals imposed by the 1988 CDTA. The new law was intended "to control the diversion of certain chemicals used in the illicit production of controlled substances such as methcathinone and methamphetamine." This title in itself offers remarkable testimony to the fear caused by CAT, which was even placed ahead of the far more prevalent methamphetamine.

Despite the early flurry of popularity, CAT never became anything more than a local fad. As table 6.1 indicates, 92 percent of lab seizures occurred in just three states, and most of that activity was concentrated in a few areas of those states, mainly in Michigan's Upper Peninsula and neighboring regions of Wisconsin. Even if we accept that CAT use genuinely was rampant in this region, the whole Upper Peninsula contains only some three percent of Michigan's nine million people. The volume of activity, too, must be put in perspective. During 1993, authorities reported eight times as many raids on methamphetamine operations nationwide as on CAT labs. Even this comparison is not entirely fair, as the laboratories required for the two substances are quite different in nature. Methamphetamine labs vary enormously in size and complexity, but the largest, especially in California, approach the character of true factories. Even the smallest methamphetamine laboratories dwarf the rudimentary facilities required for CAT (two mason jars!), and "CAT labs resemble nothing more than a high school chemistry set."[14] In the context of methcathinone, then, the term "lab seizure" often makes the criminal operation sound far more elaborate than it actually is, as a clandestine laboratory might actually be a kitchen table. This sort of lab raid should be imagined not in terms of the media stereotype of the storming of a fortified urban house defended by gangbangers armed with Uzis, but rather of an arrest in a trailer occupied by a couple of confused teenagers. A few such confiscations did not constitute evidence of a drug epidemic.

*

The popularization of CAT proceeded according to the familiar cycle of self-fulfilling prophecies. As authorities began to intervene against the new illegal drug, media reports overpraising its effectiveness stirred curiosity among sections of society with an interest in illegal stimulants, which usually meant teenagers and young adults, many of whom are skilled in computers and chemistry. Among these groups, warnings about harmful effects were discounted as a standard element of anti-drug rhetoric. Moreover, vital information about the drug's manufacture was disseminated by even sketchy media accounts of raids, which might mention that ephedrine was a crucial precursor: this information was enough to begin the successful researches of our California chemist and no doubt of others. As production and use spread, police and federal agents undertook more raids and interventions, and the drug was hyped ever more successfully in the media. Theoretically, this cycle has no necessary conclusion, except perhaps with the arrival of yet another ultimate drug to draw the attention of both users and enforcers.

Media coverage of a drug issue is crucial to the evolution of that problem, as reporting shapes actual usage. In the case of methcathinone, the mushroom growth of coverage created intense expectations about the substance and its impact and performed a remarkable job of public relations. The print media surveyed by LEXIS/NEXIS contained only three stories about methcathinone in 1992, but there were fifty-eight stories in the single year of 1993 and thirty-nine in 1994. The drug made a spectacular debut in the fall of 1992, when the *Detroit News* proclaimed, "New Drug CAT is More Addictive Than Crack."[15] Media interest in the new drug subsided a little over the next few months, but it revived vigorously the following March and rarely flagged over the following year.

Coverage was naturally most intense in the news media of Michigan and Wisconsin, where the drug was certainly present, and stories appeared regularly in newspapers like the *Detroit News,* the *Milwaukee Journal,* the *Wisconsin State Journal* and Madison's *Capital Times.* Throughout 1993 and 1994, regional papers found many opportunities to denounce CAT, such as when police reported an arrest or a laboratory raid and when politicians demanded additional resources for law enforcement or stringent legislation against methcathinone and its precursors. Apart from the dangers of an epidemic, the drug posed an environmental threat: unlike cocaine, it was manufactured on American soil, with all the consequent hazards of pollution and industrial accidents. According to one report, "These labs leave behind dangerous chemical waste which is routinely dumped into the ground. As a result . . . the sites must be cleaned up at great expense to the taxpayers."[16]

Warnings of national growth were soon appearing in media across the nation, as accounts were spread by the process of news syndication. The original 1992 *Detroit News* story was syndicated through the Gannett News Service and promptly taken up with slight variations in many other parts of the country, ensuring that a problem then strictly localized in Michigan would be seen as affecting wider areas. The *Louisville Courier-Journal* now warned that CAT was "giving police kittens," though the drug would never make more than a token appearance in Kentucky. Later stories were syndicated through the Gannett, Scripps-Howard and Knight-Ridder networks, spreading national alarm. In March 1993, the *Arizona Republic* was announcing, "U.S. Epidemic of New Drug is Feared" on the strength of a story from the *Detroit Free Press*. In June, a *Milwaukee Journal* story was reprinted in the *Chicago Tribune* and the *Houston Chronicle*, both of which declared the new drug "more powerful, addictive, than cocaine."[17]

In the electronic media, stories by local midwestern affiliates soon drew the attention of national networks. This local reporting was the source of ABC's alarmist account of conditions in the Upper Midwest that June, and in the fall, NPR made the CAT scourge the subject of an exposé that revealed how the drug was "sweeping the Midwest" and making its debut in Los Angeles and Seattle. The CAT problem was further nationalized by a story on "the new drug of choice" in *U.S. News and World Report*. By August, the *Los Angeles Times* published the first of a series of front-page pieces on the problem, headlining "Michigan Woods a War Zone Against New Drug Epidemic" and "Drug CAT is Clawing Up Michigan." The latter story claimed, "Methcathinone is spreading like wildfire in the Upper Peninsula, prosecutor says. It's less expensive than cocaine, but just as dangerous." The "Home-Grown Drug Menace" received new publicity shortly afterwards from a syndicated story cowritten by Jack Anderson.[18]

The new CAT menace bore a close resemblance to the ice that became before it. Like ice, CAT was "highly addictive," "extremely addictive" and worse than cocaine, and it could have "devastating effects." *Rolling Stone* quoted a DEA spokesman as stating that CAT users even preferred the drug to cocaine or crack: "Put a pound of coke and a pound of CAT on a table and come back in an hour. The coke will still be there." And just as ice had allegedly overwhelmed Hawaii, CAT was now sweeping Michigan, the Midwest, or even the whole "drug subculture"; indeed, it was spreading "like wildfire."[19]

Methcathinone was frequently described as uniquely addictive, but no less than "epidemic," the whole concept of addiction deserves examination. The word itself originated in Roman law, where it referred to a kind of forced servitude, usually inflicted as a judicial sentence: borrowed into English, addiction became a metaphor for slavish devotion, and only in the nineteenth century did the technical medical usage develop. Addiction certainly exists as a clinical category, both in the sense of physical and psychological dependence, and it has associated characteristics, like steadily increasing tolerance to the substance in question and a withdrawal syndrome when that substance is removed. The condition can arise from amphetamines and related drugs, including methcathinone. However, it is by no means obvious that anyone using a given drug is addicted, with all the behaviors of dependence and compulsion that implies, as so much depends on the social context of the drug and its users. As Craig Reinarman has argued, the term is often used more vaguely to suggest a loss, however temporary, of the self-control so fundamental to Western, and specifically to American, social ideology. In both the media and official statements, distinctions between recreational and compulsive users are frequently ignored, with the suggestion that anyone using a given drug is by definition an addict who fulfils the worst stereotypes conjured by that term. The concept of the nonaddicted user barely exists in the thought-world of the drug-enforcement bureaucracy or in that of the media, which rely upon that officialdom for their opinions. Legal documents and the media were referring to users as methcathinone addicts before such a medical condition had even been documented.[20]

Images of epidemic and addiction were reinforced by the familiar media tactic of verbal plays on the main keywords in the story. Feline imagery came to the fore, with implications of secretive, sinister, predatory behavior and animalistic violence. The drug "gave police kittens" when the patent office regrettably "let the CAT out of the bag." CAT was "creeping" across the Midwest; a "chemical predator" was "clawing up Michigan"; the country was facing a CAT fight, a CAT attack. Users "smell like something the CAT dragged in." These obvious metaphors and puns gave journalists an instant tag for stories seeking to contextualize the emerging problem.[21]

From the time of their initial discovery of CAT, the media demonstrated an eager willingness to accept the most negative interpretations of the new problem and its likely trajectory, and this attitude could not fail to influence the behavior of legislators and policymakers. If CAT was such a pressing threat, then political rewards were available for those who took the lead in suppressing it, while failure to act visibly would appear irresponsible. For the local politicians of the Upper Midwest, acting swiftly against CAT could be seen as a necessary social prophylactic against the danger that the urban problems of Milwaukee or Detroit would spill over into neighboring rural and suburban regions, just as suburban Pennsylvania legislators a decade earlier had reacted to contamination from the speed capital of Philadelphia. Even if legislators were personally skeptical over media claims about CAT, they gained nothing by expressing such qualms or by urging that the problem be kept in perspective. We can observe a kind of feedback loop whereby media claims about a problem stimulate official activism, which in turn generates newsworthy events in the forms of congressional hearings, debates and reports. Increased media attention stimulates awareness of the issue and its apparent importance, which further encourages legislative action. Moreover, when local politicians press for official action and federal legislation, their campaigns reinforce the idea that this is or could become a national issue, meriting the concern of all Americans.

By mid-1993, several midwestern legislators were drawing attention to the supposed CAT menace—and extracting great political benefit from it. Anti-CAT legislation was sponsored by U.S. senators Carl Levin (D-MI) and Russell Feingold (D-WI), and Levin cited this as one of his major achievements for 1993. The most visible activist, however, was Michigan Representative Bart Stupak, who pushed vigorously for the bill to regulate ephedrine as a precursor chemical.[22] Stupak had a powerful local interest in fighting CAT, as he had previously served as a state representative for the Upper Peninsula, and in 1992 he was elected to the First (U.S.) Congressional District, a sprawling rural area in northern Michigan. As he had served as a Michigan state trooper for ten years, Stupak was especially likely to be sensitive to crime issues in his region. His prominent role in the anti-CAT movement was a major item in his successful campaign for reelection in 1994, in which he became the first Democrat ever to serve successive terms in this conservative Republican district: moreover, this local triumph occurred during one of the worst elections in forty years for Democrats nationwide.

All three of the main anti-CAT congressional activists were Democrats, and partisan issues contributed to making the party especially vigilant on drug policies at this time. At the national level, the Democratic administration that took office in 1993 was attacked by Republicans for being soft on crime and drug issues, a critique owing something to the new president's brief encounter with marijuana in the 1960s. In December 1993, critics gained powerful ammunition when the controversial surgeon general Joycelyn Elders called for the limited legalization of some presently illegal drugs. Recognizing that the drug issue could be an area of potential vulnerability, the Clinton administration fervently depicted itself as just as tough on drugs as its predecessor, a message reinforced by the choice of General Barry McCaffrey as drug czar: this selection proved that the drug war would not merely continue, but would retain its military flavor. Draconian action against CAT further permitted the administration to portray itself as toughest on those illegal substances that posed a particular threat to white rural and suburban communities. This stance was all the more important to a state like Michigan, which would be vital to the electoral success of any future presidential candidate. Furthermore, the emphasis on environmental hazards enhanced the stigma attached to the drug while appealing to liberal sections of the public that might otherwise be dubious about the notion of the drug war. One of Representative Stupak's main demands was that the Superfund monies designated for environmental cleanup should be available for removing traces of methcathinone manufacture.[23] Republicans, obviously, were not likely to complain about an escalation of the anti-drug campaign, which for a decade they had regarded as their distinctive issue.

As in the case of the major parties, a strong political agenda influenced the reactions of federal law enforcement towards the new drug. Public concern about CAT reached a crescendo in mid-1994, when the DEA identified the drug as a major potential threat, alongside the more obvious problems of heroin and methamphetamine. This intensity of concern was in marked contrast to the agency's relaxed attitude to ice, but the DEA now found itself in a very different and far more perilous political environment from that of 1990. Paradoxically, the federal anti-drug bureaucracy was a victim of its own success, as the worst of the crack cocaine threat was already receding after 1992 and some of the largest international drug trafficking networks were being disrupted. At the same time, the Clinton administration was committed to restructuring and streamlining federal agencies, and one scheme under consideration involved a merger between the FBI and the DEA.[24] It was politically imperative for the DEA to justify its continued existence by stressing the danger of new substances like CAT: why should resources be poured out to fight a war that had already been won?

In August 1994, the DEA had a chance to make its case before a sympathetic audience when the House of Representatives' Subcommittee on Information, Justice, Transportation, and Agriculture held hearings on "New Challenges" in the drug world, namely heroin, methamphetamine and CAT. Undoubtedly, the prominence given to CAT reflected Representative Stupak's membership in this body. Throughout, the committee referred to CAT in the same context as methamphetamine, and "CAT and Speed" were contextualized together as the foundations of a dual epidemic. This association also served to enhance the notion that violence inevitably arose from trafficking, as the August hearing occurred only a few weeks after the death of a DEA agent in a gunfight with methamphetamine dealers in

Arizona. DEA administrator Thomas A. Constantine stressed that CAT was about to erupt on a national scale: "We thought at one point it would just be limited to Northern Michigan. It is very obvious however that this is not the case."[25] He also claimed that over half of all American homicides were drug-related, a figure that would be accepted by few authorities on violent crime. A CAT epidemic could thus be expected to have grim effects on public order and safety, not merely in the inner cities.

DEA statements buttressed media opinions about the extreme seriousness of the problem, and the volume of news reports on CAT now surged back to the levels of late 1993. New stories asserted the most extravagant claims about the drug, stating, for example, that "it has quickly become one of the biggest challenges faced by the U.S. Drug Enforcement Administration." Stories syndicated on the Scripps-Howard and Knight-Ridder news services retold the history of the drug, recounting in terms reminiscent of classical mythology how the evil had been unleashed onto the world through the evil of one man, the original Ann Arbor chemist. Once again, the *Los Angeles Times* was the most passionate prophet of an imminent national threat. Despite the law-enforcement crackdown, the paper asserted, the midwestern epidemic was swiftly spreading beyond the original home base among the "hunting cabins nestled in the birch and maple stands of the north woods."[26] According to these claims, even the controls imposed upon ephedrine had only slowed the impending disaster.

The Knight-Ridder chain's news stories about the chemical predator appeared in early 1995, but in retrospect they can be seen as marking the end of significant media concern.[27] After the awful earlier predictions, the fate of methcathinone over the next year or two proved anticlimactic. Though the actual number of news stories concerning the drug was actually higher in 1995 than in 1994, the tone of reports was quite different. Whereas the 1994 stories had often been general or analytical in nature, the following year mainly brought brief and specific notes about arrests, court proceedings or lab raids. The only spark of anything like the earlier concern was when the drug was first recorded in states in which it was previously unknown, as when a CAT lab was found in Arkansas in early 1996. And while the drug continued to be mentioned in congressional hearings, it was always in passing, as an afterthought to more genuinely popular drugs like methamphetamine and even to old staples like LSD.

After the first two months of 1995, methcathinone effectively died as an issue of concern for the national media and even for the major regional newspapers. There were no further exposés on the television networks, no features in national newsmagazines like *Time* or *Newsweek*. The virtual collapse of the CAT problem attracted little media attention, nothing like the interest paid to the rise of the supposed epidemic: in media terms, the absence of a danger is scarcely newsworthy. Only a handful of stories reported retrospectively on the disappearance of CAT, with one commenting that the drug had simply failed to achieve popularity and the other claiming that its disappearance reflected official vigilance.[28] Methcathinone also failed to compete with readily accessible supplies of cheap methamphetamine, which became available in the Midwest during 1994–95. However, it remains open to question whether the scale of production and usage of CAT genuinely declined or if the drug simply lost the attention of law-enforcement agencies and the media, who found new priorities. As in the case of ice, the supposed new epidemic ceased because no one was paying attention to it.

SEVEN

Redneck Cocaine

The Methamphetamine Panic
of the Nineties

"Crank, meth, crystal. White. Lamont used to say, 'If it ain't white, it ain't right.'"

—Marjorie Standiford in Stewart O'Nan's
The Speed Queen, 1997

Though both the ice and the CAT scares soon fizzled out, the next anti-synthetic campaign was far more successful, developing powerful legs of its own. This was the 1995–96 movement against methamphetamine, the first of the post-crack panics to begin to live up to its auspicious precedent. Though the hyperbolic language of the new movement superficially recalled the abortive scares of the early nineties, clearly something had changed: not only did the new speed menace gain instant credibility as a national threat, but it retained some resonance an impressive four years after its inception. The issue had obvious political appeal, to the extent that in 1996, President Clinton made suppressing speed a major element of his national policies on crime and justice. But why should a speed problem have achieved such success, while its predecessors languished and died?

At first sight, methamphetamine offered a much more convincing menace than CAT because it was genuinely popular in some regions. Some convincing quantitative evidence showed that both usage and availability were increasing during the early 1990s and expanding into new geographical areas, while thirty years of research plausibly linked the drug with violence and serious medical problems. And the growing availability of methamphetamine may indeed have displaced other synthetics, including methcathinone and some of the designer drugs, so this drug at least represented an authentic social phenomenon. Having said this, the speed scare involved a great deal of distortion and exaggeration, especially in terms of the potential for epidemic growth. In this case more than most, the problem was substantiated by dubious statistical criteria, especially the figures cited for drug-related deaths. These artifacts reflect the changing subjective opinions of medical examiners rather than any long-term trends in substance abuse.

The methamphetamine issue won and retained popularity because it was so vigorously supported by powerful, insider claims-makers with strong partisan and bureaucratic agendas. The white storm warning of mid-decade can largely be traced to a DEA anxious to defend and augment its resources at a time of potential political threat. In addition, the ethnic and geographical appeal of methamphetamine made it particularly disturbing for the general public and thus appealing for claim-makers. The near-total media emphasis on white users and dealers raised the question of whether something like crack had finally invaded the heartland. Moreover, the vogue for methamphetamine was largely in the West and Southwest, areas of growing electoral importance, making this a natural cause for national politicians facing crucial contests in the imminent future. With such potent interest groups backing the newly redefined problem, it is scarcely surprising that it should have taken off as impressively as it did. The rediscovery of methamphetamine was a political product par excellence.

Even before the explosion of media interest in 1995, methamphetamine stories had never been wholly absent from the mass media. Through the early 1990s, there were regular reports of raids on clandestine laboratories and seizures from criminal gangs, mainly in California and occasionally in other Sun Belt states.[1] In 1993, the California BNE seized 360 labs in that state, compared to a mere 160 raided by the DEA nationwide. Such incidents became almost commonplace in the regional news of the Southwest.[2] Indeed, when in 1993 the federal Bureau of Alcohol, Tobacco and Firearms wished to obtain support and heavy equipment from other agencies prior to its proposed attack on the compound of the Branch Davidian sect at Waco, Texas, it did so by spreading the spurious tale that the site concealed a methamphetamine lab. However ill-founded, the notion proved all too plausible in this particular region.

There were also familiar horror stories about the drug's effects on individual speed freaks, tales of the sort that had been appearing at least since the 1960s. Usually such stories told how the drug was found in individuals who had carried out heinous crimes, implying a direct cause-and-effect relationship. News stories about the speed/violence linkage followed the story of the California man who murdered several members of his family on a rampage in September 1993. The best-publicized incident of this type involved a man who was under the influence of methamphetamine when he reportedly concluded that his young son was demonically possessed, leading him to decapitate the boy on a New Mexico interstate in 1995. This incident would be much cited as evidence of the drug's disastrous effects, just as earlier stories about users on angel dust tearing out their eyes or breaking through steel handcuffs were cited. Also in 1995, a man said to be high on methamphetamine went on a rampage through the streets of San Diego while driving a hijacked army tank before being shot dead by police; in the same city, a couple using crystal meth killed a four-year-old niece by submerging her in a bathtub of scalding water. Other events pointed to the harmful effects of drug manufacture, as at the end of that year, when an explosion in a trailer-based lab killed three small children.[3]

From mid-1995, reports depicted a rising speed threat, suggesting that both production and abuse were spreading rapidly and reaching new geographical areas and social classes. Initially, methamphetamine-related stories mainly concerned conditions in California and the Southwest along the I-40 corridor. In Arizona, the rate of laboratory seizures accelerated dramatically, with some three hundred operations raided between early 1996 and mid-1998; methamphetamine-related arrests in Phoenix alone grew by 360 percent between 1992 and 1998. News items concerning this state's methamphetamine problem appeared at a rate of one or two a year during the early 1990s, then soared to an average of five a month between the start of 1995 and mid-1997. One reason for this growth was the plethora of stories following the Oklahoma City bombing of April 1995, the perpetrators of which operated in a subculture of heavy methamphetamine use. Journalists now explored "the dope-smoking, methamphetamine-swilling world of Kingman," Arizona where the bombers and their associates had spent much time, and pointed out that terrorist Timothy McVeigh had apparently been using the drug in the weeks before the attack.[4] This reporting encouraged an association between methamphetamine and what was popularly dismissed as a violent, trailer-trash world.

Yet at just about this time, the tone of coverage changed, incorporating suggestions that the drug was gaining popularity beyond its traditional homelands in the Southwest. Moving into the Midwest, speed was entering rural communities, which were the absolute antithesis of the conventional stereotype of drug abuse. From being a working-class preference, the drug was said to be finding a market among young suburbanites and professionals and in wealthier sections of cities. References to the drug began to appear in mainstream popular culture: in 1997, crystal meth was featured in a hedonistic, sexual context in the hit rock song "Semi-Charmed Life" by Third Eye Blind.[5]

From 1995, the media used the familiar epidemic script to trace the growth of meth abuse. Warning that the drug was "the poor man's cocaine," the *San Francisco Chronicle* warned of the "Kiss of Meth." The urgency of the menace was emphasized by repeated puns on the speed theme: if ice had been chilling and CAT mauling, then speed was racing. The *Christian Science Monitor* headlined, "Drugs Speed West to East," while *U.S. News & World Report* claimed, "A New Drug Gallops through the West." Its cheapness, easy availability and seductive effects would make methamphetamine the drug of the nineties. It was, more specifically, the "crack of the nineties," a phrase that was, like "poor man's cocaine," derived verbatim by the media from DEA press statements. By the end of 1995, the word "epidemic" was appearing in the headlines of the sober *New York Times,* which reported that "a startling rise in the use of methamphetamine in California and the Southwest has raised fears among law enforcement officials that the trend toward dangerous stimulants could spread across the country much as crack did in the 1980s." In the first months of 1996, methamphetamine earned star treatment in all of the major news outlets, including *Time, Newsweek,* and the *Christian Science Monitor,* as well as in the major metropolitan newspapers. Both of the main California papers, the *San Francisco Chronicle* and the *Los Angeles Times,* presented the meth story in front-page headlines.[6]

The new wave of speed coverage was long on hyperbole. As we have already seen in the case of CAT, anyone using methamphetamine was automatically portrayed as an addict, a speed freak, with all of the qualities associated with that devastating label. As the television documentary program "Meth's Deadly High" declared, "This drug is different. It is so addictive, using it one time can create an addict. . . . It's called the crack cocaine of the nineties . . . the future is methamphetamine." The program reinforced the image of meth as a lethal hard drug by focusing entirely on its use by injection, suggesting quite inaccurately that this was the preferred method of ingestion, rather than smoking or snorting. Methamphetamine was actually claimed to be *more* damaging than either heroin or cocaine because of its long-term effects on the brain, where it permanently depresses the levels of neurotransmitters, consigning the speed freak to a self-destructive life of inner slavery. Speed use was almost literally a plague: in a remarkable medical analogy, San Diego's chief of police remarked, "Abuse patterns suggest a two to four year latency period from first use to full addiction," using a concept more familiar in the context of infectious diseases like syphilis.[7]

Newspapers and television news programs recounted the familiar stories of lives ruined by addiction, tales of abandoned children and shattered families, "an epidemic of burned-out brains and broken bodies." These stories usually focused on the experiences of women users, partly in recognition of the drug's appeal to women but also in deference to the growing importance of women as a target audience for the news media. Typical accounts told of how women had not only lost jobs or property, but had abandoned their family responsibilities. The *New York Times* featured a photograph of a young Spokane woman with track marks on her arms, its caption alleging, "Users of methamphetamines are mostly white women"; the associated story recounts the experience of one user for whom the drug "wrecked her life, costing her custody of her three-year-old son." The women's magazine *Redbook* offered an inspiring story of a woman addicted to crystal meth who "had four weeks to save herself" and her children and family. As the 1997 documentary "Meth's Deadly High" stated, "Crank can rend gaping holes in a woman's life." Even the crack-baby notion surfaced once more, as the program showed one woman tending a child allegedly born addicted to methamphetamine and wondering "if drug addiction has doomed her offspring." The deepest condemnation was reserved for those who made drugs in settings where their children might be exposed to them: "These home labs bring the war on drugs into the heart of the family."[8]

As so often in the past, media coverage of the newly identified plague emphasized its potential spread. As one documentary noted, this was a new front in the war on drugs, "a front that may soon be coming to a neighborhood near you." Western police officers were quoted as saying, "Stand by . . . it's going to get a lot worse."[9] One recurrent theme was that the drug was speeding east from the Pacific Coast, initially striking the Midwest but soon to be found in the cities of the East. Of course such accounts demonstrate some amnesia about the recent past, when one such East Coast city had been proclaimed the speed capital of the world.

As noted above, new accounts stressed the extreme violence said to have been caused by the drug, with wide publicity being given to notorious crimes like the 1996 rape-murder of a girl in Ukiah, California, while she was under the influence of methamphetamine. Stories of savage violence became the staple of reporting on methamphetamine issues: *Reader's Digest* saw the drug as a "demon stalk[ing] the land" and blamed speed for an upsurge in child homicides, noting that "[c]ranksters can be paranoid, delusional and extremely violent." As in the eras of angel dust and marijuana, the drug user was depicted as a mindless monster ever spoiling for a confrontation with police. A Florida narcotics officer remarked that meth was a "drug that he says scares the hell out of him. It's a drug that can turn mild-mannered folks into hallucinating psychotics who won't hesitate to pull a gun, sometimes without the slightest provocation. . . . 'you just don't know when these [dealers] are going to snap. . . . They are just uncontrollable.'" An Arizona police officer agreed in a television news interview: "If you do encounter a suspect that is high on meth, he is extremely dangerous, because he already has a paranoid psychosis about him from the drug itself."[10]

According to news accounts, "the poor whites' crack" was spreading into rural areas and trailer parks, bringing unrestrained violence in its wake. This angle was even pursued by NPR's news program *All Things Considered,* which usually affects a responsible tone appropriate for its upscale audience. Such crimes were said to be proliferating in hitherto peaceful rural communities in midwestern states like Iowa, where the state's director of Narcotics Enforcement proclaimed, "We're in the middle of a meth epidemic." *Newsweek* used the North Dakota city of Fargo as the setting for a now-obligatory meth-in-the-Midwest story, with a photo that recalled the popular recent film *Fargo,* which had also explored random carnage in remote landscapes. In the real-life Fargo, "a meth addict who burned his house down while hallucinating, killing his own mother, pleaded guilty to manslaughter." In the state at large, "[r]esidents have been locking their doors since an elderly woman was shot to death by four teens on meth last year. Life on the prairie may never be the same."[11]

The battery of media reports stressed how incongruous it was to see images familiar from either foreign or minority settings in a white, rural context, an intrusion of the shockingly inappropriate that recalls films like *Invasion of the Body Snatchers.* The *New York Times* began a 1996 report with a bucolic image: "In this small town surrounded by corn fields, nothing but Sunday morning church bells ever made much noise, and the jail sat three-quarters empty most of the time. And then about a year or so ago, things started to go haywire. Crime began to soar, coupled with an outbreak of irrational behavior . . . some parents suddenly became so neglectful that their children were taken away; a man fled his workplace to get a gun, terrified that helicopters were coming after him; motorists in routine traffic stops greeted the police with psychotic tirades." Reporting a later case in Missouri, the same paper remarked on "a perverse vision of Middle American domesticity." *U.S. News and World Report* discussed "the Iowan Connection," recalling traditional media tags about exotic French Connections, Colombian Connections and so on, but here superimposed upon the Norman Rockwell world of Marshalltown, where "[t]he town square is the picture-postcard variety, with a vintage courthouse anchoring the center of town." The report offered a dreadful catalog of the drug's effects in the rural Iowa community of Marshall County, which was said to have become a center for Mexican-based meth syndicates: "Theft and domestic abuse were rising in the county seat of Marshalltown (population 25,000), and involuntary committals to psychiatric hospitals—previously a once-a-week occurrence—increased to as many as eight or ten a week." "It is a problem that is tearing apart this community."[12]

Images of insanity in the heartland proliferated. A CNN report entitled "High in the Heartland" used two Missouri settings, first the city of Independence, said to be the meth capital of the Midwest (or even "the methamphetamine capital of America"), and next a rural county overwhelmed by a sudden upsurge of murders and rampant paranoia. In an image that seems to have been lifted straight from the television series *The X-Files,* one AP story began with the observation, "It might seem a supernatural force has seized this remote [Missouri] county of two-lane blacktops and white oak forests. It can be found in the surge of crime. And in the inexplicable behavior." The answer, of course, is in the demonizing effects of methamphetamine on the "normal" residents of the heartland: "Where meth thrives, so does a David Lynch-ian violence." During 1997 alone, Missouri police raided an astronomical 450 meth labs, the largest total in the nation.[13]

Just as crack reporting had swiftly become a genre of news coverage in the eighties, so meth stories soon acquired a predictable shape over the next decade. One element inherited from the crack era was the literalizing of the war-on-drugs metaphor by television depictions of militarized police units raiding labs and even "crank-houses." In a typical report, journalists accompany "an elite team of anti-drug agents," dressed in black helmets and Kevlar body armor, with drawn pistols and automatic rifles, while helicopters hover overhead. Paramilitary drug warriors are then shown storming a house said to contain a suspected lab, generally a kitchen or garage attached to a tiny house or trailer. These dramatic scenes make for exciting television and are also effective in mobilizing support for drug-war policies. The militarized approach suggests, with whatever plausibility, the deadly danger to which police will be exposed from cranksters. Observing the incident through police eyes, the viewer is led to believe that a literal war zone exists in rural California or Arizona, Iowa or Missouri. Moreover, such scenes remind viewers of the incidents that were a staple of the news programs of the 1980s, when armed police used battering rams and tanks to smash into fortified urban crack houses: now the locale has shifted to the heartland, and the pathetic faces of the suspects ordered to the ground at gunpoint are white rather than black.[14]

In May 1996, the emerging portrait of the methamphetamine problem received national publicity in a potent segment of CBS's news program *48 Hours*. The program once again showed police storming drug labs and arresting alleged dealers, as well as tracing the experiences of recovering users of crystal meth who were going through a detoxification program. Police expressed their dread of paranoid speed users, and a rehabilitation counselor agreed that "the meth abuser will kill you in a heartbeat." Arizona police claimed that 70 percent of their workload was methamphetamine-related.[15] Though all of these examples were selected from conditions in Arizona (Meth Country), the program repeatedly warned that "meth is spreading through the United States" as anchor Dan Rather cited cases of overdoses and seizures as far afield as Nebraska and Texas. Just as ice was supposed to rampage outwards from its base in Hawaii, and CAT from its rural fastnesses in Michigan's Upper Peninsula, so Arizona now stood as a portent for the rest of the country.

Stories about Meth Country or an Iowan Connection established both a social and geographical location for the emerging problem, but they were by no means the only ones that could have been selected. Methamphetamine has always had a broad cross-class appeal, with pockets of usage as diverse as upscale gays, urban manual workers, college students and professional sports players, and it certainly had a presence among other racial groups, including African and Asian Americans. Nevertheless, after the first few weeks, news coverage focused almost entirely upon rural dwellers, often portrayed as white trash, with trailer-park images usually to the fore. To quote the district attorney of California's Humboldt County, "If crack cocaine is the drug of choice for poor urban blacks, methamphetamine is the drug of choice of poor rural whites."[16] The methamphetamine problem was framed in increasingly narrow terms of class and ethnicity, to the exclusion of other possible lines of inquiry.

The Missouri city of Independence became typecast as the setting for such tales of Americana-gone-bad; the community was portrayed as "Tweakville" in a *Rolling Stone* piece, adding yet another nickname for the drug. This report was characteristic in its setting of the semirural Midwest: "Walter's place, a single-story dump surrounded by cars, washing machines and lawn mowers that had been disassembled and then half put back together. A tweaker's place, with that Sanford and Son feel." Speed was popular in "[t]hese parts of Independence [which] are so Travis Tritt/pickup truck that they're known as Dogpatch, after Li'l Abner's insular, threadbare turf."[17] The real Independence bears little relation to the Dogpatch of media legend: though caricatured in terms of Ozark backwoodsmen, the actual community is a prosperous suburb of Kansas City, with an enviable commercial and retailing base and a solid tourist trade. Nevertheless, reporting of the speed problem demanded a white-trash setting, so the objective reality was distorted accordingly.

Cultural representations of methamphetamine use must be seen in the context of other equally troubling portrayals of lower-class white people in the same years. As Annalee Newitz points out, the media in these years were offering an unprecedented range of images of "White savagery and humiliation," with degenerate whites used as bizarre villains in films like *Pulp Fiction, A Time to Kill* and *Rosewood* as well as in true-crime genre shows such as *Cops.* The reasons for this are complex. At its simplest, the ethnic politics of the previous two decades had made it politically difficult to use many familiar stereotypes, and white trash or Dogpatch was one of the last such images that could be used without offending a potent interest group. Newitz further stresses the internal contradictions of racial ideology in these years, an era of "white-on-white class conflicts, fears about the unattainability of a total 'white power,' and a crippling sense of guilt caused by an (often repressed) acknowledgment of white racism." In this view, "As savage whites, poor whites in the United States and abroad become unruly children who need discipline, strict boundaries and (coercive) guidance from the upper classes."[18] Class conflicts were manifested in issues like gun control, where it became fashionable for the liberal-oriented media to depict rural whites as violence-obsessed, while moral controversies about homosexuality and abortion revived old ideas of the heartland as superstitious and intolerant.

This contemptuous racial imagery, with its vicious stereotypes, blossomed after the Oklahoma City bombing of 1995, which was initially presented as a treacherous foreign blow against the authentic American heartland. When subsequent investigation suggested that the perpetrators were themselves products of this same heartland, the media message veered sharply in more hostile directions, and the ensuing scare about right-wing militias produced countless cartoons depicting rural whites as primitive, fanatical bigots. Such media trends justified and encouraged the obsessive contemporary gaze into the world of the white methamphetamine user. And in Dale Brown's techno-thriller *The Tin Man*, the methamphetamine trade is once more linked to villainous whites, both neo-Nazis and motorcycle gangs. The drug's prevalence was used to expose the shallowness of stereotypically white values, of which a city like Independence became the epitome—"a town that likes to think of itself as the quintessential Middle America," with "its trademark aura of Midwestern rectitude."[19] Methamphetamine became a symbol of white degeneracy, of massive downward social mobility.

In serious fiction no less than in popular culture, speed became a symbol of desperation, ruined lives and brutal murder. In Robert Stone's novella *Bear And His Daughter,* the speed user is Rowan Smart, whose childhood traumas culminated in an act of incest with her father. She spends her young adult years in flight from her past, becoming a park ranger in a remote part of the West, engaging in ever more self-destructive behavior aggravated by crystal methamphetamine. "The famous ice" makes her "crazier than all get-out": the drug is after all "made by the Hell's Angels and not the Red Cross." Driven by the "crystal energy," after sharing the drug with her father, she kills both him and herself. In Kathryn Harrison's *Exposure*, likewise, a young woman uses crystal meth as a means of rejecting her emotionally and sexually abusive father, as part of a systematic rebellion that also includes crime and petty theft. Like Rowan Smart, she slides ever deeper towards paranoia and psychic collapse.

In Stewart O'Nan's *noir* novel *The Speed Queen,* the drug is the preferred stimulant of the Sonic Killers, a homicidal trio of robbers wan-
dering the Southwest, recalling the fictional white-trash killers portrayed in such recent films as *Natural Born Killers* and *Kalifornia.*
O'Nan's tale is the autobiography of Speed Queen Marjorie Standiford, whose poor white origins are suggested by the names of characters like her boyfriend, Lamont. As she recalls from Death Row, they
used to inject methamphetamine: "Crank, meth, crystal. White. Lamont used to say, 'If it ain't white, it ain't right.' That was the good
stuff. I've heard of kids making bathtub crank from muriatic acid and
Vicks inhalers. It's all junk really, the worst thing in the world for
you." But Marjorie has firm standards about which drugs she considers appropriate, and the worst are those linked to minorities: "Whatever you do, don't make us crackheads. That's just disgusting."[20]
There are some lines you do not cross.

The same official sources raising the alarm of a meth epidemic were
also shaping the regional and racial character of the discourse. By far
the most important agency was the DEA, which since mid-1995 had
identified methamphetamine as a primary threat, and most media accounts acknowledged their heavy debt to reports and testimony produced by the agency. As early as August 1995, DEA administrator
Thomas A. Constantine introduced the then-novel topic of methamphetamine in a presentation to the Senate Foreign Relations Committee on the subject of international drug trafficking organizations in
Mexico. Constantine declared, "In the last three years, these trafficking organizations have virtually saturated the western United States
market with high-purity methamphetamine, known also as 'speed' or
'crank.' In some areas of California, it has now reportedly replaced cocaine as the drug of choice. With a saturated West Coast market, these
traffickers have begun to expand their markets to the East Coast and
in the South. . . . As supplies have increased, prices have fallen, making
it a cheap alternative to cocaine. Some have called it the poor man's
cocaine." Mexican imports of amphetamine drugs were scarcely a novelty, as this problem had been highlighted by federal agencies, including the DEA, through the 1960s and 1970s, but the implication was

that the Mexican Connection now represented a novel or rising threat.[21]

The DEA produced descriptions with a sound-bite quality bound to attract the media, as in "poor man's cocaine." In October, DEA views dominated the hearings of the House Subcommittee on Crime on what was billed as the rising scourge of methamphetamine in America. Some months later, the DEA argued not merely that methamphetamine usage was rising rapidly, but that its consequences were often lethal, as a much-quoted report suggested that the number of meth-related deaths was soaring in western cities such as Los Angeles, Phoenix, San Diego and San Francisco. Constantine was the primary force in drawing together law-enforcement officials in February 1996 for a national conference on the dangers of the drug. At this gathering, Attorney General Reno was pessimistic, remarking, "When I first took office, people talked about it being a problem in the West. Let us disabuse ourselves of that notion and recognize that it is spreading across this country. . . . There should be no question, no question in anybody's mind, that methamphetamine poses a real and serious threat to the citizens of our nation."[22]

The case for an emerging meth epidemic was summarized in the DEA's March 1996 report, *The Methamphetamine Situation in the United States,* which served as the primary source for virtually all later media coverage and political statements. This document cited a vast expansion in all of the standard measures by which drug abuse can be measured—arrests, seizures, deaths and emergency-room episodes—and claimed, "In the last 3 years, there has been a 518 percent increase in the amount of methamphetamine seized in California. . . . In Phoenix, methamphetamine-related hospital emergency room episodes nearly tripled between 1992 and 1994. Likewise, methamphetamine-related deaths increased from 20 in 1992 to 122 in 1994, more than a six-fold increase. . . . Arizona's methamphetamine problem has exploded recently." Thus was Meth Country born. Later that month, Constantine told another Senate committee, "Methamphetamine use and criminal ties to Mexican organizations are now evident in areas as diverse as Iowa, Florida and Georgia."[23]

That spring, the federal government identified controlling methamphetamine as a key policy objective. DEA statements were echoed by national drug czar Barry McCaffrey and by President Clinton himself, both of whom cited as key evidence the alleged surge in meth-related fatalities. In April, the president made a speech in Florida on national drug-control strategy in which he noted that methamphetamine "is a deadly drug. It is gaining in popularity. In two years, deaths from this drug have doubled. I'm glad it's not here yet, but we have to stop it before it becomes the crack of the 1990s. And we are going after it right now" (*Applause*). The same day, General McCaffrey stressed the need to stop the drug before it became "the poor man's cocaine of the late 1990s. That's where this thing is going. So we're finding it popping up around the country. . . . It's an absolutely devastating drug. . . . And it has just got an abysmal effect on people. They're up for fifteen days straight, awake, and then crashing for five days, and getting increasingly paranoid. They're enormously dangerous to law enforcement officials under the influence of methamphetamine. . . . there's no rhyme nor reason to where methamphetamine are [*sic*] showing up, but it's cheap and incredibly dangerous."[24]

With so much support from the federal law-enforcement bureaucracy, the DEA was solidly placed to request added resources. On May 1, just two days after the speeches by Clinton and McCaffrey, Constantine offered a litany of grim illustrations when he testified to the House Appropriations Committee, stressing the now-familiar themes of drug-related deaths and the spread of usage through the Midwest and South. The depiction of an approaching menace was thoroughly successful, in that the agency received its largest budget ever in fiscal 1997, the first year in which the total exceeded a billion dollars, and 261 additional special agents were employed. Federal authorities also received sweeping new legal powers under the Comprehensive Methamphetamine Control Act of 1996, which substantially increased penalties for trafficking and possession.[25]

Armed with these new powers and resources, the DEA was wonderfully equipped to fight an ever-escalating war against methamphetamine importation from Mexico, a campaign that continued to produce sensational tales of mass arrests and seizures through the end of the decade. Though the cocaine cartels of Medellín and Cali were now removed from the national demonology, leaving a gap in the guilty-foreigners theme, shifting the focus to methamphetamine allowed the agency to construct new substitutes in the form of Mexican drug lords, such as the Tijuana-based Arellano syndicate and the Amezcua family of Guadalajara. If Americans could be convinced that methamphetamine trafficking was the work of what DEA chief Thomas Constantine has called "a very structured, tightly controlled criminal organization that impacts every citizen in the United States," then the drug war should have no difficulty sustaining itself into the indefinite future.[26]

Though the DEA has enjoyed immense success in projecting its distinctive view of the methamphetamine crisis, the claims advanced need to be evaluated carefully. The general statement about the increased usage of methamphetamine can be broadly accepted, as can the explanations offered for the easier availability of the drug. Expanded supply resulted from increased importation from Mexican laboratories and the more efficient manufacturing process based on ephedrine. Numerous recent laboratory seizures in the Midwest support the view that consumption was and is rising in that area, though none of these facilities produces at anything like the rate of the large Mexican or southern Californian plants: all labs are by no means created equal. But even if usage is growing, this does not justify speaking of a national epidemic or crime wave.

The best evidence for rising consumption derives from the DUF system, in which arrestees in various cities are tested for drug use. Generally, this is a critical and well-designed program, so we have to give credit to the 1996 finding that over the previous five years, there had been an overall increase in methamphetamine use among arrestees. Though growth was modest in the cities of highest usage, including San Diego and Phoenix, there were signs of increase in some midwestern communities, leading researchers to conclude cautiously that "sites like Denver, Omaha, and St. Louis could experience significant increases in use *if current trends continue* [my emphasis]. . . . data recently received from Denver and Omaha indicate that use may be expanding to the Midwest." In contrast to the media assertions of this time, DUF findings were warning of a possible trend, not an actual epidemic. Based on this data, the methamphetamine problem in mid-decade still remained basically what it was five or ten years ago, namely a highly regionalized issue heavily focused in the West and Southwest. In 1995, nationwide, only about 6 percent of all adult arrestees from the twenty-three DUF sites tested positive for methamphetamine, compared to 41 percent for cocaine, 28 percent for marijuana, 8 percent for opiates and about 2 percent for PCP. Speed usage was overwhelmingly concentrated in only eight cities, namely San Diego, Phoenix, San Jose, Portland, Omaha, Los Angeles, Denver and Dallas. According to the DUF report, "Other sites reported rates among arrestees at or near zero." As recently as 1998, a major federal study of drug use among arrested offenders found methamphetamine to be overwhelmingly a western and southwestern issue: while in San Diego nearly 40 percent of those arrested had the drug in their systems, the figure for Washington, D.C., was less than one-half of 1 percent.[27] A similar picture emerges from raids on manufacturing facilities. In 1993, the number of clandestine meth laboratories raided in California, Arizona and Nevada was 132, compared to less than ninety for all other states combined.

Also raising doubts about the drug galloping across the country, we should note that the data used by the federal government have serious shortcomings in tracking a drug like methamphetamine, which finds many users in rural and suburban areas. DUF reports are scrupulous in warning readers about the limitations of the system, which is based only on findings from selected metropolitan centers: this evidence cannot be extrapolated to wider populations, not even in those urban areas and still less to the nation at large. The DUF system would not detect high speed usage within rural areas or in smaller cities like Independence, Missouri, or Fargo, North Dakota. Nor indeed would information be available for any of the states that lacked one of the cities included in the program: DUF measures conditions in twenty-three cities spread over eighteen states and the District of Columbia, so that over thirty states are unrepresented.

Moreover, the DUF program originated only in 1987, so we can say little about long-term trends. We thus lack data about major regions in which subcultures might have been abusing synthetics for many years, attracting little official attention. A lack of evidence, though, does not imply an absence of a drug subculture. To take one specific example, in 1997 the DEA tried to illustrate the spread of methamphetamine by showing that speed-related deaths were rising even in Oklahoma City, a community hitherto "relatively untouched by drug abuse." In fact, this same city had had a very substantial amphetamine culture at least since the early 1960s, and some users even then were injecting methamphetamine in this particular corner of the heartland.[28] For all we know, this local drug problem may well have continued uninterrupted to the present day, though it would not show up in any of the federal drug forecasting mechanisms: because a community of that sort was presumed not to be a center of drug activity, there was no reason to track it. This example should make us wonder whether the speed problem was really exploding in Iowa and Missouri in the 1990s, or whether a preexisting situation was just being noticed afresh.

Other proof of growing methamphetamine abuse was provided by emergency-room admissions. While these data are more reliable than some other types, they too are open to interpretation. The chief source here is DAWN, which observes trends in emergency-room episodes involving various drugs, legal and illegal. The data are based on mentions of a particular drug in incidents of very different types: some might involve overdoses, but many others involve accidental injuries or car crashes, when there is no necessary implication that a given drug directly caused injury or death.[29] Another shortcoming of the data is that, like the DUF program, they mainly reflect metropolitan trends and conditions.

Yet at first sight, emergency-room data seem to confirm an explosive growth in meth use. Between 1990 and 1994, the total number of DAWN-reported episodes rose by a dramatic 37 percent, and a portion of this increase can be attributed to methamphetamine abuse. According to DAWN, "Between 1988 and 1991, there was a decrease in methamphetamine-related emergency department episodes. However, from 1991 through 1994, methamphetamine-related episodes rose 256 percent from 4,900 to 17,400. Between 1993 and 1994, methamphetamine-related episodes increased 75 percent from 9,900 to 17,400." This sounds appalling, but these raw figures are misleading, as the high 1994 figures were inflated by changes in reporting practices at two major hospitals in western areas with high methamphetamine usage. In late 1992, detoxification centers opened near these facilities, and patients seeking admission for detox had to obtain medical clearance through these hospitals, causing an artificial increase in the number of episodes reported at their emergency rooms. If we remove just those two hospitals, the national increase for 1993–94 is closer to 45 percent, not 75. Though significant growth in speed usage is attested, DAWN data encourage us to keep the problem in perspective: record-keeping changes in one or two hospitals can make an immense difference.[30]

Even in 1994–95, methamphetamine still played a minor role in the emergency rooms when set beside the medical crises caused by heroin and cocaine, and the increase in the rate of speed episodes was considerably smaller than that involving marijuana or even acetaminophen, the painkiller best known under brand names such as Tylenol. In 1994, acetaminophen was involved in a hundred thousand DAWN episodes nationwide, far more than methamphetamine, and a 1995 report found several hundred deaths directly attributable to the effects of acetaminophen. By far the largest reason for the increase in emergency-room episodes involved surging abuse in heroin, not speed.

Another type of distortion occurred when increased rates of seizure and detection were cited as if they represented rising usage rather than intensified official action. Indeed, official statements about methamphetamine demonstrated a remarkable ability to take essentially identical statistics as proof of diametrically opposite trends. In the fall of 1996, the DEA used the high rate of raids on laboratories as proof of the urgency of the problem and thus the need for greater resources. A few months later, President Clinton used a high rate of seizures to make exactly the opposite point, that law enforcement was winning enormous victories in the face of the drug menace. Addressing the U.S. Conference of Mayors, he boasted that "seizures of dangerous drug labs used to manufacture meth are up 170 percent in one year alone. . . . So this shows you that if we work together we can actually turn the tide in problem after problem after problem."[31] Though the quantitative evidence demonstrating the scale of methamphetamine abuse had scarcely changed since the previous year, the president was declaring that the issue had declined precipitously as a serious social problem.

*

Though both DAWN and DUF figures showed growing methamphetamine usage, the most powerful data employed by the DEA and the White House reported the number of deaths related to the drug. Though the sensational mortality figures were questionable, they were stressed so much in official rhetoric because they were believed to confirm an emerging public-health crisis: speed killed. In January 1996, the DEA expressed alarm in *Methamphetamine/Speed Abuse*, including figures that would often be repeated over the following year. Based on data from medical examiners in major cities across the nation, the report claimed a massive increase in methamphetamine-related deaths—145 percent nationally between 1992 and 1994. There were 1816 such deaths nationally for the period 1991–94, of which 80 percent (1459 deaths) were reported by just four western urban areas. The evidence for increasing mortality was most apparent in these communities (see table 7.1):[32] These lessons were repeatedly cited. Even the responsible *New York Times* reported simply, "In Phoenix, [methamphetamine] killed 122 people in 1994, the authorities said," while President Clinton himself claimed, "In two years, deaths from this drug have doubled." By the end of 1996, the director of NIDA announced that methamphetamine had swiftly become the third deadliest drug in California, following crack and heroin.[33]

On the surface, this looks like irrefutable evidence for a surge in speed abuse and its harmful consequences, as the data derive from medical professionals rather than criminal justice agencies. Still, the figures simply cannot be accepted at face value. It is far from clear what is being measured in such a table and whether the standards applied are consistent over time. To understand the difficulties, consider this remark: "Nationally, [methamphetamine] episodes ranked seventh among controlled substances after cocaine, heroin, codeine, diazepam, marijuana and methadone." We must be brought up short by the suggestion that more deaths were caused by marijuana than methamphetamine. Over the last sixty years, a vigorous medical debate has raged over the physical effects of that substance, and some literature argues that marijuana may cause long-term harm, such as brain damage or birth defects, but the concept of marijuana being the direct cause of death is bizarre. Is there really a single case on record in which a person has died from the direct effects of this drug? When an

Table 7.1 Methamphetamine-Related Deaths in Major Cities

City	1992	1993	1994	Increase 1992–94 (%)
Los Angeles	68	198	219	222
Phoenix	20	63	122	510
San Diego	97	110	172	77
San Francisco	48	62	69	44
TOTAL	233	433	582	150

agency did venture to list a fatal dose for marijuana in the early 1970s, the joke in the underground media was that the amount listed must have referred to the quantity dropped on one's head from a three-story building. Pot emphatically does not kill, and the inclusion of marijuana raises the critical and often intractable question of what exactly is meant by a death "related to" this or any drug.

Ideally, this phrase should be applied to an event in which a death was directly caused by the substance and would not have occurred otherwise, as in the case of a lethal overdose, but these strict criteria are not followed in the data supplied here. Instead, the term "methamphetamine-related death" is employed to describe any suspicious or violent death in which the drug is subsequently found in the victim's system, so that the question of causation is elided. If we find nicotine in the system of a deceased individual, we do not automatically classify that as a cigarette-related fatality. In fact, the concept of speed having the power to kill is open to debate: a comprehensive study of the different bodies of data available for amphetamine use in the mid-1970s suggested that there might be one death for every two million uses of the drug, making it a remarkably safe product. Methamphetamine might be expected to produce far more serious results, but even a major overdose of this drug is very rarely a direct cause of death, except in combination with substantial amounts of other substances.[34] Methamphetamine certainly can be associated with fatalities, especially if it is injected. This practice raises the specter of contaminated needles, with all that implies for the spread of AIDS and hepatitis, but this issue was not raised in all the clamor over meth-related deaths.

How exactly, then, is speed meant to kill? The DEA's report notes that, of the 1,816 deaths supposedly linked to speed, "the manner of death was predominantly reported to be accidental (47 percent), while suicide was reported in only 13 percent of the episodes." Since methamphetamine is a stimulant, a powerful upper, it is a most unlikely choice for a suicide weapon, in contrast to sedatives such as the barbiturates. Presumably, these are cases in which the drug is found in the systems of suicide victims, rather than where it was a contributory cause of death. Moreover, if accident and suicide account for only 60 percent of deaths, many of the remaining cases were presumably homicide, so that the drug is blamed when speed is found in the body of a murder *victim*, without any proof that the substance contributed to the fatality. There might be cases in which speed encouraged someone to act recklessly and aggressively, thereby provoking a violent incident, but the whole notion of victim-precipitated homicide is controversial. If it is no longer acceptable to argue that women provoke rape attacks, even in instances in which their conduct might seem irresponsible, it is difficult to see why a comparable interpretation should be tolerated in cases of murder.

The question of causation is also difficult where multiple drugs were involved, which was the situation in 90 percent of those instances: drugs found in combination with methamphetamine included alcohol (31 percent of cases), cocaine (22 percent) and heroin (18 percent). This was exactly the same statistical sleight of hand recently applied to generate the allegedly surging figures of cocaine-related deaths: as Reinarman and Levine show, the presence of cocaine, often in combination with other drugs, was repeatedly and misleadingly taken to imply that cocaine alone had caused the fatality.[35] From the figures offered in the DEA's 1996 report, it is not clear whether methamphetamine was the direct physical cause of any of the deaths noted, and still less of any significant proportion of them. Perhaps the drug did contribute in many instances—for example, in causing impaired driving—but the decision to list such a death as drug-related depends upon the subjective judgment of individual medical examiners, who were far more likely to render such an opinion in communities where the drug was recognized as a grave social problem.

In summary, what the death figures show is that in the early 1990s, medical examiners in certain cities were finding substantially more evidence of methamphetamine in the systems of people who died suddenly or violently, which might reflect increased usage among the general population. Death statistics could also reflect other changes in official practice, including a greater willingness to test for the presence of speed and a greater tendency to blame the substance for violent acts, which is perhaps an after effect of the crack experience. In any case, the rates of increase suggested by the death statistics are far higher than what can plausibly be sustained from other data, including arrestee tests and emergency-room episodes. The sixfold increase of deaths in Phoenix between 1992 and 1994 simply cannot indicate a comparable rise in the city's consumption rates during the same time period, because we find no such evidence of increase from the area's emergency rooms. And yet when reported by the media, such caveats are forgotten.

To put these figures in context, we should note that all drugs can cause adverse reactions, including perfectly legal medications properly prescribed by qualified medical personnel. The scale of such adverse reactions is amazingly high: according to a recent survey, perhaps a hundred thousand Americans die each year from the effects of legal synthetic drugs administered in hospitals, and over two million more (7 percent of all hospital patients) suffer nonlethal adverse reactions. Moreover, this survey only tracked adverse reactions in hospital settings and did not include lethal effects that might have occurred at home. The unintentional consequences of legally supplied synthetics amount to perhaps the fourth leading cause of death for Americans. In contrast to the situation with illegal synthetics, medical authorities vastly understate the damage caused by these prescribed drugs, so that only a tiny proportion of these hospital fatalities are recorded as drug-related. In a typical year, only 3,500 such events are reported to the federal government, less than 4 percent of the total. The disastrous consequences of legal drugs are understated quite as thoroughly as those of their illegal counterparts are exaggerated.[36]

Similar questions about causation and drug-related phenomena should also be applied in cases where an individual who carries out a violent act is found to have methamphetamine in his or her system, as recounting stories of notorious crimes does not indicate whether those acts would not have occurred without the presence of the drug. As with cocaine or PCP, the evidence associating methamphetamine with criminal violence is suggestive, but not conclusive.[37] If we consider the cities with the highest known usage of speed, then Phoenix certainly did experience a significant upsurge of homicides between 1992 and 1994, and much of this was linked to shifts in the organization of drug trafficking. On the other hand, San Diego experienced a marked decline in homicides at this same time. At the height of the alleged speed epidemic in 1995, both cities actually recorded declining homicide rates, though nobody drew the lesson that methamphetamine was somehow discouraging violence.[38] Based on this evidence, little or nothing can be concluded about the impact of meth trafficking on violent crime.

What can plausibly be said about the methamphetamine situation in the mid-1990s was that some evidence suggested a geographical expansion beyond the traditional centers of usage in the West and Southwest, but it was far too early to suggest any explosive growth of national popularity. As General McCaffrey accurately stated, "It's not in New York City. It's not in Miami. It's not in Washington, D.C."[39] Using the evidence of drug-related deaths not only vastly inflated the seriousness of the problem; it also made quite unwarranted suggestions about the deadly effects of the drug. The rising scourge of methamphetamine scarcely justified its billing.

The rediscovery of speed must be understood in terms of the needs and priorities of the political leaders and bureaucrats making the claims. The DEA's role is not difficult to comprehend, as bureaucratic exigencies demand that the agency find and publicize a continuing diet of new drug menaces, and a decline in one quarter is likely to be countered with growth in another. During the ice age, the agency needed no new problem, as the crack cocaine menace was more than sufficient, but matters had changed substantially by mid-decade. The agency flirted with the possibility of identifying methcathinone as the next menace before plumping for the more plausible issue of speed.

Table 7.2 Changing Murder Rates 1992–95

City	Murders Recorded, 1992–95			
	1992	*1993*	*1994*	*1995*
Phoenix	136(207)	158(229)	231(308)	214(305)
San Diego	146(245)	133(245)	113(205)	91(198)

City	Murder Rate for MSA			
	1992	*1993*	*1994*	*1995*
Phoenix/Mesa	8.8	9.6	12.4	11.9
San Diego	9.5	9.3	7.7	7.5

Figures in parentheses refer to MSA.

Methamphetamine rose to prominence at a time when the DEA was radically reformulating its political agenda. As the agency boasted in its review of highlights of 1995, "the year . . . will be remembered as an historic period in international and domestic drug law enforcement. With the arrest of six of the seven top leaders of the Cali mafia, and with the possible unraveling of the Shan United Army's dominance of the global heroin enterprise, significant enforcement gains against the world's most notorious drug traffickers were realized." But it is possible to be too successful, and the DEA was anxious to ensure that a spectacular decline in international drug threats should not be perceived as a justification for relaxing vigilance or reducing the agency's resources. The review of achievements therefore concluded with a warning against complacence: "Looking forward, 1996 promises many challenges as law enforcement pressure is focused on major trafficking organizations from Mexico, and as federal, state and local law enforcement work together to address a new epidemic of methamphetamine."[40] The new campaign was a triumph, with its height of publicity coinciding with the DEA's budget hearings for fiscal year 1997. As we have seen, the methamphetamine alarm justified a remarkable expansion in DEA resources, rather than the severe cutbacks that had been feared so recently. Challenges can become opportunities.

It was by no means obvious that methamphetamine should have been singled out as the agency's new post-crack target. The drug was not necessarily booming any more than a variety of other substances, notably heroin, which since the late 1980s had regained some of its middle-class following, initially on the West Coast but with some influence in the East. In 1994, a congressional inquiry listed the possible new challenges facing the DEA as heroin, methamphetamine and CAT.[41] Even if other drugs had slipped from the headlines, substantial markets also still existed for other synthetics, such as PCP, Ecstasy and the new party drugs, including GHB, Rohypnol and Ketamine. In contrast, methamphetamine had a particular appeal for claim-makers because of both its racial and its regional appeal. Such a definitively white drug could be presented as posing a novel threat to a large majority of the population, while an emphasis on heroin would merely reinforce existing stereotypes of drug abuse as an urban phenomenon. Methamphetamine had the potential to become a ubiquitous national phenomenon.

Moreover, the concentration of this problem in the West and Southwest was politically important. Since mid-century, American politics have been reshaped by a fundamental shift of influence to the states of the South and West, as Sun Belt states grew and acquired steadily more electoral votes, while those of their northern counterparts contracted. Between 1952 and 1992, Texas grew from twenty-three electoral votes to thirty-two, Florida from ten to twenty-five, California from thirty-two to fifty-four, and southwestern states, which in 1950 had three or four electoral votes each, now generally had six or eight. This new electoral geography does much to explain the political triumph of the Republican Party in the 1980s, as well as the growing influence of attitudes and cultural forms once considered purely southern.[42] By 1996, all electoral projections agreed on the imperative need for the winning presidential candidate to retain California, which was the focus of intense campaigning throughout these years. It made excellent political sense for the Clinton administration to demonstrate such intense concern about a regional crime problem like methamphetamine, especially when his party had been attacked by Republicans for being soft on crime and drug issues. The crusade against speed permitted the administration to portray itself as not merely tough on drugs, but as toughest on those substances that were a particular threat to the West and Southwest—to Phoenix and San Diego, Dallas and Los Angeles. By late 1995, any potential voter in California or Arizona who paid the slightest attention to the news media would have fully accepted the contention that speed was a direct and immediate threat to the community.

This political context helps explain the potent environmental subtext in media attacks on methamphetamine. Even more than in the recent encounter with CAT, drug manufacture was presented as a dreadful hazard to neighboring communities, through immediate dangers such as fire and explosion as well as long-term contamination. Every meth lab, even a tiny operation in a garage, was "a mini-toxic waste site" that might take several thousand dollars to clean up.[43] This theme of toxic hazard enhanced the stigma attached to the drug, while environmental sentiment generally has greater electoral appeal in the western and southwestern states. The display of Democratic concern about issues affecting the region helped the 1996 Clinton-Gore campaign carry the states of California, Oregon, Washington, Arizona, New Mexico and Nevada, and Clinton became the first Democratic candidate to win Arizona since 1976.

Another related agenda was at work here, in that during 1995 and 1996, several states experienced lively campaigns to legalize the use of marijuana for medical purposes, the first attempt in many years actually to reduce penalties for an illegal drug. The DEA repeatedly denounced this measure in press statements and congressional testimony. In April 1995, the agency warned of "The Cruel Hoax of Legalization," and in September, another statement declared, "Legalization Is a Surrender." Bureaucratic activism intensified during 1996, when marijuana initiatives appeared on the ballots of several states, including California and Arizona: these were, of course, the regions in which methamphetamine was most popular and that had, rightly or wrongly, been most frequently associated with drug-related mayhem. The emphasis on speed permitted anti-drug campaigners to reinforce warnings against legalization in precisely those jurisdictions most directly threatened.[44] At many levels, the methamphetamine menace was an invaluable political issue for the mid-1990s.

The white storm warning originated in the federal anti-drug bureaucracy, but once established, the claims had great potential for further dissemination and growth. Federal campaigns promised substantial dividends for state and local agencies in terms of both resources and ideological advancement, often appealing to smaller states not traditionally seen as overly concerned with drug issues. Still, much was at stake. The drug war declared by the Reagan and Bush administrations had promised extensive support to governments and law-enforcement agencies in regions designated as facing a particularly serious narcotics problem, which in practice referred to major urban communities. The new emphasis on methamphetamine, however, promised the same cornucopia of resources to virtually any rural or suburban area that could be presented as a center for that drug.

Thus the methamphetamine scare now justified appeals for federal largesse to these smaller states. In Iowa, for instance, both Democratic senator Tom Harkin and his Republican challenger were pressing in 1996 for legislation to designate five midwestern states as a High Intensity Drug Trafficking Area, a concept previously applied to metropolitan regions like South Central Los Angeles.[45] Now the designation was sought, and won, for Iowa, Missouri, South Dakota, Nebraska and Kansas. The incentive for demanding such a grim label was, of course, the federal funding that would flow to assist police and prosecutors in such an afflicted area, which totalled $8 million in the first year of designation: in fact, this was the motive that had inspired cities a decade previously to vie for the title of "speed capital." And identifying an area as drug-intensive (or as a speed capital) provided extra fuel to the continuing perceptions of a crisis. Resources granted for increased investigation would cause a dramatic rise in arrests and lab seizures, which would in turn supply evidence for an epidemic and justify demands for still more federal assistance.

Like all of its synthetic predecessors, methamphetamine gained notoriety in 1995 not because it posed a new or growing danger, but because it was phenomenally useful, a valuable resource for a variety of political, rhetorical and bureaucratic causes. Partly by manipulating racial fears, claim-makers succeeded in constructing a convincing successor to the crack scare. But at every stage, the new image of the "kiss of meth" was flawed: though the drug was certainly popular in some western areas, it is far from clear whether it was spreading rapidly into new regions or whether long-standing activity was just being noticed afresh. Also, the widely quoted figures purporting to trace the drug's impact by means of deaths and hospital admissions were largely statistical quirks that did not reflect real changes in drug usage.

For all of its symbolic power, methamphetamine was by no means the only synthetic to attract attention in the mid-1990s. In these same years, generational and sexual tensions opened the way to a revival of the designer-drug panic, focusing on substances believed to pose a danger to young teenagers, particularly to women.

EIGHT

Rave Drugs and Rape Drugs

You had to let them know that in spite of their best efforts to
make you like them, to make you dead, you were still alive.
　　　　—Irvine Welsh, "Lorraine Goes to Livingston," 1996

Just as publicity concerning methamphetamine was cresting in the
summer of 1996, a new synthetic menace was looming in the form of
rave or party drugs. Over the last four decades, successive youth cultures have adopted very different tastes in music, dress and dance
styles, but through all of these waves, illegal drugs have remained a
constant presence. In the last few years, several different synthetics
have become popular as party or rave drugs, and these substances have
provided the foundation for a new wave of designer-drug panics. The
dance/party cultures have been highly localized, so that one substance
might have a powerful vogue in the clubs of one city while being unknown in a neighboring state. Anti-drug crusaders mobilized public
opinion by depicting regional vogues as a portent of a national fad,
perhaps even a nascent epidemic. Through the 1990s, the media have
avidly reported on such alleged breakout drugs as Ecstasy, ketamine
(Special K), GHB and even a supposedly revived LSD.

The coverage in each case has been almost interchangeable, with
the common theme of homemade synthetics posing a deadly danger
to the young. The atmosphere for the renewed drug panics has been
made possible by demographic changes in the society at large, as a
large baby-boom audience that experimented freely with illegal drugs
is now prepared to be alarmed by the supposed dangers to its own off-

spring. The exposés about clubland drug use by teenagers, or baby-busters, are perhaps what we should expect from the much older society of the 1990s: the median age of the U.S. population rose sharply from twenty-eight in 1970 to thirty-three in 1990; Americans aged fourteen through seventeen represented almost 8 percent of the population in 1970, but only 5.3 percent by 1990.

Coverage of party drugs has been closely linked to the concept of rape drugs—the use of GHB, Rohypnol and other synthetics to render women unconscious for sexual purposes. As so often occurs in emerging social problems, the media establishes the significance of a supposed danger by giving it a human face, personalizing the story in a way that will make it comprehensible to a mass audience; the rape-drug menace found its martyr in an innocent young Texan girl supposedly killed in a botched chemical seduction. Though subsequent evidence showed that drugs probably did not play a part in her death, the myth continued to be recycled as a potent political weapon. Though drugs like Rohypnol have been used to facilitate sexual assaults, the coverage of these incidents in the late 1990s implied a pervasive threat from rape drugs, with the media advocating defensive measures that appear grossly excessive. Once again, synthetics became a public nightmare not so much because of any objective threat they posed, but because they came to symbolize underlying fears, in this case fears of rape and sexual molestation. These charges became so important because they gave such a powerful added incentive to the suppression of the party drugs.

Though prohibited in the mid-1980s, Ecstasy would return as one of the most important of the new wave of youth-culture drugs.[1] By far the greatest impact was seen in Europe, where the drug became the basis of a subculture. In the mid-1980s, Ecstasy became popular in cosmopolitan Mediterranean resorts like Ibiza, or XTC island, where it appealed to hedonistic nightclubbers as well as to New Age seekers: it was especially popular with followers of the Indian cult leader Bhagwan Shree Rajneesh. Ecstasy proved an all-purpose chemical companion. Seekers used it for promoting visions and elevated states of consciousness, partygoers for providing a whole new dimension to all-night dance events and others for enhancing sexual encounters. Young people brought these new fashions back to their home countries in Northern Europe, and the resort party scene was reproduced in Great Britain, the Netherlands, Belgium and Germany.

By the late 1980s, all-night, Ecstasy-fueled parties had come to be known as raves, which were associated with a revolution in popular music. Raves were held in so-called acid-houses, where Ecstasy fulfilled the functions served by LSD in the 1960s. Gatherings were also known as warehouse parties, as the events were simply too large to be held in regular dance clubs, and the associated culture and music were known as "house." In British popular mythology, the summer of 1988 occupies an exciting and liberating role similar to that of the 1967 Summer of Love in San Francisco. By 1990, it was estimated that perhaps half a million people in Great Britain had tried Ecstasy, which inspired "the most vibrant and diverse youth movement Britain has ever seen. Ecstasy culture . . . is the best entertainment format on the market, a deployment of technologies—musical, chemical and computer—to deliver altered states of consciousness."[2] The idea of integrating biological, chemical and electronic technologies to enhance pleasure and consciousness owes much to science fiction, especially to the cyberpunk genre begun by William Gibson's novel *Neuromancer* (1984): Gibson's characters are equally expert with computer hacking and the latest synthetic drugs, each of which opens gateways to new types of virtual reality, mediated by technology.

The rise of rave culture provoked a flood of popular and scholarly studies, which presented British youth of the nineties as a chemical generation in much the same way as their American counterparts had been depicted thirty years before. Ecstasy-trafficking occupied center stage in British popular-culture treatments of the youth drug culture in films like *London Kills Me* (1991) and theatrical productions like *Beyond Ecstasy* and *Shopping and Fucking* (both 1998). The Ecstasy theme attracted novelists such as Douglas Rushkoff, whose 1997 work *The Ecstasy Club* depicted the transplantation of a British-style rave club to San Francisco.

Ecstasy was the title of a volume of tales of chemical romance by popular Scottish author Irvine Welsh, best known as the author of the novel (and film) *Trainspotting*. His young, working-class characters live in a world dominated by the quest for raves and the drugs needed to participate in them. These are usually Es, or Ecstasy, sold under myriad brand names suggesting cosmopolitan sophistication (such as "Amsterdam Playboys"). The drug produces feelings of joy, satisfaction and sexual desire, offering a few hours of subversive pleasure in a life of grey squalor and pervasive poverty. As one character recalls, "I went to go to the toilet to see myself in the mirror. I didn't seem to walk but to float through within my own mystical aura. All those beautiful people were smiling and looking like I was feeling." "I was going to take every drug known to the human race and shag anything that moved." In short, "You'll just feel good about yourself, and the rest of the world for a while. There's nothing wrong with that." Welsh's characters persist in their habits despite a barrage of warnings and advice from politicians and media experts. Users recognize that "[Ecstasy] kills you, but so does everything, every piece of food you ingest, every breath of air you take. It does you a lot less damage than the drink."[3] Warnings about drugs and health hazards were scarcely to be believed when stemming from an officialdom that lied systematically about virtually everything and which was intimately allied with the legal drug pushers of the multinational pharmaceutical corporations.

Faced with a massive upsurge of illegal drug use, European governments tried to suppress Ecstasy, supported by a mass media that linked the substance to deaths and brain damage. The evidence of harm caused by these "dances of death" is controversial. Some fifteen deaths were reported in the United Kingdom over a two-year period, but in no case was the death associated with an overdose: problems arose when the drug raised body temperature, which often occurred in the overheated setting of a poorly ventilated dance club. Death thus occurred from dehydration and heat exhaustion. However, the media used each succeeding incident to stigmatize the drug and the surrounding culture, a process aided by celebrity admissions of drug misuse. As in the United States, critics used the drug's chemical relationship to methamphetamine to recall the worst propaganda surrounding speed and to suggest that MDMA started an individual on a slippery slope culminating in meth use. The decisive event in Britain was the 1995 death of a teenager named Leah Betts, ostensibly following a single tablet of Ecstasy, the first and only one she had ever taken. The media account was misleading in almost every particular, but whatever the actual circumstances, the idea that Ecstasy kills fostered even tougher legal action. Betts's parents led a public campaign against the drug, which led directly to a 1997 law that allowed licensing authorities, acting on the advice of local police, to revoke the licenses of clubs that failed to deal effectively with their drug problems. Further tarnishing the image of Ecstasy was the linkage with organized crime, which inevitably became involved in the aftermath of legal repression. In such settings, Ecstasy travelled far from its therapeutic and yuppie origins to provide the motive for gutter-level ripoffs and intimidation.[4]

Ecstasy use followed a very different course in the United States, where it had gained a following in the mid-1980s, but it was slower to win mass appeal. Instead, the drug retained its niche following among selected communities, including New Agers and especially Deadheads, the cultish followers of the Grateful Dead. By 1989, it was popular among yuppies and clubgoers in cities such as Atlanta, Dallas and New Orleans and was gaining ground on certain college campuses. In one survey of the mid-1980s, almost 40 percent of Stanford undergraduates reported having tried MDMA at least once. Some users also turned to a milder, nonscheduled analog, MDEA, or EVE.[5]

In the early 1990s, European expatriates introduced the rave concept and the associated drugs into the night-club cultures of New York and San Francisco. "Partygoers—attired in Cat in the Hat-hats and psychedelic jumpsuits—pay $20 at the door to dance all night to heavily mixed, electronically generated sound, surrounded by computer-generated video and laser lightshows. They pay another $3 to $5 for 'smart drinks'—amino acid-laced beverages that reputedly enhance energy and alertness. And for another $20, those so inclined can purchase an Ecstasy tablet." Reinforcing the sixties nostalgia of such events, some Los Angeles raves were hosted by the son of Timothy Leary, a man legendary for his promotion of LSD in that earlier epoch. Worried reports of the vibrant club scene on both sides of the Atlantic appeared in professional publications like the Journal of the American Medical Association (*JAMA*) as well as in the popular media, which in turn served to advertise both the culture and its attendant drugs. Though Ecstasy never acquired the same enormous vogue in the United States as it did in Manchester or Amsterdam, it was successfully repackaged as part of a voguish culture. Soon, furious local debates ensued as American cities tried to regulate or suppress raves.[6]

Ecstasy was not the only new rave drug. Another popular substance was GHB, or gamma-hydroxy-butyrate, a concentrated version of an amino acid that occurs naturally in the brain, praised by advocates for its wide-ranging effects on mood and metabolism. Throughout the 1980s, the substance was sold legally in health food stores and was popular with bodybuilders.[7] In 1990, the FDA officially reclassified GHB as a drug rather than a nutrient, making it subject to more stringent regulation so that it was no longer available over the counter. Still, GHB's career was only beginning. It may have been through the bodybuilding link that it gained a foothold in the gay social circuit and later in club life in general. As one anonymous enthusiast wrote on the Web, "All but replacing Ecstasy (MDMA), it's now on the forefront of what seems like a new drug revolution." Though hostile publicity about the drug and its effects mounted in the early 1990s, the drug remained legal under federal rules, so that its manufacture was regulated only by the FDA, not the DEA.

Another new synthetic was ketamine hydrochloride, popularly named Special K or Vitamin K, an anesthetic intended primarily for veterinary use with dissociative effects comparable to those of PCP.[8] Its effects were described at some length in the 1970s in the work of Dr. John Lilly, whose experiments with various psychedelic substances made him a hero in the drug subculture. As with other synthetics, it initially gained popularity in the gay dance party world, where the drug was esteemed as a safe high, lacking the perils of better-known drugs. Ketamine became popular at fashionable gay events such as Washington's Cherry Jubilee and Miami's White Party. These circuit parties used Special K alongside old favorites like crystal methamphetamine. The drug acquired an impressive social cachet: a 1997 account of the wealthy gay circles of New York and Miami described "the young, hip, up-for-anything set that reveres Versace, works out at the trendiest gym, dances bare-chested at the hottest club, knows all about (and sometimes takes) the latest designer drugs, such as Ecstasy,

Special-K, or crystal meth." K received intense publicity following the mid-1996 closure of two fashionable New York City clubs, Limelight and the Tunnel: a DEA investigation alleged the existence of "'a drug supermarket' where 'massive amounts' of Ecstasy, as well as cocaine, the animal tranquilizer ketamine and the depressant Rohypnol were used as 'promotional tools to lure patrons to the club.'"[9] The club owner was eventually acquitted of drug charges following a lengthy trial, but this catalog does provide an accurate listing of the favored drugs of the American rave culture in New York and other cities. By 1997, the drug's breakout into a wider market was reflected in an upsurge of references in rock music, in the film *Scream II* and on *The X-Files.*

Like GHB, ketamine was not initially regulated in such a way as to expose it to DEA sanctions or controls, and thus it existed in a semilegal netherworld. Unlike GHB, though, ketamine had widely accepted medical and veterinary uses and was distributed by major pharmaceutical companies such as Parke-Davis, which made the drug more resilient in the face of prohibition attempts. When in 1998 U.S. Senator Joseph Biden proposed a bill to declare ketamine a Schedule I controlled substance, he was defeated by industry efforts, though individual states did pass more stringent laws.

Information about new designer drugs had spread easily enough in earlier decades, but the pace of dissemination was made immensely faster by new computer technologies, which spread information to the remotest corners of the country. And though Internet usage can be tracked, most users feel a much greater sense of anonymity with this medium than they would with a mail-order bookseller, whose records could be subpoenaed. The rise of the Internet has revolutionized the world of synthetic drugs, although the new environment is scarcely familiar to either media people or anti-drug authorities. Most journalists fall far behind high school and college students in understanding the potential of the Internet, and thus they fail to appreciate just how easily information about illicit stimulants can be accumulated. When the *New York Times* published a headline story warning, "A Seductive Drug Culture Flourishes on the Internet," the main problem discussed was purely political rather than technical, namely the use of the

Internet to promote policies of drug legalization.[10] In reality, once young and reasonably well-educated people are alerted to the presence of a hot drug, it is then a simple matter to find more information about it through the World Wide Web.

An hour on the Internet can give even a fairly inexperienced person a series of consumer reports on drugs both familiar and arcane, often with detailed manufacturing instructions. This information is amazingly accessible, even if one only knows the name of a newly popular drug. To illustrate this, in late-1998, I put myself in the position of someone knowing nothing whatever about illegal drugs who was intrigued by a news report mentioning the existence of potent chemicals called GHB and ketamine. Using the Web search engine Infoseek to find references to the single word ketamine, I found a substantial 1,658 hits (and GHB produced 1,997 results, with 4,126 for MDMA). Ketamine is difficult to synthesize in amateur labs and most supplies are obtained from the clandestine diversion of legitimate products, so that most of the Internet references to the drug concerned experiences of its use rather than details of its manufacture.[11]

Internet sites also produced many suggestions for finding near analogues and alternatives users might try in addition to ketamine. A productive resource here is the newsgroup alt.drugs, to which makers and consumers post their hints and recipes. One item from 1994 notes that since PCP and ketamine derive from the same general group of chemicals, "MK-801 (dizocilipine? or something like that), which is another of the same class of NMDA/sigma agents, should have a similar set of effects."[12] A follow-up questions whether dizocilpine would indeed be as potent or as interesting as ketamine, but adds encouragingly, "If you wish to list other dissociative agents, you should certainly include tiletamine, the N-ethyl, thienyl analog of ketamine. In admixture with a benzodiazepine, it is known as Telazol, and is used as an animal anesthetic." Despite their apparent technical expertise, such postings are not reviewed for accuracy by any external source, and it is conceivable that the recommended drugs might be wholly ineffective, or indeed lethal. But someone is bound to experiment with them, and, assuming he or she survives, we will no doubt have a report on the experience available through the Internet.

Entering the search term GHB is equally successful, and one can easily find a GHBInfo home page. From just the first ten references offered, the Web-surfer can promptly find two separate means for synthesizing the drug. The easiest gives a simple list of ingredients, including "60 grams of NaOH, 120 ml of gamma-butyrolactone, and a liter of 95 percent alcohol." The only possible obstacle to easy manufacture is the difficulty of finding gamma-butyrolactone, though "several companies sell it on the Net—make a search using *Dejanews*. Other companies sell complete kits for preparing GHB." Other materials are straightforward, including funnels, mason jars and coffee filters, and the manufacturing process is presented comprehensively. By 1997, Web-based entrepreneurs were offering complete GHB manufacture kits for prices ranging from $60 to $160.[13] By this stage of our search, we might be developing a new respect for the former FBN head Harry Anslinger, who rejected the idea of drug education in schools on the grounds that any exposure to the world of narcotics would simply invite young people to become curious and experiment; he died long before the emergence of the Web.

Any search for a specific drug is also likely to produce leads about other psychedelic or stimulant substances of which the researcher might not hitherto have heard. From the first few references in a GHB search, we find a posting about "a most excellent trip report about a 2C-B + GHB combo," which will introduce the novice to the mild psychedelic about which Alexander Shulgin had waxed so lyrical in *PIHKAL*, and further suggest how GHB can be used in combination with other drugs. Following a link on that trip report will bring a Web-surfer to the Lycaeum, one of the richest sites for drug-related information, with its Drug Information Archives and chat rooms. The Lycaeum's main index offers information on magic mushrooms, on naturally occurring psychedelics like Ayahuasca and *Salvia Divinorum* and on DXM (dextromethorphan), and moreover it offers links to sites on Ecstasy and the amphetamines.[14] If we take this last connection, we come to the Hive, "your global resource center for the advancement and exchange of Ecstasy and amphetamine chemical knowledge"—and we are still only four or so mouse-clicks away from the initial Infoseek search on GHB, from which we began.

The Hive is a fascinating site, though by no means the only one of its kind. A prospective clandestine chemist finds here a comprehensive and user-friendly environment that presents information for the callowest novice: "Having trouble understanding synthesis? Don't know what a reagent is? What are the effects of MDMA? Maybe you don't know anything about chemistry or biology. Here's some links, books, whatever, to help." The archive at the site includes references or links to such technical resources as Chemical Abstracts On-Line and the Medline Database, and to printed works including *Advanced Practical Organic Chemistry*, the *Journal of Forensic Science*, *Psychedelic Chemistry*, and, of course, *PIHKAL*.[15] There are also links to suppliers of psychedelic-related literature, like Mind Books and Loompanics. For anyone still discouraged by the cornucopia of information, there is a link to "*Chemistry Quickly*—the hardcore caffeine-fueled chemistry course . . . recommended for beginners!!!" The Hive includes a message board, where manufacturers and users post picayune technical queries as well as consumer reports, which incidentally are frank about the possible harmful effects of the various substances. A few minutes more of surfing will bring the user to the Web site for the Multidisciplinary Association for Psychedelic Studies, which "offers access to all its past newsletters, searchable by keyword. Through this feature, you can review the history and current status of research into MDMA, psilocybin, DMT, ibogaine, ayahuasca, marijuana, LSD, ketamine, and other drugs." This site is cross-referenced to the WWW Psychedelic Bibliography, "a searchable electronic bibliography of scientific papers related to psychedelic drugs."

The number of potential substances is almost limitless, and most will remain untapped unless or until some well-meaning journalist or politician anoints one drug as hot, a drug of choice, whereupon the search for effective analogs will begin in earnest. As such analogues are not generally subject to strict legal prohibitions, they stand a good chance of acquiring a vogue until they in turn are publicized and forbidden, whereupon the cycle begins afresh.

The U.S. media discovered the new party culture during 1993, though initially the main perceived drug problem was that of LSD rather than the newer synthetics. Partly, this reflected observations of the San Francisco area, where LSD had remained popular since the 1960s and where most of the labs were still to be found. Rave culture in the Bay Area therefore used LSD in addition to Ecstasy, and the American public first encountered rave in early 1993 as part of a general warning in what the news program *48 Hours* called "LSD Return Trip." According to this report, "experts say that more teenagers are now using LSD and other illegal hallucinogens than cocaine, the scourge of the eighties," while the DEA was struggling "to prevent LSD becoming the drug epidemic of the nineties." LSD usage was indeed rising at this time, with high school seniors recording usage at levels unparallelled since the mid-1970s, but prophecies of epidemics were as spectacularly inaccurate as contemporary charges about the ferocious CAT attack. Extrapolating unpardonably from San Francisco conditions, the program warned parents that "there's a good chance your children know all about [LSD]." Raves, meanwhile, were "coming to a town near you."[16]

Early reports of the supposed LSD revival largely missed the role of the newer rave drugs, but this neglect soon ended, as a renewed scare about synthetics revived the fears of the mid-eighties, bringing the mythology of designer drugs back into the headlines. The turning point came on Halloween 1993, when twenty-three-year-old actor River Phoenix died shortly after collapsing outside a Los Angeles nightclub. The event was shocking because of Phoenix's youth and the fact that he was a rising romantic star recently featured in films including *My Own Private Idaho* and *Running on Empty*. The media suspected a drug connection with the death, and during the first week of coverage, the culprit was identified as GHB, which in some cases has been associated with nausea, coma and seizures: as Web postings stress, it is perilous when consumed with alcohol. The Phoenix affair inspired exposé stories about the drug, which was presented as almost as bad as fentanyl, the drug serial killer responsible for several deaths in the early nineties.[17] The drug's rumored association with Phoenix's death survived for years afterwards, although subsequent autopsies showed that GHB had not contributed to the event. The young star had in fact been consuming dangerous quantities of heroin, morphine and cocaine in hazardous combination with alcohol.

As the "stealth assassin of the nineties," GHB became almost as demonized as Ecstasy had a decade previously, and with as little justification. A mainstay of the emerging rave scene, the drug attracted various nicknames suggesting not only its potency, such as liquid ecstasy, but also its familiarity, such as Georgia Home Boy. The intimidating nickname Grievous Bodily Harm (a near-acronym of GHB) was conceived by anti-drug authorities, or perhaps by the media, in the wake of the Phoenix case. Inevitably, the drug also became the subject of parlous warnings about possible side effects, and in 1997, the Centers for Disease Control issued a severe statement about GHB, claiming that in a single year, it had been associated with one death and sixty-nine cases of overdose. All occurred in Texas and New York, which may be evidence of the localized character of usage but may also mean merely that medical authorities elsewhere were failing to detect the drug's use.[18]

In 1996, the anti-GHB campaign found a new martyr in the curious case of Texan teenager Hillory Janean Farias, who lost her life that August, allegedly after drinking a Sprite soft drink said to have been laced with GHB. This was a shocking incident, since Hillory was so definitely a "good girl" from a loving family, an able student and a sports star, rather than a wayward teenager on the streets. The implication was that she had been given the drug surreptitiously by some ill-intentioned person, possibly just as a prank but perhaps with the intention of disabling her for sexual purposes. The impact of the case was all the greater because it occurred in the large media market of Houston.

In the immediate aftermath of the Farias affair, GHB was attacked with all the zeal once mobilized against PCP. The *Houston Chronicle* reported the Farias case with a front-page headline that referred simultaneously to the drug's character as both a rape drug and a death drug: "The 'Mickey Finn of the Nineties' Labeled a Killer." Shortly afterwards, *Time* informed a national audience of the growing problem in "Liquid X—A Club Drug Called GHB May Be a Fatal Aphrodisiac." The story emphasized the sexual danger, which was fresh in the public mind after the spate of rape-drug stories throughout that summer: as one doctor was quoted as saying, "A substance that knocks out the victim and leaves her with amnesia makes the perfect agent for date rape." *Time* concluded, "Unfortunately . . . the dose required to knock someone out isn't much lower than the one that kills."[19] GHB was painted as the ideal weapon for callous rapists who scarcely cared whether their victims lived or died.

The Farias case was far less simple than it initially appeared, and Hillory may have been no more a victim of a GHB-induced fatality than was River Phoenix. The medical examiner was slow to determine the presence of GHB, and the amount of the drug in her system was by no means enough to have caused death: some have even questioned whether she had consumed any GHB whatever, as the quantities detected could have been naturally present in the system of any human being. Moreover, a friend of hers who had shared the supposedly lethal drink reported no ill effects, and later medical comments on the case have been contradictory. It may well be that Hillory succumbed to a congenital heart defect unrelated to any drug use, either licit or illicit. Some months after the original furor, the Farias family publicized a contradictory medical report that raised disturbing questions about how Hillory's death had been exploited for anti-GHB propaganda. Following the whole panic over so-called rave drugs, authorities in some areas have become far too ready to accept the role of these vogue substances in suspicious deaths. In one 1997 case, police in Georgia's Douglas County promptly assumed that GHB had caused the sudden death of a sixteen-year-old boy, who subsequently proved to have perished from a congenital birth defect under the influence of neither drugs nor alcohol.[20] GHB may perhaps have caused harm to some individuals, but its homicidal qualities remain controversial, and the associated legends are a poor basis for policy-making.

From mid-1996, the new synthetics formed the basis of a new wave of anti-drug polemics on the television news shows. CNN now broadcast a special report under the title "Trendy Drug Goes Club Hopping," a model example of a warning that could not fail to entice young people hitherto ignorant of the drug's existence. "GHB, or liquid Ecstasy, is sweeping the club and bar scene. It's fairly easy to get and relatively cheap. But experts warn: It's also very dangerous. . . . And at the raves, it's becoming the rage." Noting the fondness for GHB on the rave scene, the report told of recent overdoses and possible deaths, but such negative stories could not undermine the provocative message that the drug was trendy, what everyone was doing. As a later CNN documentary claimed, GHB was "quite the rage with the glamour crowd in the party spots and the nightclubs," part of "life in the fast lane": all in all, quite a commercial.[21]

Most at risk from the new drug culture were the young and white. The exposure of young Florida teens to synthetics was the theme of a *Time* article in 1997, which asked in a characteristically hair-raising manner, "Is Your Kid on K?" The following report interviewed youngsters of fifteen and sixteen who were enthusiastic about the drug, and the magazine reported that "K has exploded in the past few months onto the suburban drug scene." Some months later, ABC's *20/20* covered teen raves, which appealed to youngsters aged ten to eighteen. Despite their youth, all those interviewed claimed easy access to a panoply of drugs that included Ecstasy, Special K and heroin. As with the exposés of the so-called rape drugs in these same months, these programs offered viewers a portrait of illegal drug use radically different from the stereotypes of a decade previously, as users and dealers depicted were white or Hispanic, and their social settings ranged from respectable lower-middle class to very prosperous. In the words of a *20/20* report on illicit Rohypnol use in a Florida suburb, the teenagers involved lived "amidst neat lawns, clean streets and comfortable homes." As *Time* declared, "a hot new high hits Main Street," and users were "suburban," that is, white.[22]

Characteristic of the new genre of synthetic exposés was a CNN exposé on the dangers of GHB under the evocative title "Daughters, Drugs and Death." This special was typical in taking a local problem from the Southeast and presenting it as if it represented national concerns. Throughout, the major experts and police authorities interviewed were from Georgia, in close proximity to the network's geographical base, and the conditions described were those of the Atlanta club scene. The drug was regarded as so dangerous because it was made in "Backroom bathtubs," as "the moonshine of the drug world." Of the two horror stories offered concerning the drug, one involved a young woman from the west Georgia community of Carrollton, who had suffered incurable brain damage and coma, allegedly following a single disastrous encounter with the drug. The centerpiece of the CNN report was, however, a wrenching account of the Hillory Farias case: the segment showed her friends and family visiting her grave, which was marked with a stone commemorating the "precious angel." Her death was depicted as a form of murder, though the report was made several months after the reconsideration of the medical evidence, which had raised doubts about whether GHB was even involved in the incident. This was too powerful a story to spoil with facts.

In response to these supposed atrocities, the program praised authorities in Georgia and several other states that had made GHB a schedule I controlled substance, possession or sale of which carried a mandatory minimum sentence of thirty years; this term is, incidentally, much longer than the sentence for first-degree murder in most European nations. GHB was portrayed as a growing nightmare: as a DEA official commented, "It's spreading, it's not under control," and federal officials were said to be slow to classify it as a dangerous drug: "Protection isn't coming from Washington."[23] But federal legislators would soon climb on the bandwagon, and a proposal to make GHB a Schedule I controlled substance was included in a federal "Hillory J. Farias Date Rape Prevention Drug Act." In 1998, GHB was the subject of hearings before the U.S. House Subcommittee on Crime, at which the substance was blamed for at least fifteen deaths: witnesses included the uncle of Hillory Farias. The event gave the national news media a tag for renewed claims about GHB "cutting a swathe through the nation."

Such media exposés repeatedly alerted prospective users to the potential of the new rave drugs. ABC's nightly news offered an egregious example of advertising just before Christmas 1997, at the height of the party season, when an item billed as "Hot Drug" addressed the spread of ketamine. Anchorman Peter Jennings began by noting, "Kids are into yet another exotic drug," and a user confirmed its appeal: it was "very, like, trendy and hip—you know, it's up there." The drug was said to be particularly dangerous, with "an addictive potential that's greater than any of the other psychedelics"—a curious remark, given that few psychedelics have any addictive qualities at all, whatever their other harmful effects. The segment then discussed the scale of usage with a remarkable sleight of hand that contrived to give a misleading impression of a national upsurge. Of course, "no one is certain how much ketamine is being abused nationwide, but there are clear signs that it is becoming an increasingly popular drug."[24]

The rise of a national problem was substantiated by a tendentious series of maps, which followed each other in rapid sequence. The first showed several East Coast states in which veterinary clinics had reported thefts or burglaries of the drug. A second noted that "significant quantities" had been seized in drug raids in Maryland and Massachusetts, while in Minnesota, according to the voice-over, ketamine had recently been identified as one of the new drugs of choice. Finally, another map showed the nine states, mainly in the South and Southwest, that had recently boosted penalties for possession or sale of the drug, though without indicating whether there was any objective justification for such a response. It would have taken an alert viewer to note that the only solid statement implying significant usage for the drug was about the (unspecified) large seizures in two states. The assertion about Special K becoming anybody's drug of choice was belied by the accompanying graphic, which quoted a document as reporting that the drug had first been *identified* in the Minneapolis/St. Paul area, which is an entirely different matter. And the fact that legislatures are moving against a given drug says nothing about whether it has ever been recorded in that state. Even so, the report had managed within the space of half a minute or so to make verbal or visual reference to all regions of the country. Of such are national menaces born.

Apart from death and physical harm, the new party culture was also believed to pose a grave sexual danger, and between 1996 and 1998, one of the most intense contemporary drug scares grew out of charges that unscrupulous men were using chemical knockout drops to facilitate rape. This concern was linked to the broader issue of party drugs because a major suspect in the rape cases was GHB, while the sexual incidents often grew out of encounters at drug-laced parties or dances. In fact, one of GHB's several nicknames is Easy Lay, which originally referred to its role in enhancing sexual desire and pleasure, but which was wrongly taken to have rape-drug implications. In fact, virtually none of the Internet materials concerning GHB pay any attention to its potential for disabling women, and it is unlikely that this silence reflects discretion about possible legal problems: rape fantasies are easily accessible on the Web for anyone who wishes to find them. GHB was not seen as a rape drug by the overwhelming majority of its users, whose only interest lay in enhancing their own moods.

The idea of drugs being used for sexual purposes was far from new. It certainly dates back to the opium scare of the late nineteenth century, when sinister Chinese were said to use the drug to coerce white women into sexual slavery. Again in the Progressive Era, one of the most emotive social problems of the day was white slaving, or involuntary prostitution. Many poor and immigrant women were undoubtedly employed as prostitutes against their will, but the white slaving issue expanded with claims that middle-class girls were drugged and abducted against their will and sold to brothels at home or abroad. A persistent urban legend told of a well-intentioned girl assisting an elderly woman across a busy street, only to have the woman inject her surreptitiously with a disabling chemical. The victim then found herself in a brothel in a Latin American country, adding an element of racial violation to the sexual danger. Such rumors stirred a political furor, and in 1910 the United States acquired in the Mann Act one of the very first criminal statutes that permitted action by federal law enforcement to eliminate the supposed moral menace.[25] Though the abduction stories are apocryphal, the use of micky finns or knockout drops was a common practice in shady bars or clubs through the first half of the century, usually to permit the robbery of wealthy patrons. The preferred drug in such situations was a solution of alcohol and chloral hydrate, a drug synthesized as far back as 1832.

The concept of drugs as a rape weapon was virtually unknown in popular culture before the mid-1990s, though knockout chemical technologies were still known and presumably used illicitly from time to time. PCP developed this reputation in the 1970s, and this drug also offered criminals the advantage of producing a degree of amnesia in the victim. The substance used in the vast majority of recorded date-rape incidents is alcohol, though as always, alcohol's legal status immunizes it from consideration alongside other drugs: indeed, the phrase "candy is dandy but liquor is quicker" has long been quoted as a sophisticated witticism. Rape drugs returned forcefully to the headlines in the mid-1990s with an amazing spate of stories concerning such crimes.

By far the main weapon was the drug Rohypnol, nicknamed roofies. Rohypnol is a brand name for flunitrazepam, a benzodiazepine, part of a chemical family of sedatives/hypnotics that also includes Valium. Rohypnol was manufactured legally by the mammoth pharmaceutical concern Hoffman-La Roche, and it was used in sixty countries as a powerful sleeping drug, said to be ten times more powerful than Valium. Though it was not approved by the FDA, travelers were allowed to bring in moderate quantities for personal use.[26] By the end of the 1980s, the drug gained some underground popularity as a "parachute" to help users descend from highs caused by other stimulants.

In the clandestine culture of substance abuse, Rohypnol was originally publicized as a party drug. The first national media reports surfaced in mid-1995 on programs such as NPR's *All Things Considered,* which described Rohypnol as the fastest-growing drug of abuse in South Florida and other parts of the Sun Belt, where it appealed to "club-goers, cocaine and heroin addicts, and recreational drug aficionados." The drug was popular chiefly because of its reputation for safety, as it was sold in its original commercial wrapping and was presumably safe from tampering: in the reported words of one Florida teenager, "You don't hear anything bad about it like heroin or crack, where people die or anything." The following year, the DEA reported that "flunitrazepam is used widely in Texas where it is popular among high school students. Flunitrazepam is reported to be readily available in the Miami area, and epidemiologists from that area have stated that it is South Florida's fastest growing drug problem." "At just $1 to $5 a pill," the DEA continued, "the drug is especially popular with teens, who like to combine it with alcohol for a quick punch-drunk hit. The 'lunch money' high has also caught on with gangs and the rave crowd."[27] The drug gained a celebrity connection when rock star Kurt Cobain was put into a coma by a combination of roofies and champagne.

Remarkably, in view of later developments, these early reports said little or nothing about the rape-drug concept. A lengthy 1995 report in the *New York Times* briefly mentioned the drug's use in date-rape situations in Florida, but put little stress on this and devoted most of the story to a characteristic portrait of a teen fad. Matters soon changed, as the rape issue gave the media a powerful new tag. The number of press stories concerning Rohypnol grew from three in 1993 to twenty-five in 1994 to 854 in 1996, and the rape-drug crisis reached new heights over the following year. The turning point was apparently a story *Newsweek* published in early 1996, which covered familiar territory in terms of the drug's growing regional popularity and which merely alluded to cases of alleged rape. The title of the article, nevertheless, was "Roofies: The date-rape drug," and the story concluded by stressing the idea of involuntary doping: "Despite these efforts, the roofie wave probably hasn't even crested yet. So, experts say, quiz your kids. And don't take your eyes off your drink."[28] Other professional and popular pieces followed, and by March, importation of the drug was banned.

The media feeding frenzy on the date-rape theme occurred that summer, with coverage in all major urban and regional newspapers. In June and July alone, the *Washington Post* headlined "Banned date rape drug is linked to six assaults in area," the *Los Angeles Times* declared "Crackdown sought on date rape drug," the *San Francisco Chronicle* warned "Drug zaps memory of rape victims," and the *St. Louis Post-Dispatch* complained "Rape is only thing that this drug is for." Most reported incidents occurred in southern states, especially in college situations, such as Spring breaks in beach resorts. The danger was publicized through treatments in magazines aimed at women and teenage girls, such as *Seventeen* and *Sassy*, which coined the term "date rape in a bottle." The fact that the newsworthy drug was imported even meant that it briefly became an issue of foreign policy: in July, the US Senate's Foreign Relations Committee held hearings on Rohypnol, at which several rape victims testified, while senators demanded stricter official action against the drug. At least as important as official media in spreading news of the drug and its effects spread through college campuses were E-mail messages, a lively rumor network and stories disseminated by feminist groups.[29]

Federal and state action was soon forthcoming, as state legislatures strengthened penalties for illegal possession or use of Rohypnol. Many moved the drug into the prohibitive Schedule I of their respective controlled substances laws, suggesting that its dangers massively outweighed any conceivable medical benefits, so that it could not be used legally in any circumstances. Remarkably enough, given its normal hair-trigger response to perceived drug threats, the DEA came under attack for its slowness to suppress Rohypnol: the headline for a typical story in the *Detroit News* complained, "Slow DEA Action Gives Women No Relief from the Threat of New Date-Rape Drug."[30] The agency soon followed the lead of the states, urging a move from the medically controlled Schedule IV to the prohibitive Schedule I. In the fall, proposed federal legislation added up to twenty years to the sentences of convicted rapists who used the drug to immobilize victims.

Even with Rohypnol under official condemnation, the rape-drug problem continued and even became a mainstay of popular culture. On television, the issue was featured in major reports on all of the networks during the 1997–98 period, with both GHB and Rohypnol targeted. CNN began the trend with its 1997 feature, "Daughters, Drugs and Death," and shortly afterwards, ABC's *20/20* followed with a story called "Watch What You Drink," which suggested that rape drugs might be lurking at virtually any social gathering (August 1, 1997). The feature began with the question "Could someone you know be the next victim of the perfect crime?" and there followed several case studies of women who recounted being raped under the influence of Rohypnol, which had been surreptitiously slipped into their drinks at bars or parties. Though all of the stories were set in South Florida, the problem was said to be "very widespread," and each of the victims was presented as a respectable, middle-class woman: as in all stories on synthetics, all were of course white. The show's host, Hugh Downs, enthusiastically praised the response by states like Florida, which now imposed thirty-year prison terms for the mere possession of the drug.

Similar themes emerged from ABC's *Primetime Live,* which reported the case of a serial rapist who used Rohyponol to render his victims unconscious. The story told of an offender who was "preying upon them [the women] like a wild animal" and whose deeds "smacked of necrophilia." Rohypnol also appeared in fictional treatments, including an episode of *Beverly Hills 90210* in which a character finds that she has been drugged and raped.[31] This show appeals particularly to teens and young adults, for whom the date rape threat was a particular concern. In a related treatment, the crime series *Millennium* depicted a sexual predator who uses Ecstasy-based synthetics as an aphrodisiac bait for victims encountered at raves: after they have fulfilled his sexual fantasies, he kills them. And roofies were even featured in the cartoon show *South Park*.

The nature of this coverage is epitomized by an episode of the *Oprah Winfrey Show*, which warned of a pervasive threat to women. The program began with a report of a Los Angeles case in which GHB had been the primary weapon of a pair of serial rapists, who had retained souvenirs of their crimes in the forms of nude photographs of victims. In this case, there was no doubt that rape drugs had been used by sex criminals, but the program implied that such cases were commonplace: as Oprah Winfrey claimed, "there are rape drug predators on the prowl. . . . This drug is a perfect crime in a pill." Throughout, the emphasis was on such good girls and decent women such as Hillory Farias, and the program assured the audience that such disasters could happen to any one of them.[32]

If the threat was ubiquitous, then women everywhere had to act on the assumption that men in social situations were rapists unless proved otherwise. When one rape victim reported that she had asked a man at a bar to hold her drink, Winfrey quickly interjected, "Never do that!" A representative of the Santa Monica Rape Treatment Center enunciated new rules women would have to observe for their own protection, rules that, if followed, would constitute a revolution in social interactions and everyday life. Women, in effect, were to regard themselves as living in a state of sexual siege from predatory males, who might be lurking anywhere, but particularly at social gatherings and parties. Women were instructed never to drink from punch bowls, whether or not the drink in question was alcoholic. They should try no new drinks, drink nothing with an unusual taste or appearance and take their own drinks to parties. Women should drink nothing, alcoholic or otherwise, opened by another person, and should never leave a drink unattended: if they turn their backs for a moment, they should assume that the drink has been spiked and abandon it. The Santa Monica list of rape prevention warnings was now publicized in pamphlets from rape crisis centers and reproduced in full in the syndicated

Dear Abby column.[33] The views of one small group were thus portrayed as a national orthodoxy.

Such appalling accounts made the rape drugs quite indefensible, especially as they undermined the long-established argument that substance abuse was purely a consensual and victimless crime with which the state should not interfere. Here, there clearly were victims, and the drugs presumably should be regulated as certainly as if they were poisons. Who could possibly defend something called a rape drug? Though the charges of rape are extremely serious, none of the various scare stories in these years offered the slightest idea of the scale of the problem in terms of the number of cases in which the drug was used to permit rape. Nor, incidentally, was there any suggestion of the number of times a drug like GHB was used as a party stimulant voluntarily by a consenting individual, rather than as a tool to harm another person. Oprah Winfrey's program spoke vaguely of "thousands" of women being raped, meaning that the claims-makers had not the slightest clue of the extent of the problem but wished to make it appear immense. There is no warrant whatever for the wild charge that rape drugs have become so prevalent as to demand that women adopt a siege mentality and regard themselves as living in a hostile bandit territory, subject to daily assault by men.

The acute concern surrounding the rape drugs is rich testimony to the changing marketplace for claims about social problems. We might speculate about how such a rape-drug problem would have been treated in the media twenty or thirty years ago; presumably, charges would have been seen as a source of humor as much as of official concern or panic. Since that point, of course, women have gained much greater economic and political power and have succeeded in bringing sexual threats much more centrally into public debate. Since the mid-1980s, campaigns against rape, stalking, child abuse and workplace harassment have succeeded in giving a vastly higher political profile to all of these issues. Partly this reflects the realization by the mass media of the economic importance of the female audience and the urgent need to respond to their presumed needs and interests. In television news, this has meant a greater prominence for medical and family-oriented stories that would once have been dismissed as soft or even trivial lifestyle items. In the case of drugs, the feminization of the media audience has been reflected in a new emphasis on the experiences of women as users and addicts, which was so obvious in the case of methamphetamine coverage. Contrary to thirty or forty years ago, the harm caused by drugs is presented in terms of families and children, most glaringly in the case of babies supposedly born addicted to crack or speed.

For all of their inaccuracies, media reports about Rohypnol and GHB had an overwhelming impact on public perceptions of the substances, which were now irrevocably labeled rape drugs. This label was all the more threatening, and newsworthy, at a time when serial sexual predators were so much in the news and when most states had recently passed special laws to defend women and children against their depredations. When two suburban Pennsylvania teenagers attempted a kitchen synthesis of GHB, the *Philadelphia Inquirer* headlined, sensationally, "Date-rape drug from Internet puts two boys into comas," though there was no indication that the boys had any intention of committing a sexual crime. The ensuing story dwelt heavily upon rape-related themes and the analogy with Rohypnol (though GHB was "far scarier"), with a rape crisis counselor as the main authority cited on the phenomenon. The report even raised yet again the drug's spurious association with the death of Hillory Farias. Henceforward, whenever GHB labs were discovered, the press immediately announced the find in terms of a date-rape drug factory, inviting suitably severe measures by police and prosecutors.[34] This was a stigma far more powerful than anything that could be imposed by thousands of pseudo-expert scare stories about the alleged effects of the drug on a particular user. Users and makers of these drugs were now portrayed as potential sex criminals, and the drugs themselves were indefensible. This was a dramatic rhetorical victory for anti-drug activists wishing to undermine the argument that illicit drug-taking was simply a consensual, victimless crime.

NINE

The Next Panic

That humanity at large will ever be able to dispense with Artificial
Paradises seems very unlikely.

—Aldous Huxley, 1954

Since the mid-1970s, synthetic panics have erupted with striking regularity in the United States, and they have generally followed very
similar patterns and been based on extremely dubious claims. Similar
assertions will unquestionably be heard in the near future, perhaps
concerning substances presently unknown outside academic departments of chemistry. With so many precedents at hand, it should be
possible to frame a typical model of the panic cycle in operation, with
the goal of encouraging both the media and policymakers to acquire
greater caution and scepticism in such matters, lest the spurious quest
for the next crack cocaine become an endlessly recurring process. The
importance of such a defensive effort becomes all the more pressing
when we consider the impact of successive panics and drug wars on
the wider society: controversies over synthetics raise in an acute form
the whole rationale of drug prohibition and its distressing effects. The
cumulative effects of anti-drug campaigns are so damaging that they
can only be justified if they prevent worse alternatives, and it is far
from clear that they do so. The unbending approach that has characterized anti-drug prohibitionism in recent years is a manifestation of
a narrowly puritanical view of drugs and medicines that severely limits their potential usefulness for human well-being. The emphasis of

drug policy urgently needs to shift from policing to medicine, from zero tolerance to harm reduction.

In order to understand how to defuse a prospective panic, we first need to know how such events are constructed in the first place and the means by which a drug is demonized. Let us imagine the administrator of an agency with a vested interest in drug regulation, one who has to report to an investigative or official body about some newly popular synthetic substance: perhaps we might call it Ultra. How might that person go about convincing an audience that the issue was worthy of concern and that the agency in question deserved resources to research and confront it?

Several obvious rhetorical tactics come to mind.[1] The administrator would want to present the problem in terms that would be readily familiar to that audience, to assert that new drug X is closely comparable to established drug Y and would have roughly the same effects. He or she would try to make the substance seem as dangerous as possible, ideally by a catchy label that would lend itself to imaginative permutations in news headlines. The account would emphasize the notorious features of drug abuse already well cultivated in the public consciousness—aspects such as a high potential for addiction, toxicity, devastating effects on families and communities and enhanced personal aggression. These images would be substantiated by impressive statistics illustrating rapid and uncontrollable growth. Throughout, the problems said to be posed by the drug would be illustrated by horrifying case studies of extreme violence or personal devastation, tailored as closely as possible to strictly contemporary concerns: whether the hot social issue of the time involves sex crime or illegal immigration, cults or terrorism, the new drug would somehow be implicated as a player in this wider problem. In short, the rhetorical indictment would be much like that constructed against PCP in the 1970s, designer drugs and Ecstasy in the 1980s, methamphetamine and CAT in the 1990s.

Past experience suggests that such an account would be accepted quite uncritically by the media, which views its role in such matters as essentially stenographic—recording the fact that a new drug epidemic is in progress and seeking to enhance the charges without critically examining whether they have the slightest validity. But if they ever did choose to apply a skeptical approach, critical observers would find grave flaws at every stage of the presentation.

Law Enforcement Experts Claim . . .

The first question must apply to the source from which claims arise. By definition, agencies whose primary mission is the control or suppression of illegal drugs have a vested interest in portraying those substances as threatening and ubiquitous. This is true for the DEA especially; its *raison d'être* depends on finding and combating drug abuse, preferably with a regular infusion of issues that are sufficiently new and distinctive to grab the attention of media and political leaders, who face many rival demands for resources. Any statement from such a body must be taken with that agenda in mind. Given the nature of bureaucracies, no drug-enforcement agency is ever likely to present Congress with a statement asserting that the illegal drug menace is under control or largely defeated, as this would invite either a dismantling of the agency or a large reduction of its resources. The same is true for state agencies, like California's BNE.

An English Victorian statesman once bemoaned the self-serving nature of expert advice: "If you believe the doctors, nothing is wholesome. If you believe the theologians, nothing is innocent. If you believe the soldiers, nothing is safe."[2] And as he might have added, if you believe the drug warriors, the nation is always suffering from a drug epidemic or about to face a new one. When approaching such claims, it is always helpful to bear in mind the question, *Cui bono?* Who benefits?

The Serial Killer of Drugs . . .

A presentation intended for a mass audience will frame the new problem through the use of threatening metaphors and other rhetorical devices. Rape drugs, the serial killer of drugs, zombie drug users, the crack of the nineties: all are wonderful grabbers for media stories, but in what sense, if any, do these phrases correspond with reality? It is dangerous to assume that the metaphors developed to tout a given drug are accurate reflections of its destructive qualities—for example, that CAT is clawing up a region, that ice is chilling officials or that methamphetamine is preparing to speed across the nation. And even if a substance is dubbed a rape drug, we cannot presume that everyone possessing it has rape in mind. A little historical perspective permits us to see a term like "the new drug of choice" as the empty cliché it is.

Epidemic . . .

The concept of an epidemic is one such metaphor, however often it seems to be employed in an objective medical or scientific sense. In fact, the term begs several key questions, not least the harmful effects of the substance concerned. To speak of an epidemic of drug X automatically assumes that the substance is a health menace comparable to an infectious disease. Medical analogies ipso facto presume that the subject under discussion is pathological, an impression reinforced by the use of pseudomedical language like "latency periods."

And the word epidemic poses other difficulties. In western society, the most familiar epidemic of recent times is the AIDS outbreak that began in the early 1980s; in the aftermath of this experience, to speak of a drug epidemic suggests that the behavior observed is likewise a brand new phenomenon that has seemingly come from nowhere. Claims of a drug epidemic are often made without adequate evidence that the behavior in question has really grown: if we know accurately neither how many people were using a drug ten years ago nor how many are using it today, we can make no accurate statement concerning growth or decline of usage.

To speak of an epidemic further assumes that growth in drug usage can be measured accurately, with the model familiar from infectious diseases, but in reality, usage itself is effectively invisible. All we can measure is behavior that is either reported or observed, and it is difficult to extrapolate from that to judge the actual scale of a drug phenomenon. Because illegal drug use is a private behavior that can attract severe sanctions, its scale cannot be determined by the usual means devised to judge the popularity of a television program or a type of margarine. That statement may seem obvious, but its implications are easily ignored when we confront claims about the alleged popularity of a given drug. People often fail to respond accurately to surveys, and that difficulty is all the greater when dealing with illegal conduct, so that agencies must resort to techniques of extrapolation that are controversial at best, ludicrous at worst. Estimates of, say, the number of habitual cocaine users in the United States at any given time in the mid-1990s were variously put at 582,000 and 2.2 million, and in fact one government report presented each of these wildly divergent figures within a few pages of each other.[3] There are no plausible grounds for believing that any of these figures reflects objective reality, any more than we can find grounds to believe the stratospheric, multibillion-dollar figures occasionally hazarded for the financial damage caused by drugs to the national economy.

Drug usage can be quantified in terms of persons arrested, amounts of drugs seized or numbers of laboratories raided, but in all of these cases, what we are measuring is the intensity of official reaction and not the changing volume of drug usage. If a state believes that it has a problem with drug X, its police forces will go looking for it, prosecutors will be more likely to press charges concerning it and medical examiners will tend to look keenly for its role in violent incidents: all of the leading indicators will therefore soar, regardless of whether actual usage is rising or falling. Furthermore, a society that grows less tolerant of drugs will have more arrests and seizures, so that higher statistics for official action may in fact coincide with declining drug usage, as occurred nationwide during the late 1980s.

Soon to Sweep the Nation . . .

It is tempting for the mass media to illustrate a looming drug crisis by taking one area in which a drug is indeed very popular and suggesting that these conditions will soon become generalized, so that the whole nation will soon share the experience of San Jose with PCP, northern Michigan with CAT, Hawaii with ice or Arizona with methamphetamine. The only difficulty is that these extrapolations are virtually never justified by events. If the problem is at present strictly localized, are there any plausible signs of usage spreading, absent the massive free publicity provided by media and legislators?

More Addictive Than Crack Cocaine . . .

No less than "epidemic," other standard terms in the law-enforcement lexicon concerning drugs are deceptive in suggesting an objective scientific quality. Yet, in fact, these terms are malleable and unreliable, owing more to rhetoric than to objective science. "Designer drugs" itself is such a phrase, as is the distinction between so-called "hard" and "soft" drugs. In the case of designer drugs, the term is used to cover both potent substances like fentanyl and far milder ones like Ecstasy, both of which have been subjected to equal official stigma.

"Addiction" is another of these flexible words. As long ago as 1946, the famous medical writer Paul De Kruif denounced the FBN's tendency to conclude that a given drug was addictive or damaging based only on anecdotal evidence, on "the unscientific, uncontrolled reports that flow into the files of governmental bureaus dabbling in science."[4] Matters have changed little in the last half-century, and most of the so-called science remains mere dabbling. Police forces and drug-enforcement agencies like to use scientific-sounding rhetoric concerning drugs (as in "epidemiologists . . . have stated that it is South Florida's fastest growing drug problem"), but we should never forget that these statements are taken from political documents that would not conceivably pass muster if reviewed by neutral medical or social scientific observers. As used by politicians and law-enforcement agencies today, the term "addict" often becomes synonymous with "user," or even with a person who has had only one or two contacts with the substance in question and is not addicted by any medical criterion. Whenever claims are made that a given substance is severely addictive, it is crucial to ask how addiction is being defined. The nature and severity of chemical dependency is subject to great debate among professionals, and any claim that a substance produces addiction after a single use should be viewed skeptically: such a claim is so bizarre and improbable that it should raise doubts about other statements made by the same source.

Over the last decade, too, highly questionable charges about the nature of addiction have been made in the context of possible drug effects on babies born to users—the infamous crack-baby phenomenon and its later imitators. As in the case of instant addiction, stories of babies born addicted to any given substance should be treated with great scepticism, especially when all possible pathologies and symptoms suffered by the child are attributed to the influence of that drug.

The Addict Will Kill You in a Heartbeat . . .

Claims about new drugs have a dreadful track record in matters of accuracy and credibility. A century of anti-drug rhetoric has regularly drawn on a rather limited repertoire of images, which have successively been applied to many different drugs bearing no obvious connection. One familiar script suggests that a drug transforms a user into a soulless, drug-lubricated killing machine, a model variously applied over the years to cocaine, marijuana, PCP and methamphetamine. This concept is illustrated by tales of savage murders, sex attacks and mutilation, which acquire an urban legend quality as they are repeatedly retold in successive drug panics. If these earlier scripts are now known to have been thoroughly inaccurate regarding well-known substances like marijuana, is there any reason to suppose that they are likely to be truthful when applied to new or emerging menaces? A hypothetical substance might indeed have a devastating effect on an individual, but as in the case of stories about instant addiction and addict babies, a long record of bogus claims has necessarily shifted the burden of credibility firmly onto the claim-makers themselves.

Drug-Related Deaths . . .

One yardstick used to substantiate the seriousness of a drug problem is the number of deaths associated with a given substance. As a rhetorical tactic, this is an obvious means of both attracting public attention and contradicting the view that drugs are a harmless, individual vice. But what is a drug-related death? In a particular case, can the given death plausibly be shown to result from the usage of the drug itself, as opposed to, say, a conflict between traffickers? The fact that an individual died while showing traces of a drug in his or her body does not of itself establish causation. The notion of a drug-related death is not implausible in itself, as alcohol, heroin, nicotine and other drugs can certainly cause or contribute to fatalities, but this does not mean that claims about the volume of damage should be accepted without further evaluation.

Ruined Lives . . .

Claim-makers illustrate the harmful nature of a given phenomenon by giving it a human face, providing case studies of individuals whose lives were devastated by a particular drug. These stories have to be used with caution, especially if, as is so often the case, they portray desperate users in treatment programs and imply that this self-selected sample is representative of every individual who has tried the drug. Such accounts fail to acknowledge that users in such programs are often there under court mandate as an alternative to lengthy prison terms, so they have a powerful incentive to present the starkest possible contrast between their previous drug abuse and their recent progress towards sobriety. The drug users whose lives we can observe are not necessarily representative of nonaddicted consumers. We must beware what Reinarman and Levine term "the routinization of caricature—worst cases framed as typical cases, the episodic rhetorically recrafted into the epidemic."[5] The use of illegal drugs can ruin lives, but often the harm arises less from qualities intrinsic to the drug itself than from its legal consequences.

. . . Roads Not Taken

Those promoting concern over drug problems frame issues in particular ways, so that for instance the methamphetamine problem of the nineties was chiefly seen in terms of rural and suburban white users, while the rave-drug phenomenon was portrayed as a subset of the sexual endangerment of women. Each of these issues could, however, be viewed with equal plausibility in quite a different way; the topics omitted from official statements and media coverage are as significant as those included. Though new synthetics have often been popularized within the gay clubs, especially the gay dance circuit, no media exposé has ever discussed the problem as one of "gay drugs." Presumably, journalists and editors reasonably feel that such coverage would tend to increase the existing stigma on homosexuality by associating gays with irresponsible and illegal behavior. Whatever the reason, the decision to select one area of an issue rather than another must always be recognized as a subjective one, reflecting political and cultural concerns of the moment. Why does a particular problem acquire the shape it does? How is it made to mean what it does?

The need for such a critical and even debunking approach becomes apparent when we consider the harm wrought by past drug wars and the certainty that they will recur. Much has been written since the early 1980s about the grim social effects of the drug war in terms of mass incarceration, the increasingly militarized ethos of law enforcement, and the disproportionate burden placed upon minority communities.[6] The drug war must take much of the blame for the abysmal state of police-community relations during the 1980s and 1990s and the depths of mutual hatred that became apparent during the wave of urban violence in Los Angeles and elsewhere in 1992. Drug-related prosecutions are largely responsible for the fact that several million Americans now find themselves under the supervision of the state, if not through institutional confinement then through the mechanisms of probation and parole. Meanwhile, the reach of the penal system has expanded to affect ever-new categories, from the youngest to the oldest, women as well as men. The drug war went far in reversing the gains in civil liberties made during the due process revolution of the Warren Court years, and a host of new drug-related cases provided judges with the opportunity to roll back the rights of suspects and prisoners.

Perhaps most troubling is the fact that these trends have no logical or predictable end, in the sense of being a period of unfortunate travail that must be endured before the drug problem is somehow solved and social peace reigns once more, at however great a cost. To adapt the famous saying, even creating a desert will not bring peace. Deterrence can have some effect—the number of people using illegal drugs has fallen since the late 1970s—but the fact that so many millions continue to run the appalling legal risks of the drug-war era suggests that they constitute an irreducible core population. The vision of a drug-free America is a chimera. Even if we imagine that, by some miracle, foreign supplies of illegal drugs had been altogether suppressed and no byproduct of the poppy or the coca leaf ever crossed the American frontier (a ludicrous supposition), the drug war would not abate. The appearance of successive new panic waves in the 1990s shows that the emphasis would shift instead to the synthetic products of domestic laboratories. The anti-drug bureaucracy will continue to wage its destructive campaigns ad infinitum, or at least until some administration acquires the political will to order a halt.

The drug war is a perfect example of what criminologist Jeffrey Reiman once termed a Pyrrhic defeat.[7] The familiar concept of Pyrrhic victory refers to a struggle in which the winner suffers such appalling damage that, in practice, he loses the war. In contrast, a Pyrrhic defeat refers to a battle in which one wins by losing, in the sense that the perpetual failure to eliminate drugs brings a never-ending stream of new resources to law enforcement, which is extolled at length for its heroic struggles against the vast menace. When it appears, however briefly, that a victory might be gained, as in the struggles against heroin and cocaine in the early 1990s, new and still more fearsome foes must be found or concocted.

Though most Americans may not consider themselves directly affected by these events, successive anti-drug movements have in fact had a widespread impact, causing serious harm to millions of mainstream individuals whose direct exposure to illegal narcotics has been slim or nonexistent. Among other things, the fear of abuse has resulted in the removal from the medical arsenal of some highly effective pharmaceuticals, especially those that control pain.[8] In illnesses like terminal cancer, drugs such as heroin are by far the most effective for relieving pain and are commonly used for this purpose in most other advanced countries. In the United States, by contrast, patients are notoriously undermedicated, ostensibly because doctors fear the effects of addiction, as if that were a realistic concern for the terminally ill. In reality, heroin and its analogues are underused because of the overwhelming campaign against them by the anti-drug bureaucracies. A sophisticated health care system thus expects patients to endure excruciating pain, to a degree that would be utterly unacceptable in a less nervous and more humane environment.

The issue recalls another pressing controversy in which the ideological purity of anti-drug politics came into conflict with medical necessity: the matter of needle exchange programs. As the AIDS problem grew worse in the 1980s, activists proposed to offer drug addicts clean needles to prevent the danger of transmitting this and other diseases, including hepatitis, and thereby to save several thousand lives each year. While drug users themselves might conceivably be seen as morally culpable, this would not be true of their spouses and sexual partners, who would also be protected from deadly diseases. Yet, in 1989, the federal government prohibited financing for such programs on the grounds that they might be seen as supporting or acquiescing in drug use. This prohibition was renewed in 1998, despite furious lobbying by public-health experts and AIDS activists. During the 1998 controversy, the argument that proved decisive in influencing the Clinton White House was made by drug czar Barry McCaffrey, who declared that clean needle programs would send the wrong message to children about drugs: the symbolic facade of absolute prohibition must be maintained, even when it kills.[9]

Legislatures over the years have granted sizable resources to the anti-drug bureaucracies, not realizing that in so doing, they were entrusting to these police agencies a de facto supervision over the American medical profession. The right to regulate drugs is in large measure the right to shape medical policy. The resulting overextension of police powers became apparent in the mid-nineties, when several states debated the legalization of physician-assisted suicide and a law allowing it was passed in Oregon. The Oregon measure was swiftly put on hold when DEA chief Thomas Constantine warned that any doctor using drugs for this purpose would be prosecuted for violations of controlled substances laws, as his agency had determined (under pressure from conservative politicians) that assisted suicide did not constitute a "legitimate medical purpose." In this instance, an embarrassed Justice Department overruled the DEA, but the agency's ham-fisted intrusion into delicate ethical debates is still startling.[10]

Apart from such extreme cases, sporadic panics have removed a number of effective drugs from general access. While the classification of drugs into the various CSA schedules is ostensibly based on a rational scientific evaluation of their costs and benefits, this is in reality a highly politicized process in which symbolic and cultural factors play a major part: the result is a systematic tendency towards over-restrictive classification. Contrary to the polemics of recent years, drugs like Rohypnol do have purposes other than merely facilitating rape, as they are effective sedatives when used in pre-anaesthesia situations. When the drug was used for criminal purposes, the manufacturer responded promptly by adding safeguards, so that when slipped into a drink it would color the resulting mixture, thereby alerting a potential victim. However, the anti-rape-drug campaign had become so intense and uncompromising that yet another valuable pharmaceutical was placed off limits. This same process not only removed marijuana from the legitimate pharmacopoeia, but even prevented its return in individual states that democratically expressed their support for such a move in repeated referenda. As in the assisted suicide controversy, drug-enforcement policy implies a substantial shift towards federal authority over social issues.

The campaign against useful medicaments had its widest effects on everyday life when major retailers cooperated with the DEA to remove from store shelves any substance that might conceivably be used in making methamphetamine or methcathinone. The policy initially affected asthma sufferers, but soon had an impact on virtually everyone with a need for an over-the-counter cough and cold medication. In many regions, the ban was extended from ephedrine to bulk sales of pseudephedrine, which is found in many familiar brand-name products.[11] By this standard, it will perhaps not be long before the whole category of over-the-counter medicines ceases to exist, all as part of the desperate endeavor to prevent the unauthorized manufacture of chemicals that someone, somewhere, has labeled a designer drug. The movement to prohibit supposedly harmful substances leads inexorably to a spreading net of proscription, which increasingly takes in harmless and even beneficial drugs and medicines.

Apart from the evidence of collateral damage and social harm, a powerful philosophical argument can be made that the state should not limit an individual's right to consume substances that might harm him or her. The classic text of libertarian thought is John Stuart Mill's *On Liberty*, published in 1859 in direct response to the American movement to prohibit alcohol. Mill argued for a right for individuals to undertake potentially self-destructive behaviors so long as those did not harm other people, a criterion that certainly extended to substance abuse. There are, of course, cases in which drug abuse ceases to be merely victimless crime, and an argument for regulation can be justified in terms of the potential of harm to nonconsenting individuals, as with the so-called rape drugs. Indeed, Mill specifically took account of the question of poisons, which were freely available in Victorian England, and even this arch-libertarian had no difficulty with the prospect of controlling or registering the sale of poisons to prevent crimes. By analogy, the restriction or registration of potential rape drugs is a legitimate role for government, though active suppression is more questionable, and the element of public protection should not altogether overwhelm individual rights. But where there is no threat to innocent parties, a libertarian position should oppose any unnecessary restrictions upon the behavior of responsible adult citizens.

Such an approach is far removed from the moral and political assumptions of contemporary drug policy, in which the idea of individual rights is countered by claims about the interests of children or by varieties of communitarian rhetoric. Regardless of the scientific rhetoric with which decisions are buttressed, the absolutist principles of prohibitionism are based on a distinctive kind of conservative morality, with a traditional, even archaic, puritanical hatred of anything smacking of hedonism. Ecstasy, for instance, was tolerated while it had a limited therapeutic use, but suppressed when it acquired a reputation as a party drug; it was condemned as much by this social context as by the studies suggesting that it might pose health risks.

The example of Ecstasy also raises crucial questions about the criteria employed to prohibit any drug. Even assuming that the scientific evidence for brain damage from Ecstasy is widely agreed to be credible (which it is not), we should recall that all drugs and medicines, even those in most common nonprescription use, can have harmful effects on some individuals in some circumstances: we have already noted that adverse reactions to legal drugs administered in hospitals kill perhaps a hundred thousand Americans each year. The use of legal drugs and medicines is permitted because their benefits vastly outweigh the marginal possibility of harm to a few. To put this in non-drug terms, Americans who travel by air are well aware that hundreds of people die each year as a result of aviation-related fatalities, but they accept the risk because it is tiny in comparison to the possible advantages. Moreover, it is a risk that they consciously, voluntarily, choose to accept. Why should the same principle not apply to synthetic drugs? Why should a drug like Ecstasy not be permitted, despite its possible risks, in view of the mental and spiritual elevation so widely reported by willing users? Why should a chemical not be used for recreational purposes?

The answer, regrettably, is self-evident. None of the regulating agencies accepts that a drug should have as its primary goal the elevation of mood, the giving of pleasure, the enhancement of sexual feeling or the refining of consciousness, at least for normally functioning people (as opposed to the clinically depressed). If none of these features is accepted as desirable or even tolerable, then the slightest evidence of harm automatically outweighs the (supposedly nonexistent) benefits of a given chemical, and it falls under a legal taboo as stringent as that imposed by any religion. It sounds eminently reasonable to say that the benefits of a given drug should outweigh its possible costs, but if one category of benefits is always counted as worthless, if one side of the equation is always set at zero it will always be countermanded by the costs. In this severe view, any use of the given substance constitutes abuse.

To be permissible, then, chemicals can have, must have, no association with pleasure, and still less with ecstasy. The central dilemma here, of course, is that throughout recorded history, humanity has used drugs to alter mind and mood, and the principle of such experimentation is deeply rooted in human cultures. To quote Aldous Huxley once more, "The universal and ever-present urge to self-transcendence is not to be abolished by slamming the currently popular Doors in the Wall." Or as Dr. Ronald Siegel has observed, "Unless you want to defoliate the entire planet and pave it over, and outlaw the science of chemistry and cooking, you'll probably never stop the use of synthetic drugs or natural drugs in the search for ecstasy and altered states."[12] In the last quarter-century, science has evolved a sophisticated understanding of the human brain that should in theory open the doors to any number of new drugs with enormous potential to enhance pleasure and expand consciousness. Yet all are certain to meet diehard opposition from the inflexible doorkeepers of drug enforcement.

In chemistry, as in computing, creativity is usually several steps ahead of the capacity of legislators and policymakers to comprehend the challenge they face in seeking to enforce orthodoxy, much less to present effective countermeasures. Like generals throughout history, they are usually fighting the last war, or even the one before that. The battle to suppress ecstasy in all its forms has always been an unequal one, but now the balance of forces has shifted dramatically to the side of experimentation, which can only be suppressed by increasingly rigid laws and ever more intrusive police supported by a willfully obscurantist media. As neurochemistry and chemical technologies advance, the stage is set for persistent confrontations between an entrenched anti-drug bureaucracy and the demonized phantom chemists, the evil scientific masterminds. The outcome, in short, will be recurrent synthetic panics.

ABBREVIATIONS IN NOTES

The following abbreviations are used in the notes:

ADAMHA Alcohol, Drug Abuse and Mental Health Administration
AJP *American Journal of Psychiatry*
AR *Arizona Republic*
BG *Boston Globe*
CDT *Centre Daily Times* (State College, PA.)
CSM *Christian Science Monitor*
CT *Chicago Tribune*
DAWN Drug Abuse Warning Network
DEA Drug Enforcement Administration
DHHS Department of Health and Human Services
DN *Detroit News*
DUF Drug Use Forecasting System
FEER *Far Eastern Economic Review*
GPO U.S. Government Printing Office
JAMA *Journal of the American Medical Association*
JPAD *Journal of Psychoactive Drugs*
JPD *Journal of Psychedelic Drugs*
LAT *Los Angeles Times*
NIDA National Institute on Drug Abuse
NIJ National Institute of Justice
NYT *New York Times*
PHS United States Public Health Service
RS *Rolling Stone*
SFC *San Francisco Chronicle*
USNWR *U.S. News and World Report*
WP *Washington Post*
WSJ *Wall Street Journal*
WWW World Wide Web

NOTES

Notes to Chapter 1

1. *Designer Drugs: Hearing before the Committee on the Budget,* Senate, 99th Cong., 1st sess., July 18, 1985 (Washington, D.C.: GPO, 1985), 42. This will be cited throughout as *Designer Drugs.*

2. For examples of the excellent standard works on illegal drugs that say virtually nothing about the synthetics, see Eric L. Jensen and Jurg Gerber, eds., *The New War on Drugs* (Cincinnati: Anderson, 1998); Craig Reinarman and Harry G. Levine, eds., *Crack in America* (Univ. of California Press, 1997); Jill Jonnes, *Hep-Cats, Narcs and Pipe-Dreams* (New York: Scribner, 1996); Alfred W. McCoy and Alan A. Block, eds., *War on Drugs* (Westview, 1992); David Musto, *The American Disease,* 2d ed. (Yale Univ. Press, 1987).

3. Paul Glastris, "The New Drug in Town," *USNWR,* April 26, 1993, 20–21; Matt Bai, "White Storm Warning," *Newsweek,* March 31, 1997, 66–67.

4. Erich Goode and Nachman Ben-Yehuda, *Moral Panics* (Oxford: Blackwell, 1994); Henry Brownstein, *The Rise and Fall of a Violent Crime Wave* (Guilderland, NY: Harrow and Heston, 1996); Craig Reinarman, "The Social Construction of Drug Scares," in Patricia A. Adler and Peter Adler, eds., *Constructions of Deviance,* 2d ed. (Belmont, CA: Wadsworth, 1997), 97–108.

5. Aldous Huxley, *The Doors of Perception* (London: Penguin, 1959), 52.

6. Musto, *The American Disease;* Edward M. Brecher, *Licit and Illicit Drugs* (Boston: Little Brown, 1972), 310–34; Troy S. Duster, *The Legislation of Morality* (New York: Free Press, 1970); compare William Weir, *In the Shadow of the Dope Fiend* (North Haven, CT: Archon Books, 1995); Craig Reinarman and Harry G. Levine, "The Crack Attack," in Joel Best, ed., *Images of Issues,* 2d ed. (Hawthorne, NY: Aldine De Gruyter, 1995), 147–86.

7. All emphases in the original: Stuart Hall, Chas Critcher, Tony Jefferson, John Clarke and Brian Roberts, *Policing the Crisis* (London: Macmillan, 1978); see also Stanley Cohen, *Folk Devils and Moral Panics* (London: MacGibbon and Kee, 1972); Philip Jenkins, *Intimate Enemies* (Hawthorne, NY: Aldine de Gruyter, 1992); idem, *Using Murder* (Hawthorne, NY: Aldine de Gruyter, 1994).

8. William H. Brock, *The Norton History of Chemistry* (New York: W. W. Norton, 1993).

9. This account is chiefly drawn from M. Weatherall, *In Search of a Cure* (New York: Oxford Univ. Press, 1990).

10. These fears are related to the idea of the cyborg, the being created through a fusion of humanity and machine. Over the last decade or so, the cyborg image, at once tempting and terrifying, has been a source of fascination in cultural studies of science: see for example Donna J. Haraway, *Simians, Cyborgs, and Women* (New York: Routledge, 1991).

11. The Allen Ginsberg quote is from H. Wayne Morgan, *Drugs in America* (Syracuse Univ. Press, 1981), 156. The quotes from the 1985 hearings are in *Designer Drugs*, 35, 42. Sharon Cohen, "Drug Craze Takes Foothold in Midwest," AP wire story published in *CDT,* March 9, 1997; "Meth's Deadly High," Television program broadcast on A&E Network's *Investigative Reports,* August 16, 1997; Kenneth Goddard, *The Alchemist* (New York: Bantam, 1985).

12. *Designer Drugs,* 62. Compare Jon Turney, *Frankenstein's Footsteps* (Yale Univ. Press, 1998).

13. Aldous Huxley, *Brave New World* (1932; reprint, London: Penguin Books, 1955), 53.

14. John C. Lilly, *The Scientist,* rev. ed. (Berkeley, CA: Ronin, 1996).

15. Quoted in Brecher, *Licit and Illicit Drugs,* 414.

16. Robin Cook, *Acceptable Risk* (New York: Berkley Books, 1994).

17. Ruth Frankenberg, *White Women, Race Matters* (Minneapolis: Univ. of Minnesota Press, 1993); Matt Wray and Annalee Newitz, eds., *White Trash* (New York: Routledge, 1997); Nicole Hahn Rafter, ed., *White Trash* (Boston: Northeastern Univ. Press, 1988).

18. Musto, *American Disease,* 244–45.

19. Joseph R. Gusfield, *Symbolic Crusade* (Urbana, IL: Univ. of Illinois Press, 1963); Musto, *American Disease;* R. Bonnie and C. Whitebread, *The Marijuana Connection* (Charlottesville, VA: Univ. Press of Virginia, 1974).

20. Erich Goode, *Drugs in American Society,* 4th ed. (New York: McGraw-Hill, 1993), 246.

21. When in 1986 the President's Commission on Organized Crime published a substantial volume on illegal drugs, this work devoted barely twenty-five of its eight hundred pages to all of the synthetics combined: *America's Habit: Drug Abuse, Drug Trafficking and Organized Crime, Report to the President and the Attorney General of the President's Commission on Organized Crime (The Kaufman Commission)* (Washington, D.C.: GPO 1986).

22. Ralph A. Weisheit, *Domestic Marijuana* (Westport, CT: Greenwood, 1992).

23. Jimmie Lynn Reeves and Richard Campbell, *Cracked Coverage* (Durham, NC: Duke Univ. Press, 1994); compare Patrick T. MacDonald and Rhoda Estep, "Prime Time Drug Depictions," *Contemporary Drug Problems* 12 (1985): 419–38; Jock Young, "Drugs and the Media," *Drugs and Society* 2 (1971): 14–18.

24. Compare Jane Gross, "Speed's Gain in Use Could Rival Crack," *NYT*, November 27, 1988; Reinarman and Levine, "The Crack Attack"; Brownstein, *The Rise and Fall of a Violent Crime Wave*; Reinarman, "The Social Construction of Drug Scares"; Cynthia Kuhn, Scott Swartzwelder and Wilkie Wilson, *Buzzed* (New York: W. W. Norton, 1998).

25. For glue-sniffing, see Brecher's account, "How to Launch a Nationwide Drug Menace," in *Licit and Illicit Drugs*, 320–34; the Canadian investigation is quoted in ibid, 292. For crime and the media, see Ray Surette, *Media, Crime, and Criminal Justice* (Pacific Grove, CA: Brooks/Cole, 1992); Gregg Barak, ed., *Media, Process, and the Social Construction of Crime* (New York: Garland, 1995); and Jeff Ferrell and Clinton R. Sanders, eds., *Cultural Criminology* (Boston: Northeastern Univ. Press, 1995).

26. Paul Cotton, "Medium Isn't Accurate Ice Age Message," *JAMA* 263 (May 23, 1990): 2717; Marcia R. Chaiken, "The Rise of Crack and Ice: Experience in Three Locales," in *NIJ Research in Brief*, March 1993; and idem, "Identifying and Responding to New Forms of Drug Abuse," in *NIJ Issues and Practices*, Office of Justice Programs, September 1993.

27. Howard Becker, *Outsiders* (New York: Free Press, 1963), 145.

28. Joseph Gusfield, *The Culture of Public Problems* (Chicago: Univ. of Chicago Press, 1981); Joel Best, *Threatened Children* (Chicago: Univ. of Chicago Press, 1990), 11–13.

29. Peter D. Kramer, *Listening to Prozac* (New York: Viking, 1993).

Notes to Chapter 2

1. Gail Sheehy, *Speed Is of the Essence* (New York: Pocket Books, 1971), 59.

2. Sources used throughout this chapter include Edward M. Brecher, *Licit and Illicit Drugs* (Boston: Little Brown, 1972); David E. Smith and Donald R. Wesson, eds., *Uppers and Downers* (Englewood Cliffs, NJ: Prentice Hall, 1973); Oriana Josseau Kalant, *The Amphetamines: Toxicity and Addiction*, 2d ed. (Toronto: Univ. of Toronto Press, 1973); Lester Grinspoon and Peter Hedblom, *The Speed Culture* (Cambridge, MA: Harvard

Univ. Press, 1975), 40–60; John Caldwell, ed., *Amphetamines and Related Stimulants* (Boca Raton, FL: CRC Press, 1980); James V. Spotts and Carol A. Spotts, *Use and Abuse of Amphetamine and Its Substitutes*, Department of Health, Education and Welfare, PHS/ADAMHA (Washington, D.C.: GPO, 1980); Khursheed Asghar and Errol De Souza, eds., *Pharmacology and Toxicology of Amphetamine and Related Designer Drugs*, DHHS/PHS/ADAMHA/NIDA (Washington, D.C.: GPO, 1989); Arthur K. Cho and David S. Segal, eds., *Amphetamine and Its Analogs* (San Diego: Academic Press, 1994); Hilary Klee, ed., *Amphetamine Misuse* (Amsterdam: Harwood, 1997); and Darryl Inaba, William E. Cohen and Michael E. Holstein, *Uppers, Downers, All Arounders*, 3d ed. (Ashland, OR: CNS Publications, 1997). Some chemical purists dislike the term "amphetamines" as a collective word for a large family of psychostimulants. Amphetamine as such is more properly described as phenyl-isopropylamine or methyl-phenethylamine. For the neurotransmitters, see Larry J. Siever and William Frucht, *The New View of Self* (New York: Macmillan, 1997) and Richard M. Restak, *Receptors* (New York: Bantam, 1994).

3. *Amphetamine Abuse among Truck Drivers: Hearing before the Subcommittee on Alcoholism and Narcotics*, U.S. Senate. 92nd Congress, 1st sess., Oct. 1, 1971. (Washington, D.C.: GPO, 1971).

4. The quote about over-achievers is from Harvey Cohen, *The Amphetamine Manifesto* (New York: Olympia Press, 1972), 4; and see James M. Graham, "Amphetamine Politics on Capitol Hill," in William J. Chambliss and Milton Mankoff, eds., *Whose Law? What Order?* (New York: John Wiley, 1976), 107; Grinspoon and Hedblom, *The Speed Culture*, 11–39; and Richard Hughes and Robert Brewin, *The Tranquilizing of America* (New York: Harcourt Brace Jovanovich, 1979). For drugs in schools, see *Federal Involvement in the Use of Behavior Modification Drugs on Grammar School Children: Hearing before a Subcommittee of the Committee on Government Operations*, House, 91st Cong., 2d sess., September 29, 1970 (Washington, D.C.: GPO 1970).

5. John D. Griffith, "Psychiatric Implications of Amphetamine Abuse," in J. Robert Russo, ed., *Amphetamine Abuse* (Springfield, IL: Charles Thomas, 1968), 15–31; Everett H. Ellinwood, "Amphetamine Psychosis," *JPD* 2 (1969): 42–60; Charles O. Jackson, "The Amphetamine Inhaler," in David E. Smith et al., eds., *Amphetamine Use, Misuse, and Abuse* (Boston: G. K. Hall, 1979): 35–45; John D. Griffith, "A Study of Illicit Amphetamine Traffic in Oklahoma City," *AJP* 123 (1966): 560–68; Kitty Dukakis, *Now You Know* (New York: Simon and Schuster, 1990). For the scale of pill abuse, see Grinspoon and Hedblom, *The Speed Culture*, 11; *Crime in*

America: Why Eight Billion Amphetamines? Hearings, Select Committee on Crime, House, 91st Cong., 1st sess. November 18, 1969 (Washington, D.C.: GPO, 1970).

6. John A. Newmeyer, "The Epidemiology of the Use of Amphetamine and Related Substances," *JPD* 10 (1978): 293–302; idem, "The Epidemiology of Amphetamine Use," in Smith et al., eds., *Amphetamine Use, Misuse, and Abuse*, 55–58.

7. Adapted from *Sourcebook of Criminal Justice Statistics*. Compare Lloyd D. Johnston, Patrick M. O'Malley and Jerald G. Bachman, *Drugs and American High School Students, 1975–1983* (Washington, D.C.: GPO, 1984); Lloyd D. Johnston, Patrick M. O'Malley and Jerald G. Bachman, *Drug Use among High School Seniors, College Students and Young Adults, 1975–1990* (Washington, D.C.: GPO, 1991).

8. These look-alike drugs were advertised freely in the pages of adult magazines and in drug-related publications such as *High Times. Look-Alike Drugs: Hearing before the Subcommittee on Crime of the Committee on the Judiciary*, House, 98th Cong., 1st sess. October 14, 1981 (Washington, D.C.: GPO, 1983); *Further Investigation of Look-Alike Drugs: Hearing before the Select Committee on Narcotics Abuse and Control*, House, 97th Cong., 2d sess., August 12, 1982 (Washington, D.C.: GPO, 1983); John P. Morgan and Doreen Kagan, "Street Amphetamine Quality and the Controlled Substances Act of 1970," *JPD* 10 (1978): 303–18.

9. *National Household Survey on Drug Abuse: Population Estimates, 1991*. NIDA (Washington, D.C.: GPO, 1991); *National Household Survey on Drug Abuse: Highlights, 1990*, NIDA (Washington, D.C.: GPO, 1991).

10. Hunter S. Thompson, *Hell's Angels* (New York: Ballantine, 1967), 273–74. J. Phipps and R. Robinson, "Sleeping Pills and Pep Pills," *Reader's Digest*, November 1963, 103–107; H. A. Davidson, "Confessions of a Goof Ball Addict," *AJP* 120 (1964): 750–56; Frederick Lemere, "The Danger of Amphetamine Dependency," *AJP* 123 (1966): 569–71; "D-Men on the Road: Illegal Peddling of Amphetamine Tablets," *Time*, May 5, 1967, 69; "Speed Demons: Treacherous Pep Pills," *Time*, October 31, 1969, 18; Brecher, *Licit and Illicit Drugs*, 254–55; John P. Morgan, "The Clinical Pharmacology of Amphetamine," in Smith et al., eds., *Amphetamine Use, Misuse, and Abuse*, 4.

11. Griffith, "Illicit Amphetamine Traffic in Oklahoma City." For the discovery of the pill problem in the early 1960s, see Bill Davidson, "The Thrill-Pill Menace," *Saturday Evening Post*, December 4, 1965, 23–28; *Drug Abuse Control Amendments, 1965*, Proceedings of a panel discussion held as part of the Sixth Annual Conference of the International Narcotics Enforcement

Officers Association, Miami Beach, September 29, 1965, (Philadelphia: Smith Kline & French Laboratory, 1966) 3.

12. John C. McWilliams, *The Protectors* (Newark, DE: Univ. of Delaware Press, 1990). *Non-Narcotic Drug Abuse,* Proceedings of a panel discussion held as part of the Fifth Annual Conference of the International Narcotics Enforcement Officers Association, San Francisco, October 13, 1964, (Philadelphia: Smith Kline & French Laboratories, 1964) 18. A few books of the 1950s did recognize amphetamine and barbiturate pills as part of the larger drug problem: see for example Victor V. Vogel and Virginia E. Vogel, *Facts About Narcotics* (Chicago: Science Research Associates, 1951).

13. *White House Conference on Narcotic and Drug Abuse, 1962: Proceedings* (Washington, D.C.: GPO, 1963).

14. Davidson, "The Thrill-Pill Menace," 24, 27; compare Lemere, "The Danger of Amphetamine Dependency."

15. *Drug Abuse Control Amendments, 1965.*

16. This account is based on Grinspoon and Hedblom, *The Speed Culture;* Brecher, *Licit and Illicit Drugs,* 278–301; and Roger Craig Smith, "The Marketplace of Speed" (Ph.D. diss., Univ. of California, Berkeley, 1969); compare Roger Smith in *Alcoholism and Narcotics: Hearings before the Committee on Labor and Public Welfare, Subcommittee on Alcoholism and Narcotics,* U.S. Senate, 91st Cong., 1st and 2d sess. September 26, 1969– (Washington, D.C.: GPO, 1970), 68–85. William S. Burroughs, Jr., *Speed* (London: Olympia Press, 1970), 119. For media attacks, see "Unsafe at Any Speed: Methedrine," *Time,* October 27, 1967, 54; A. Rosenfeld, "Drugs That Even Scare Hippies," *Life,* October 27, 1967, 81–82; "Speed Kills: Methedrine," *Newsweek,* October 30, 1967, 67; J. Shepherd, "Cruel Chemical World of Speed: Methedrine," *Look,* March 5, 1968, 53–59; and J. Black, "Tempting Siren Called Speed," *Reader's Digest,* October 1970, 153–57. British users, like American, graduated to injecting methamphetamine during these years: see D. V. Hawks, M. Mitcheson, A. Ogbourne and G. Edwards, "Abuse of Methyl-amphetamine," *British Medical Journal* 2 (1969): 715–21.

17. "Uncle Fester," *Secrets of Methamphetamine Manufacture,* 4th ed. (Port Townsend, WA: Loompanics Unlimited, 1996), 229; John C. Kramer, "Introduction to Amphetamine Abuse," *JPD* 2 (1969): 1–13.

18. Peter Wilkinson, "America's Drug: Postcards from Tweakville," *RS,* February 19, 1998: 49–53+.

19. Cohen, *Amphetamine Manifesto,* 5, 7–8.97; Frankie Hucklenbroich, *Crystal Diary* (Ithaca, NY: Firebrand Books, 1997), 147: all punctuation *sic.* "Where has this been all my life?" is quoted in Brecher, *Licit and Illicit Drugs,* 283.

20. Brecher, *Licit and Illicit Drugs,* 292; Grinspoon and Hedblom, *The Speed Culture,* 25; Jay Stevens, *Storming Heaven* (New York: Atlantic Monthly Press, 1987).

21. Michael Newton, *Raising Hell* (New York: Avon, 1993), 132; for the Weathermen, Ron Jacobs, *The Way the Wind Blew* (London: Verso, 1997).

22. The quote beginning "Last month" is from Sheehy 1971, 21–22; the other quotes in this paragraph are from Gail Sheehy, "The Amphetamine Explosion," *New York Magazine,* July 21, 1969. Compare B. M. Angrist and Samuel Gershon, "Amphetamine Abuse in New York City," *JPD* 2 (1969): 84–91.

23. Anthony R. Lovett, "Wired in California," *RS,* May 5, 1994, 39.

24. Smith, "Marketplace of Speed"; James T. Carey and Jerry Mandel, "A San Francisco Bay Area Speed Scene," *Journal of Health and Social Behavior,* June 1969; Stephen F. Asnis and Roger C Smith, "Amphetamine Abuse and Violence," in Smith et al., eds., *Amphetamine Use, Misuse, and Abuse,* 205–17.

25. "Meth is death" is quoted from Lemere, "The Danger of Amphetamine Dependency," 571; the *Village Voice* is quoted in Angrist and Gershon, "Amphetamine Abuse in New York City," 85; Rosenfeld, "Drugs That Even Scare Hippies." For Leary, see Jill Jonnes, *Hep-Cats, Narcs and Pipe-Dreams* (New York: Scribner, 1996), 325; Ginsberg is quoted in H. Wayne Morgan, *Drugs in America* (Syracuse Univ. Press, 1981), 156. Compare David E. Smith, et al., *Speed Kills: The Amphetamine Abuse Problem* (New York: American Social Health Association/Amphetamine Research Project, 1969), 5.

26. Uncle Fester [pseud.], *Secrets of Methamphetamine Manufacture,* 3, 229.

27. Hucklenbroich, *Crystal Diary,* 157; Cohen, *Amphetamine Manifesto,* 9; Sheehy, "The Amphetamine Explosion," emphasis in original.

28. Russo, ed., *Amphetamine Abuse;* Smith et al., *Speed Kills;* Everett H. Ellinwood and Sidney Cohen, eds., *Current Concepts on Amphetamine Abuse: Proceedings of a Workshop, Duke University Medical Center, June 5–6, 1970* (Rockville, MD: NIMH, 1972).

29. Graham, "Amphetamine Politics on Capitol Hill"; David Smith, in *Alcoholism and Narcotics: Hearings,* 45–58; Sheehy, *Speed Is of the Essence,* 58.

30. Black, "Tempting Siren Called Speed"; W. Cole, "Beware the Amphetamines: Speed Kills," *Parents,* November 1971, 74–75+; M. English, "Speed: Downhill All the Way," *Look,* June 1, 1971, 88–89; R. Loving, "Putting Some Limits on Speed," *Fortune,* March 1971, 99+. For congressional investigations, see *Crime in America: Why Eight Billion Amphetamines?; Drug Abuse Control Amendments: Hearings before the Subcommittee on Public Health and*

Welfare, House, 91st Congress, 2d sess. February 3-March 3, 1970, (Washington, D.C.: GPO, 1970); *Amphetamines: Report to the Select Committee on Crime,* House, 91st Cong., 2d sess., January 2, 1971 (Washington, D.C.: GPO, 1971); *Amphetamine Legislation, 1971: Hearings, Investigation of Juvenile Delinquency in the United States,* Senate, 92d Congress, 1st sess., July 15 and 16, 1971 (Washington, D.C.: GPO, 1971); *Diet Pill (Amphetamines) Traffic, Abuse and Regulation: Hearing before the Committee on the Judiciary, Subcommittee to Investigate Juvenile Delinquency,* Senate, 92d Congress, 1st [i.e., 2d] sess., February 7, 1972 (Washington, D.C.: GPO, 1972). For the role of motorcycle gangs, see *Manufacture of Methamphetamine and Other Restricted Dangerous Drugs: A Report to the 1971 Legislature* (Sacramento, CA: California Department of Public Health, 1971).

31. *Proper and Improper Use of Drugs by Athletes: Hearings before the Committee on the Judiciary, Subcommittee to Investigate Juvenile Delinquency,* Senate, 93rd Cong., 1st sess., June 18 and July 12–13, 1973 (Washington, D.C.: GPO, 1973); Arnold J. Mandell, "The Sunday Syndrome," in Smith et al., eds., *Amphetamine Use, Misuse, and Abuse,* 218–27; idem, *The Nightmare Season* (New York: Random House, 1976); Tom Donohoe and Neil Johnson, *Foul Play* (Oxford: Blackwell, 1986).

32. Graham, "Amphetamine Politics on Capitol Hill."

33. Hunter S. Thompson, *Fear and Loathing in Las Vegas* (New York: Fawcett, 1971), 202. Though Methedrine was a brand name, the term came to be used as a synonym for methamphetamine, especially in the context of "crystal meth." Figures for declining legal usage of amphetamines are quoted in Erich Goode, *Drugs in American Society,* 4th ed. (New York: McGraw-Hill, 1993), 109; William H. McGlothlin, *Amphetamines, Barbiturates, and Hallucinogens* (Washington, D.C.: DEA, 1973); *Abuse of Dangerous Licit and Illicit Drugs—Psychotropics, Phencyclidine (PCP), and Talwin: Hearings before the Select Committee on Narcotics Abuse and Control,* House, 95th Cong., 2d sess., August 8–October 6, 1978 (Washington, D.C.: GPO, 1979), 106; Scott E. Lukas, *Amphetamines: Danger in the Fast Lane* (New York: Chelsea House, 1985).

34. John A. Newmeyer, "The Epidemiology of Amphetamine Use," in Smith et al., eds., *Amphetamine Use, Misuse, and Abuse,* 67; Marissa A. Miller and Juana Tomas, "Past and Current Methamphetamine Epidemics," in *Epidemiological Trends in Drug Abuse* DHHS (Washington, D.C.: GPO, 1989); Jane Gross, "Speed's Gain in Use Could Rival Crack," *NYT,* November 27, 1988; Michael Isikoff, "Rural Drug Users Spur Comeback of Crank," *WP,* February 20, 1989; Paul Weingarten, "Profits, Perils, Higher for Today's Bootleggers," *CT,* Sept. 14, 1989.

35. *Report to the President and the Attorney General of the President's Commission on Organized Crime (The Kaufman Commission)* (Washington, D.C.: GPO, 1986). Individual Kaufman volumes include *The Impact: Organized Crime Today,* 59–73; and *America's Habit,* 157–59.

36. This section is based on Philip Jenkins, "Narcotics Trafficking and the American Mafia," *Crime, Law and Social Change* 18 (1992): 303–18; idem, "The Speed Capital of the World: Organizing the Methamphetamine Industry in Philadelphia, 1970–1990," *Criminal Justice Policy Review* 6 (1992): 17–39; and "Meth," Segment on CBS's *60 Minutes,* April 22, 1990. For Philadelphia organized crime, see Donald Cox, *Mafia Wipeout* (New York: Shapolsky, 1989); Frank Friel and John Gunther, *Breaking the Mob* (New York: McGraw Hill, 1990); and Joseph Salerno and Stephen J. Rivele, *The Plumber* (New York: Knightsbridge, 1990). For more recent activity in the "speed capital," see for example Jeffrey Brodeur, "Fourteen Charged with Running Area Drug Ring," AP story in *CDT,* April 12, 1997; Melanie Burney, "Authorities Break Up $15 Million Drug Ring," AP story in *CDT,* May 17, 1997; Joseph A. Slobodzian, "U.S. Grand Jury Accuses Nine Philadelphia Men of Operating Drug Labs," *Philadelphia Inquirer,* November 20, 1998.

37. The DEA spokesman is quoted in *Illicit Methamphetamine Laboratories in the Pennsylvania/New Jersey/Delaware Area: Hearing before the Select Committee on Narcotics Abuse and Control,* House, 96th Cong., 2d sess., July 7, 1980 (Washington, D.C.: GPO, 1980).

Notes to Chapter 3

1. "PCP: A Terror of a Drug," *Time,* December 19, 1977.

2. The *Newsweek* article is quoted in Jill Jonnes, *Hep-Cats, Narcs and Pipe-Dreams* (New York: Scribner, 1996), 304–308. Lester Grinspoon and James B. Bakalar, *Cocaine* (New York: Basic Books, 1985); Albert Goldman, *Disco* (New York: E. P. Dutton, 1978); Andrew Holleran, *Dancer from the Dance* (New York: William Morrow, 1978).

3. See Harry Shapiro, *Waiting for the Man* (New York: William Morrow, 1988), for the influence of drug themes on popular music.

4. *Decriminalization of Marihuana: Hearings before the Select Committee on Narcotics Abuse and Control,* House, 95th Cong., 1st sess., March 14–16, 1977 (Washington, D.C.: GPO, 1977). David Musto, *The American Disease,* 2d ed. (Yale Univ. Press, 1987), 251–77.

5. Philip Jenkins, *Moral Panic* (Yale Univ. Press, 1998).

6. *Phencyclidine (PCP or Angel Dust): Joint Hearings before the Subcommittee to Investigate Juvenile Delinquency of the Committee on the Judiciary,*

Senate, 95th Cong., 2d sess., June 7 and 21, 1978 (Washington, D.C.: GPO, 1978), 61. This report will be cited throughout as *Phencyclidine (PCP or Angel Dust)*. Judianne Densen-Gerber and Michael Baden, *The Doctor Talks to You about Cocaine, Angel Dust (PCP) and Other Drugs* (Bayside, NY: Soundwords, 1981), sound recording.

7. Kody Scott, *Monster* (New York: Atlantic Monthly Press, 1993).

8. Harvey W. Feldman, "PCP Use in Four Cities," in Harvey Feldman, Michael Agar and George Beschner, eds., *Angel Dust* (Lexington, MA: Lexington Books, 1979), 29–31; A. Reed and A. W. Kane, "Phencyclidine (PCP): Another Illicit Psychedelic Drug," *JPD* 5 (1972): 8–12.

9. Tim Cahill, "Moonwalk Serenade," *RS*, July 13, 1978, 39.

10. Peter Koper, "Angel Death," *New Times*, March 20, 1978.

11. For the demographics of the PCP market, see Feldman et al., *Angel Dust*; Katherine A. Carlson, "PCP From the Other Side," *JPD* 11 (1979): 231–41; *Abuse of Dangerous Licit and Illicit Drugs—Psychotropics, Phencyclidine (PCP), and Talwin: Hearings before the Select Committee on Narcotics Abuse and Control*, House, 95th Cong., 2d sess., August 8–October 6, 1978 (Washington, D.C.: GPO, 1979), 25. This report will be cited as *Abuse of Dangerous Licit and Illicit Drugs*. Holleran, *Dancer from the Dance*, suggests the drug's popularity in the gay club world. The Washington user is quoted from Alice Bonner, "Angel Dust: Schizophrenia Epidemic Here Linked to Youths' Use of PCP," *WP*, June 11, 1977. The remark about "a drug women love" is from *Phencyclidine (PCP or Angel Dust)*, 247; the San Jose woman is quoted in Cahill "Moonwalk Serenade," 44.

12. These figures are drawn from John A. Newmeyer, "The Epidemiology of PCP Use in the Late 1970s," *JPD* 12 (1980): 211–15; E. Don Nelson, Leonard T. Sigell, Roger E. Parker and Janiece Hestness, "Epidemiology of PCP Use: The Midwestern Perspective," *JPD* 12 (1980): 217–22; *Abuse of Dangerous Licit and Illicit Drugs*, 25, 106. For the problems associated with DAWN data, see below, chapter 7.

13. Data for PCP-related deaths are from *Phencyclidine (PCP or Angel Dust)*, 101. The quotation is from "Angel Dust Devils," *Manchester Guardian*, August 14, 1977.

14. *Sourcebook of Criminal Justice Statistics*.

15. For various claimants to the "PCP Capital" title, see for example Robin De Silva, "PCP: Killer Weed Is Status Drug," *WP*, July 3, 1977; *Phencyclidine (PCP or Angel Dust)*, 246; *Designer Drugs: Hearing before the Committee on the Budget*, Senate, 99th Cong., 1st sess., July 18, 1985 (Washington, D.C.: GPO, 1985), 1.

16. All figures for Los Angeles are from *Phencyclidine (PCP or Angel*

Dust), 101. Darryl F. Gates and Diane K. Shah, *Chief: My Life in the LAPD* (New York: Bantam, 1992).

17. Greg Krikorian, "Sixteen Accused of Making, Selling $30 Million Worth of PCP," *LAT*, July 31, 1997.

18. The study of PCP reporting in the media is John P. Morgan and Doreen Kagan, "The Dusting of America," *JPD* 12 (1980): 195–204. Compare Brent Q. Hafen and Kathryn J. Frandsen, *Phencyclidine ("Angel Dust")* (Center City, MN: Hazelden, 1980). The "Cobra" quote is from *Abuse of Dangerous Licit and Illicit Drugs*, 2–3; for PCP as "dynamite," see *Phencyclidine (PCP or Angel Dust)*, 77; for "death on the installment plan," see Feldman et al., *Angel Dust*, 1; the reference to "the most devastating drug of modern times" is from Edward W. Oglesby, Samuel J. Faber and Stuart J. Faber, *Angel Dust*, 3d ed. (Los Angeles: Lega-Books, 1982), 128.

19. Bonner, "Angel Dust"; David Black, "Angel Dust: The Devil Drug That Threatens Youth," *Woman's Day*, June 14, 1978; Koper, "Angel Death"; "PCP: A Terror of a Drug"; P. Chargot, "The Cheap Street Drug PCP," *Detroit Free Press*, January 15, 1978. For the "underground mindwares," see De Silva, "PCP: Killer Weed Is Status Drug"; compare Marcia Kramer, "Angel Dust," *Daily News*, February 23–24, 1978 (two-part series). Compare Morgan and Kagan, "The Dusting of America." The dangers of PCP are enumerated in Oglesby et al., *Angel Dust*, 47–49. The Washington statistics are from Bonner, "Angel Dust."

20. Hunter S. Thompson, *Fear and Loathing in Las Vegas* (New York: Fawcett, 1971), 101–102; Morgan and Kagan, "The Dusting of America," 210–11. The quote about how "[PCP] can knock out an elephant" is from De Silva, "PCP: Killer Weed Is Status Drug." Other Washington cases are from Bonner, "Angel Dust." The examples of self-mutilation are from *Phencyclidine (PCP or Angel Dust)*, 103; Koper, "Angel Death"; and Morgan and Kagan, "The Dusting of America." The cases of "behavioral toxicity" are from Cahill, "Moonwalk Serenade," 39.

21. This account of the Peters case is from "Angel Dust Devils," 1977; the remark about PCP users destroying the home is from *Abuse of Dangerous Licit and Illicit Drugs*, 91. The Ribicoff case is described in Marvin J. Wolf and Katherine Mader, *Fallen Angels* (New York: Ballantine, 1986), 313–19.

22. "Angel Dust/PCP," Segment on CBS's *60 Minutes*, October 23, 1977. The quote about San Jose is from *Abuse of Dangerous Licit and Illicit Drugs*, 36.

23. "PCP: A Terror of a Drug"; "PCP," Segment on NBC's *Today Show*, February 21, 1978; compare Matt Clark and Susan Agrest, "The Deadly Angel Dust," *Newsweek*, March 13, 1978.

24. Cahill, "Moonwalk Serenade"; Tom McNichol, "PCP—The Cheap Drug With a High Price," *RS*, March 24, 1988, 82–85+.

25. See for instance "PCP: Infernal Angel Dust," Editorial, *WP*, February 27, 1978. The episode is from Oglesby et al., *Angel Dust*, 14–15, 55–65; *Phencyclidine (PCP or Angel Dust)*, 101–103.

26. Oglesby et al., *Angel Dust*, 49, 60. For Representative Dornan, see *Abuse of Dangerous Licit and Illicit Drugs*, 41.

27. Musto, *American Disease*, 7.

28. "Defense Attorneys: Rodney King 'PCP-Crazed,'" *WP*, January 21, 1993; compare Claire Spiegel, "Effects of PCP: Myth vs. Reality," *LAT*, June 17, 1991; Richard Lacayo, "Anatomy of an Acquittal," *Time*, May 11, 1992, 30.

29. Darryl F. Gates and Diane K. Shah, *Chief: My Life in the LAPD* (New York: Bantam, 1992), 215. E. D. Wish, "PCP and Crime," *NIDA Research Monograph Series* 64 (1986): 174–89; M. Brecher, B. W. Wang, H. Wong and John P. Morgan, "Phencyclidine and Violence," *Journal of Clinical Psychopharmacology* 8 (1988): 397–401; A. M. Khajawall, T. B. Erickson and G. M. Simpson, "Chronic Phencyclidine Abuse and Physical Assault," *AJP* 139 (1982): 1604–1606.

30. The Dornan story is from *Abuse of Dangerous Licit and Illicit Drugs*, 41. Koper, "Angel Death"; Morgan and Kagan, "The Dusting of America."

31. Koper, "Angel Death."

32. Newmeyer, "The Epidemiology of PCP Use in the Late 1970s," 215.

33. Robert C. Petersen and Richard C. Stillman, *Phencyclidine (PCP) Abuse*, Department of Health, Education and Welfare, PHS/ADAMHA/NIDA (Washington, D.C.: GPO, 1978); *Phencyclidine Use among Youths in Drug Abuse Treatment*, Philadelphia Polydrug Research Project, Department of Health, Education and Welfare, PHS/ADAMHA (Washington, D.C.: GPO, 1978); *Phencyclidine (PCP or Angel Dust)*; *Abuse of Dangerous Licit and Illicit Drugs*.

34. For Mineta's testimony, see *Abuse of Dangerous Licit and Illicit Drugs*, 5, 91. The idea of seven million *daily* users is from Representative Benjamin Gilman of New York, R–26th District, in ibid, 3, my emphasis. The "one-way ticket to immediate self-destruction" is also ibid, 3.

35. Ronald K. Siegel, "PCP and Violent Crime," *JPAD* 12 (1980); Oglesby, et al., *Angel Dust*; compare Timothy W. Kinlock, "Does Phencyclidine (PCP) Use Increase Violent Crime?" *Journal of Drug Issues* 21 (1991): 795–816. Anne J. D'Arcy, *PCP: Angel Dust, Number One Teen Killer* (Centerville, OH: Pamphlet Publications, 1980); Ronald L. Linder, Steven E. Lerner and R. Stanley Burns, *PCP, The Devil's Dust* (Belmont, CA: Wads-

worth, 1981); Marilyn Carroll, *PCP: The Dangerous Angel* (New York: Chelsea House, 1985). Articles from the mid–1980s include William L. Chaze, "The Deadly Path of Today's PCP Epidemic," *USNWR,* November 19, 1984, 65–67; Joshua Fischman, "The Angel Dust Connection," *Psychology Today,* July 1986, 68–69; and McNichol, "PCP—The Cheap Drug with a High Price."

36. Advertisement in *LAT,* October 25, 1979.

37. *Phencyclidine (PCP or Angel Dust),* 30.

38. Todd Strasser, *Angel Dust Blues* (New York: Coward, McCann and Geoghegan, 1979), 157, 204.

39. Robert E. Allen, O. Aniline, Ferris N. Pitts, Andrew F. Pitts and Lane S. Yago, "The Urban Epidemic of Phencyclidine," *Biological Psychiatry,* 15 (1981): 813–17; compare Doris H. Clouet, ed., *Phencyclidine,* DHHS/PHS/ADAMHA/NIDA (Washington, D.C.: GPO, 1986); Dennis L. Thombs, "A Review of PCP Abuse Trends and Perceptions," *Public Health Reports* 104 (1989): 325.

Notes to Chapter 4

1. Quoted in *Designer Drugs: Hearing before the Committee on the Budget,* Senate, 99th Cong., 1st sess., July 18, 1985 (Washington, D.C.: GPO, 1985), 60. This will be cited throughout as *Designer Drugs.*

2. SOURCE: Material here is taken from the NEXIS "ALLNEWS" database. In the case of "designer drugs," the search requested references in which the separate words occurred within two words of each other. It should be noted that the data presented here draw from news sources in several countries besides the United States, so the patterns suggested may reflect panics arising in other nations, like Great Britain.

3. *Designer Drugs,* 8, 15, 29; M. M. Kirsch, *Designer Drugs* (Minneapolis: CompCare Publications, 1986). For fentanyl abuse among medical personnel, see Randy Kennedy, "Death Highlights Drug's Lethal Appeal for Doctors," *NYT,* November 11, 1995.

4. *Designer Drugs,* 77.

5. Ibid, 15, 24, 45.

6. Ibid, 41; Robert Buderi, "Dr. Detective," *California,* February 1985, 129; J. William Langston and Jon Palfreman, *The Case of the Frozen Addicts* (New York: Pantheon Books, 1995); "The Case of the Frozen Addict," NOVA television documentary, produced by WGBH, 1986.

7. The remark about the "problem of the future" is from "PCP: A Terror of a Drug," 1977. Kirsch, *Designer Drugs;* Allen C. Church and Frank

Sapienza, eds., *Proceedings of Controlled Substance Analog Leadership Conference*, DEA, Office of Diversion Control (Washington, D.C.: GPO, 1986); Hal Strauss, "From Crack to Ecstasy," *American Health*, June 1987, 50–54; Graeme P. Dowling, Edward T. McDonough and Robert O. Bost, "Eve and Ecstasy: A Report of Five Deaths Associated with the Use of MDEA and MDMA," *JAMA*, March 27, 1987, 1615–17; John P. Morgan, Donald R. Wesson, Karoline S. Puder and David E. Smith, "Duplicitous Drugs," *JPAD* 19 (1987): 21–31; Isabel S. Abrams, "Legal But Lethal Designer Drugs," *Current Health* 14 (March 1988): 19–21; *Designer Drugs*, 15, 45; Michele McCormick, *Designer Drug Abuse* (New York: Franklin Watts, 1989); Richard Seymour et al., *The New Drugs* (Center City, MN: Hazelden, 1989); Gene Barnett and Rao S. Rapaka, "Designer Drugs," in Kinfe K. Redda, Charles A. Walker and Gene Barnett, eds., *Cocaine, Marijuana, Designer Drugs* (Boca Raton, FL: CRC Press, 1989), 163–74.

8. The quote about the horse and buggy is from Jack Shafer, "The Designer Drug Market," *DN*, June 13, 1985. The drug user is quoted on NBC's *Nightly News*, February 19, 1985. Characteristic of the press coverage in these months are stories like these: Jack Shafer, "Designer Drugs an Enforcement Nightmare," *WSJ*, March 8, 1985; Sandra Blakeslee, "California Addicts Use Legal Synthetic Narcotics," *NYT*, March 24, 1985; "Death by Design," *Time*, April 8, 1985; and Jeff Leen, "Cheap, Legal, Deadly: Designer Drugs a Frightening Trend," *CT*, April 21, 1985. Jack Shafer, "Designer Drugs," *Science '85*, March 1985, 60–67; Ronald K. Siegel, "Chemical Ecstasies," *Omni*, August 1985, 29; "Designer Drugs—Murder by Molecule," *USNWR*, August 5, 1985, 14; Winifred Gallagher, "The Looming Menace of Designer Drugs," *Discover*, August 1986, 24–35; T. Ziporyn, "A Growing Industry and Menace," *JAMA* 256 (1986): 3061–63.

9. *Designer Drugs*, 17, 20, 61; Gary L. Henderson, "Fentanyl-Related Deaths," *Journal of Forensic Sciences* 36 (1991): 422; and idem, "Street and Designer Drugs," *Patient Care* 26 (1992): 118.

10. *Designer Drugs*, 1–2: remarks of Lawton Chiles. Compare *Designer Drugs, 1985: Hearing before the Subcommittee on Children, Family, Drugs, and Alcoholism of the Committee on Labor and Human Resources*, Senate, 99th Cong., 1st sess., July 25, 1985. (Washington, D.C.: GPO, 1985). The quotation about "aggressive lonewolf chemists" is from Shafer, "The Designer Drug Market."

11. *Designer Drugs*, 55.

12. These remarks are quoted from *Designer Drugs*: "Frankenstein's Monster," 5; "These phantom chemists are experimenting . . . " 56; "they are

turning young people into zombies," 42; and "human guinea pig," 36. For the Kidston case, see ibid, 30–35.

13. *Designer Drugs*, 2.

14. "As California Goes" is from *Designer Drugs*, 66. See *Clandestine Laboratories/Designer Drugs, California Legislature, Senate Select Committee on Drug and Alcohol Abuse, Senate* (Sacramento, CA: Joint Publications Office, 1985).

15. Frank Monastero, "Recommendations for the Regulation of Selected Chemicals and Controlled Substance Analogs," in Appendix G of *America's Habit: Drug Abuse, Drug Trafficking and Organized Crime, Report to the President and the Attorney General of the President's Commission on Organized Crime (The Kaufman Commission)* (Washington, D.C.: GPO, 1986); *Designer Drug Enforcement Act of 1986: Report, U.S. Congress, House, Committee on the Judiciary* (Washington, D.C.: GPO, 1986); *Designer Drugs: Hearing before the Subcommittee on Crime of the Committee on the Judiciary*, House, 99th Cong., 1st sess., May 1, 1986 (Washington, D.C.: GPO, 1986); Malcolm W. Browne, "Problems Loom in Effort to Control Use of Chemicals for Illicit Drugs," *NYT*, October 24, 1989; M. Klein et al., eds., *Clandestinely Produced Drugs, Analogues and Precursors* (DEA, 1989); *Control of Chemical Precursors and Essential Chemicals: Hearings before the Subcommittee on Crime of the Committee on the Judiciary*, House, 100th Cong., 1st sess. September 16 and October 15, 1987 (Washington, D.C.: GPO, 1989); *Controlling Chemicals Used to Make Illegal Drugs*, in *NIJ Research in Brief*, January 1993.

16. Maryann Ziemer, *Quaaludes* (Springfield, NJ: Enslow Publishers, 1997); Jack Mendelson and Nancy Mello, *Quaaludes: The Quest for Oblivion* (New York: Chelsea House, 1985); Marilyn Carroll and Gary Gallo, *Methaqualone: The Quest for Oblivion* (London: Burke, 1988); Mathea Falco, *Methaqualone: A Study of Drug Control* (Washington, D.C.: Drug Abuse Council, 1975); *Methaqualone (Quaalude, Sopor) Traffic, Abuse and Regulation: Hearings*, Senate, 93rd Cong., 1st sess., March 28–29 and April 6, 1973 (Washington, D.C.: GPO, 1973); *Drug Abuse: Quaaludes, Hearing before the Subcommittee on Investigations and General Oversight of the Committee on Labor and Human Resources, on examination of the increased use of certain drugs, focusing on Quaaludes*, Senate, 97th Cong., 2d sess., May 13, 1982 (Washington, D.C.: GPO, 1982); *Drug Legislation: Hearings before the Subcommittee on Health and the Environment of the Committee on Energy and Commerce, on drug labeling and advertising*, House, 98th Cong., 1st sess. (Washington, D.C.: GPO, 1983); *Rescheduling of Methaqualone: Report (To Accompany H.R. 4201)* (Washington, D.C.: GPO, 1983).

17. "The potential of the psychedelic drugs . . . " is from Alexander T. Shulgin and Ann Shulgin, *PIHKAL: A Chemical Love Story* (Berkeley, CA: Transform Press, 1991), xvii; for 2C-B, see pages 218, 503–506. 2C-B is more fully 4-Bromo–2,5-dimethoxy-phenethylamine. Alexander T. Shulgin, *TIHKAL: The Continuation* (Berkeley, CA: Transform Press, 1997). See also Richard A. Glennon, "Phenylakylamine Stimulants, Hallucinogens, and Designer Drugs," *NIDA Research Monograph* 105 (1990): 154–60 and idem, "Stimulus Properties of a New Designer Drug, 4-Methylaminorex (U–4-E-uh)," *Pharmacology, Biochemistry and Behavior* 35 (1990): 517.

18. Matthew Collin, *Altered States* (London: Serpent's Tail, 1997); Jerome Beck and Marsha Rosenbaum, *In Pursuit of Ecstasy* (Albany, NY: State Univ. of New York Press, 1994); Bruce Eisner, *Ecstasy: The MDMA story*, 2d ed. (Berkeley, CA: Ronin, 1994); Grinspoon and Hedblom, *The Speed Culture*. DOM is 4-Methyl–2,5-dimethoxy-amphetamine; MDA is 3,4-methylene-dioxy-amphetamine.

19. Uncle Fester, [pseud.], *Secrets of Methamphetamine Manufacture*, 4th ed. (Port Townsend, WA: Loompanics Unlimited, 1996), 197–98; Shulgin and Shulgin, *PIHKAL*, 69, 733–9; Alexander T. Shulgin, "The Background and Chemistry of MDMA," *JPAD* 18 (1986): 291–304; Alexander T. Shulgin, *Controlled Substances*, 2d ed. (Berkeley, CA: Ronin, 1992); Douglas Rushkoff, *The Ecstasy Club* (London: Scepter, 1997), 57. The remark about "totally in control" is from Shulgin and Shulgin, *PIHKAL*, 187; the penicillin analogy is from ibid, 74.

20. For the therapist, Shulgin and Shulgin, *PIHKAL*, 187; compare Myron J. Stolaroff, *The Secret Chief* (Multidisciplinary Association for Psychedelic Studies, 1997); John R. Neill, "More Than Medical Significance," *JPAD* 19 (1987); S. Adamson, *Through the Gateway of the Heart* (San Francisco: Four Trees Publications, 1985).

21. Dowling et al., "Eve and Ecstasy."

22. Jerry Adler, "Getting High on Ecstasy," *Newsweek*, April 15, 1985, 96; Joe Klein, "The New Drug They Call Ecstasy: Is It Too Much to Swallow?" *New York*, May 20, 1985, 38–43; Jack Shafer, "MDMA: Designer Drug Faces Regulation," *Psychology Today*, May, 1985, 68–69; Anastasia Toufexis, "A Crackdown on Ecstasy," *Time*, June 10, 1985, 64–65; Kathryn Gertz, "Hug Drug Alert: The Agony of Ecstasy," *Harpers Bazaar*, November 1985, 210+; Marjory Roberts, "MDMA: Madness Not Ecstasy" *Psychology Today*, June 1986, 14–15; Ronald K. Siegel, "MDMA—Nonmedical Use and Intoxication," *JPAD*, October–December 1986: 349–54. The Doonesbury strips are from August 15–17, 1985.

23. Marilyn Elias, "Fad Drug May Harm the Brain," *USA Today*, January

16, 1989; "Ecstasy Drug Tied to Brain Damage," *NYT,* January 17, 1989; Michael Perlstein, "Ecstasy: Designer Drug Has a Harsh Downside," *Times-Picayune,* November 20, 1989; Stephen J. Peroutka, ed., *Ecstasy: The Clinical, Pharmacological and Nerotoxicological Effects of the Drug MDMA* (Boston: Kluwer Academic, 1990); Peter Aldhous, "Rave Drug May Damage the Brain," *New Scientist,* September 2, 1995, 14; Anne Alvergue, *Ecstasy: The Danger of False Euphoria* (New York: Rosen Publishing, 1997).

24. *Designer Drugs,* 60, 104; Kirsch, *Designer Drugs;* Michele McCormick, *Designer Drug Abuse* (New York: Franklin Watts, 1989).

25. Peter D. Kramer, *Listening to Prozac* (New York: Viking, 1993); Clark E. Barshinger, "Christian Faith in the Age of Prozac," *Harper's,* December 1995, 16–18; "Better Than well," *The Economist,* April 6, 1996, 87.

26. For attacks on Prozac, see Peter Breggin and Ginger Ross Breggin, *Talking Back to Prozac* (New York: St. Martin's, 1994) and Mark Nichols, "Questioning Prozac," *Maclean's,* May 23, 1994, 36–41. Compare Lauren Slaker, *Prozac Diary* (New York: Random House, 1998). For the interpretation of "drug-related" death and violence, see Erich Goode, *Drugs in American Society,* 4th ed. (New York: McGraw-Hill, 1993), 274–78, and also chapter 7 below.

27. Stephen Fried, *Bitter Pills* (New York: Bantam Doubleday Dell, 1998); Thomas J. Moore, *Prescription for Disaster* (New York: Simon and Schuster, 1998).

28. Jonathan Hibbs, Joshua Perper and Charles L. Winek, "An Outbreak of Designer Drug Related Deaths in Pennsylvania," *JAMA,* February 27, 1991, 1011–13; Bruce A. Lodge, "Canadian Designer Drugs," *Journal of Psychiatry and Neuroscience* 16 (1991): 239–; M. Martin, "China White Epidemic," *Annals of Emergency Medicine* 20 (1991): 158–; A. James Ruttenber, "Stalking the Elusive Designer Drugs," *Journal of Addictive Diseases* 11 (1991): 71–87; "Fentanyl Analogs: Deadly Designer Drugs," *Emergency Medicine* 23 (1991): 75–; Sherry Rapp, "Designer Drugs: The Look That Kills," *Pharmacy Times* 57, no. 6 (1991): 53–; Diane K. Beebe and Elizabeth Walley, "Substance Abuse: The Designer Drugs," *American Family Physician* 43, no. 5 (1991): 1689–; David Evanko, "Designer Drugs: Treating the Damage Caused by Basement Chemists," *Postgraduate Medicine* 89 (1991): 67–; George L. Sternbach and Joseph Varon, "Designer Drugs," *Postgraduate Medicine* 91 (1992): 169–; Michael Hedges, "DEA nabs 2 for making ultralethal drug Fentanyl," *Washington Times,* February 6, 1993; David Zucchino, "Halting Heroin's Savage Clone," *Philadelphia Inquirer,* February 15, 1993; Lawrence Clayton, *Designer Drugs* (New York: Rosen, 1994); Paul R. Robbins, *Designer Drugs* (Springfield, NJ: Enslow Publishers, 1995).

29. Karen Schoemer, "The New Allure of Heroin," *Newsweek,* August 26, 1996. *Remarks by the President at U.S. Conference of Mayors, May 21, 1997,* WWW site of the White House, 1997.

30. *The Re-Emergence of Methamphetamine: Hearings before the Subcommittee on Narcotics Abuse and Control,* House, 101st Cong., 1st sess., October 24, 1989 (Washington, D.C.: GPO, 1990), 25, 90–91; Frank Monastero, "Recommendations for the Regulation of Selected Chemicals and Controlled Substance Analogs"; *Illicit Methamphetamine Laboratories in the Pennsylvania/New Jersey/Delaware Area: Hearing before the Select Committee on Narcotics Abuse and Control,* House, 96th Cong., 2d sess., July 7, 1980 (Washington, D.C.: GPO, 1980).

Notes to Chapter 5

1. *The Re-Emergence of Methamphetamine: Hearings before the Subcommittee on Narcotics Abuse and Control,* House, 101st Cong., 1st sess., October 24, 1989 (Washington, D.C.: GPO, 1990), 59. This will be cited throughout as *Re-Emergence of Methamphetamine.*

2. The quotes are from Craig Reinarman and Harry G. Levine, eds., *Crack in America.* Univ. of California Press, 1997), 20, 28; *"Crack" Cocaine: Hearing before the Permanent Subcommittee on Investigations of the Committee on Governmental Affairs,* Senate, 99th Cong., 2d sess., July 15, 1986 (Washington, D.C.: GPO, 1986); *The Crack Cocaine Crisis: Joint Hearing before the Select Committee on Narcotics Abuse and Control and the Select Committee on Children, Youth, and Families,* House, 99th Cong., 2d sess., July 15, 1986 (Washington, D.C.: GPO, 1987); Katherine Beckett and Theodore Sasson, "The Media and the Construction of the Drug Crisis," in Eric L. Jensen and Jurg Gerber, eds., *The New War on Drugs* (Cincinnati: Anderson, 1998), 25–44.

3. Darryl F. Gates and Diane K. Shah, *Chief: My Life in the LAPD* (New York: Bantam, 1992), 286.

4. Jensen and Gerber, eds., *New War on Drugs,* 19.

5. "Text of President's Speech on Drug Control Strategy," *NYT,* September 6, 1989.

6. Fox Butterfield, "Defying Gravity, Inmate Population Climbs," *NYT,* January 19, 1998.

7. Matthew Costigan, "Go Directly to Jail, Do Not Pass Go, Do Not Keep House," *Journal of Criminal Law and Criminology* 87 (1997): 719–50; the case in question is *United States v. Ursery,* 116 S. Ct. 2135 (1996). Henry J.

Hyde, *Forfeiting Our Property Rights* (Washington, D.C.: Cato Institute, 1995).

8. Jimmie Lynn Reeves and Richard Campbell, *Cracked Coverage* (Durham, NC: Duke Univ. Press, 1994).

9. Gordon Witkin, "The New Midnight Dumpers," *USNWR*, January 9, 1989; Michael Isikoff, "Rural Drug Users Spur Comeback of Crank," *WP*, February 20, 1989; Paul Weingarten, "Profits, Perils, Higher for Today's Bootleggers," *CT*, September 14, 1989; Pamela S. Zurer, "Federal Officials Plot Strategy to Stop Methamphetamine Spread," *Chemical and Engineering News*, November 6, 1989, 20–21. For instruction manuals, see Uncle Fester [pseudo.], *Secrets of Methamphetamine Manufacture*, 4th ed. (Port Townsend, WA: Loompanics Unlimited, 1996); Jack B. Nimble, *The Construction and Operation of Clandestine Drug Laboratories*, 2d ed. (Port Townsend, WA: Loompanics Unlimited, 1994).

10. *Re-Emergence of Methamphetamine*, 39.

11. The quote from Bob Burgreen is in *Re-Emergence of Methampheta-mine*, 110; the BNE official is quoted in M. M. Kirsch, *Designer Drugs* (Minneapolis: CompCare Publications, 1986), 122. *Profile of Organized Crime, Mid-Atlantic Region: Hearings before the Permanent Subcommittee on Investigations of the Committee on Governmental Affairs*, Senate, 98th Cong., 1st sess., February 15, and 23–24, 1983 (Washington, D.C.: GPO, 1983); Bob Wiedrich, "San Diego Has Become National Center for Manufacture of Methamphetamine," *CT*, April 20, 1987; *Organized Crime in California: Annual Report to the California Legislature* (Sacramento, CA: State of California Department of Justice, 1989); *Re-Emergence of Methamphetamine*, 37, 46; *Arrestee Drug Use—Drug Use Forecasting Series, NIJ—Research in Action* (Washington, D.C.: GPO, 1990–98); *Impact of Clandestine Drug Laboratories on Small Business: Hearings before the Subcommittee on Regulation and Business Opportunities of the Committee on Small Business*, House, 100th Cong., 2d sess., Eugene, Oregon, May 13, 1988 (Washington, D.C.: GPO, 1988); John P. Morgan, "Amphetamine and Methamphetamine During the 1990s," *Pediatrics in Review*, 13 (1992): 330–; Marcia R. Chaiken, "The Rise of Crack and Ice" in *NIJ Research In Brief*, March 1993; idem, *Identifying and Responding to New Forms of Drug Abuse*, in *NIJ Issues and Practices*, Office of Justice Programs, September 1993. For the limitations of the DUF system, see chapter 7 below.

12. "The typical methamphetamine user" is described in *Re-Emergence of Methamphetamine*, 87; ibid for conditions in San Diego (111); the opinions of the Texas police officer are found on 39 and 106–107.

13. For conditions in Honolulu, see *Re-Emergence of Methamphetamine,* 6–7, 9; ibid, 75, for the drug's popularity among women (quoting Douglas Gibb). Karen A. Joe-Laidler and Patricia Morgan, "Kinship and Community," in Hilary Klee, ed., *Amphetamine Misuse* (Amsterdam: Harwood, 1997), 163–179.

14. The graffiti wall is quoted from Eric Brazil, "Deaths Rising from Meth Abuse," *San Francisco Examiner,* December 3, 1996; Francis Anderton, "Inside Story," *The Guardian,* September 15, 1997; and Dominick Frosch, "Sexual HIV Risk among Gay and Bisexual Male Methamphetamine Abusers," *Journal of Substance Abuse Treatment* 13 (1996): 483–86.

15. Uncle Fester [pseud.], *Secrets of Methamphetamine Manufacture,* 209.

16. This account draws on Philip Jenkins, "The Ice Age," *Justice Quarterly* 11 (1994): 7–31. Arthur K. Cho, "Ice: A New Dosage Form of an Old Drug," *Science,* August 10, 1990, 631–34; Susan Pennell, "Ice: DUF Interview Results from San Diego," *NIJ Reports* (summer 1990): 12–13. For the Asian context of the drug problem, see Ian Buruma and John McBeth, "An East Side Story," *FEER,* December 27, 1984/January 3, 1985; David E. Kaplan and Alec Dubro, *Yakuza* (Reading, MA: Addison-Wesley, 1986), 198–200; Gerald L. Posner, *Warlords of Crime* (New York: McGraw Hill, 1988); Karl Shoenberger, "South Korea Seen as Major Source of Ice Narcotic," *LAT,* October 14, 1989; John McBeth, "The Junkie Culture: Supercharged Speed is Scourge of Manila's Smart Set," *FEER,* November 23, 1989; B. Savadove, "High Society: Growing Drug Abuse Reflects Economic Changes," *FEER,* September 12, 1991; Robert Delfs, "Cocaine Surge," *FEER,* November 21, 1991; *Re-Emergence of Methamphetamine,* 5, 11, 99. For the revival of methamphetamine use in East Asia during the mid–1990s, see Bertil Lintner, "The Dream Merchants," *FEER,* April 16, 1998, 26–27.

17. H. G. Reza, "Raids Shut 23 Drug Labs," *LAT,* March 20, 1989; "US Reports Drug Raids on Speed Makers," *BG,* March 20, 1989; Andrea Ford, "Federal, Local Police Raid House in San Diego," *LAT,* July 26, 1990; *Re-Emergence of Methamphetamine,* 70–72; *Drug Crisis in Hawaii: Hearing Before the Select Committee on Narcotics Abuse and Control,* House, 101st Cong., 2d sess., January 13, 1990 (Washington, D.C.: GPO, 1990), 56, 74–75, 205, 215. This will be cited as *Drug Crisis in Hawaii.*

18. Miles Corwin, "Potent Form of Speed Could Be Drug of 90s," *LAT,* October 8, 1989; Pamela S. Zurer, "Federal Officials Plot Strategy to Stop Methamphetamine Spread," *Chemical and Engineering News,* November 6, 1989, 20–21; "Drugs: Ice Overdose," *Economist,* December 2, 1989, 29–30; Jack Anderson and Dale Van Atta, "Big Plane Junket for Hill Spouses," *WP,*

January 10, 1990; Cardwell C. Nuckols, *The Ice Storm* (Center City, MN: Hazelden, 1990); Leslie E. Moser, *Crack, Cocaine, Methamphetamine, and Ice* (Waco, TX: Multi-Media Productions, 1990); "Illicit Methamphetamine: Street Drug on the Rise," *Emergency Medicine,* June 30, 1991.

19. Katherine Bishop, "Fear Grows over Effects of a New Smokeable Drug," *NYT,* September 16, 1989; Peter J. Howe, "Ice Worse Than Crack, Officials Warn," *BG,* October 1, 1989; Corwin, "Potent Form of Speed Could Be Drug of 90s"; Susan Essoyan, "Use of Highly Addictive Ice Growing in Hawaii," *LAT,* October 16, 1989; Nora Zamichow, "Navy Hopes Drug Test Will Detect, Deter Meth Users," *LAT,* October 16, 1989; Larry Thompson, "Ice: New Smokeable Form of Speed," *WP,* November 21, 1989; Michael L. Lerner, "The Fire of Ice" *Newsweek,* November 27, 1989; Mark Curriden, "Police Chilled by New In Drug," *Atlanta Constitution,* November 30, 1989; Mary Tabor, "Ice in an Island Paradise," *BG,* December 8, 1989; Brook Larmer, "Ice Chills US Anti-Drug Officials," *CSM,* December 8, 1989.

20. The remark that ice "has escalated in such leaps and bounds" is from Tabor, "Ice in an Island Paradise"; compare *Re-Emergence of Methamphetamine* 2; the story of the New York City Korean gang is from ibid, 8; Douglas Gibb's remark about "only a matter of time" is from ibid, 77. Representative Stan Parris is quoted in ibid, 19; compare *Drug Crisis in Hawaii* 3; Curriden, "Police Chilled by New In Drug: Ice"; Howe, "Ice Worse Than Crack, Officials Warn"; Christopher Durso, "Powerful Drug 'Ice' Is Found at Lab," *Philadelphia Inquirer,* August 14, 1992; Mike Sager, "The Ice Age," *RS,* February 8, 1990, 53–57.

21. The Dallas police officer, Rick Hatler, is quoted in *Re-Emergence of Methamphetamine,* 39–40.

22. U.S. Attorney Daniel Bent is quoted in *Re-Emergence of Methamphetamine,* 5; Tom Lewis in ibid, 17; Rangel and Currie in ibid, 1, 44.

23. *Re-Emergence of Methamphetamine,* 3, 77; Sager, "The Ice Age"; David Holley, Elizabeth Venant and Susan Essoyan, "The Ice Age," *WP,* May 9, 1991; compare Dominick A. LaBianca, "The Drug Scene's New Ice Age," *USA Today: the Magazine of the American Scene,* January 1992, 54–56; Larmer, "Ice Chills U.S. Anti-Drug Officials."

24. Donald R. Wesson, David E. Smith and Susan C. Steffens, *Crack and Ice* (Center City, MN: Hazelden, 1992); "Illicit Methamphetamine: Skeer Drug on the Rise." Akaka is quoted in *Re-Emergence of Methamphetamine,* 3; "It doesn't make any difference . . . " is from Representative Tom Lewis in ibid, 17; Bent, in ibid, 64; Akaka's question is in ibid, 54.

25. Bennett is quoted in Erich Goode, *Drugs in American Society,* 4th ed.

(New York: McGraw-Hill, 1993), 55. Laura Gomez, *Misconceiving Mothers* (Philadelphia: Temple Univ. Press, 1997); Loren Siegel, "The Pregnancy Police Fight the War on Drugs," in Craig Reinarman and Harry G. Levine, eds., *Crack in America* (Univ. of California Press, 1997), 249–59; John P. Morgan and Lynn Zimmer, "The Social Pharmacology of Smokeable Cocaine," in ibid, 151–52; Inger J. Sagatun-Edwards, "Crack Babies, Moral Panic, and the Criminalization of Behavior during Pregnancy," in Jensen and Gerber, *New War on Drugs,* 107–21; *Re-Emergence of Methamphetamine,* 66, 76; *Drug Crisis in Hawaii,* 2, 226–33; "A Mother's Drug Use, An Infant's Death, and Then a Conviction," *NYT,* September 11, 1994, 36; Joanne Jacobs, "Debunking the Crack Baby Myths," Knight-Ridder News Service story, reprinted in the *CDT,* August 11, 1991.

26. Ardis Carthane, "Will New Drug 'Ice' Freeze Hope in Black Communities?" *Jet,* December 18, 1989; *Methamphetamine Abuse in the United States,* Rockville, MD: DHHS, ADAMHA (Washington, D.C.: GPO, 1989); Marissa A. Miller and Nicholas J. Kozel, *Methamphetamine Abuse: Epidemiological Issues and Implications,* Rockville, MD: DHHS, ADAMHA (Washington, D.C.: GPO, 1991); Lisa Holland, "All About Ice: New Drug Nice Kids Can Get Hooked On," *Good Housekeeping,* February 1990, 215–16.

27. Bob Benenson, "Democrats Reassert Primacy in Hawaii Politics," *Congressional Quarterly,* October 12, 1991; Zachary A. Smith and Richard C. Pratt, eds., *Politics and Public Policy in Hawaii* (Albany, NY: State Univ. of New York Press, 1992).

28. Wallace Turner, "Hawaii Criminal's Pledge to Talk Seen as Door to Underworld," *NYT,* July 24, 1984; idem, "Inquiry on Murders in Hawaii Brings Governor and Prosecutor into Conflict," *NYT,* August 28, 1984.

29. "Hawaiian Politics: Ethnic Pineapple Salad," *Economist,* October 20, 1990; Robert Reinhold, "Hawaii Race Tests Democratic Hold," *NYT,* November 1, 1990; Keith B. Richburg, "For Hawaii Democrats, Anxiety Over Safe Seats," *WP,* November 1, 1990.

30. Kaplan and Dubro, *Yakuza;* D. Burstein, *Japan's New Financial Empire and its Threat to America* (New York: Simon and Schuster, 1988); C. Prestowitz, *Trading Places* (New York: Basic Books, 1989); Pat Choate, *Agents of Influence* (New York: Alfred Knopf, 1990); G. Friedman and M. Lebard, *The Coming War with Japan* (New York: St. Martin's Press, 1991).

31. SOURCE: Information is from the NEXIS "ALLNEWS" database, searching references in which the separate words "crystal" and "methamphetamine" occurred within two words of each other. I make no great claims for the validity of this table: as the data presented here draw from news sources in

several countries besides the United States, the patterns indicated may also reflect panics arising in other nations, like Great Britain or Taiwan.

32. *Re-Emergence of Methamphetamine, 76, 7–8.* See also chapter 7 for discussion of the notion of drug-related deaths.

33. *Re-Emergence of Methamphetamine,* 17.

34. The head of DEA's Honolulu office is quoted in *Drug Crisis in Hawaii,* 76; Pennell, "Ice: DUF Interview Results from San Diego"; David Lauderback and Dan Waldorf, "Whatever Happened to Ice?" (paper presented to the American Society of Criminology meetings, New Orleans, LA, November 1992).

Notes to Chapter 6

1. William J. Bailey, "Methcathinone, aka CAT," Indiana Prevention Resource Center, 1995, WWW.

2. *ABC World News Tonight,* June 29, 1993. *New Challenges Facing the DEA: Heroin, Methamphetamine, and CAT: Hearing before the Information, Justice, Transportation, and Agriculture Subcommittee of the Committee on Government Operations,* House, 103rd Cong., 2d sess., August 2, 1994 (Washington, D.C.: GPO, 1994). This will be cited throughout as *New Challenges Facing the DEA.*

3. Richard A. Glennon, M. Yousif and P. Kalix, "Methcathinone: A New and Potent Amphetamine-Like Agent," *Pharmacology, Biochemistry and Behavior,* 26 (1987): 547–51; compare M. S. Goldstone, "CAT: Methcathinone—A New Drug of Abuse," *JAMA* 269 (May 19, 1993): 2503; "Drug Agents Uncover Khat Smuggling in Newark," *NYT,* November 27, 1994; Henry Kirch, "Qat," *International Drug Prevention Quarterly* 2 (1993): 3; Elissa Silverman, "Khat Calls," *Washington City Paper,* November 13, 1998.

4. *New Challenges Facing the DEA,* 9–10; "CAT and LSD, Designer Drugs," *Current Health* 21 (1994): 13–; James McGivney, "The New and Potent Methcathinone," *Police Chief,* April 1994, 20–24. The reference to users becoming "very stinky" is from Uncle Fester [pseudo.], *Secrets of Methamphetamine Manufacture,* 4th ed. (Port Townsend, WA: Loompanics Unlimited, 1996), 194.

5. Cynthia L. Webb, "Patent Office Lets CAT out of the Bag," *Rocky Mountain News,* August 8, 1994; "Student Aided Spread of Methcathinone," *CT,* January 23, 1995; Jim Schaefer, "Chemical Predator," *Orange County Register,* January 29, 1995 and idem, "Chemistry Student Unleashes Dangerous Drug," *Times-Picayune,* February 5, 1995.

6. *New Challenges Facing the DEA,* 45.

7. *New Challenges Facing the DEA,* 34–36; "Man Admits Bringing Drug CAT to Michigan," *CT,* October 29, 1993; T. S. Emerson, "Methcathinone: A Russian Designer Amphetamine Infiltrates the Rural Midwest," *Annals of Emergency Medicine* 22 (1993): 1897; Goldstone, "CAT: Methcathinone—A New Drug of Abuse."

8. Bonnie Hayes, "Internet Drug Recipe Raises Officials' Fears," *LAT,* October 22, 1997. For the drug formula as a "cookie recipe": ABC's *World News Tonight,* June 29, 1993.

9. "The Methcathinone Project," n.d. (WWW).

10. Hayes, "Internet Drug Recipe Raises Officials' Fears"; compare Uncle Fester [pseudo.], *Secrets of Methamphetamine Manufacture,* 193–96, 240–44.

11. *New Challenges Facing the DEA,* 10–11; *United States v. Lawrence E. Vold and Joel R. Cox,* US Court of Appeals for the Seventh Circuit, 95–1521 and 95–1522, (1995).

12. For "your local hardware store," Representative Gary A. Condit in *New Challenges Facing the DEA,* 2. Sarah Ellis, "Explosion reveals new designer drug," *Denver Post,* November 2, 1993.

13. *United States v. Vold and Cox,* 1995; *United States v. Edward Lee Mahaffey,* U.S. Court of Appeals for the Seventh Circuit, 94–1287 (1995); "Police Raid Lab Used to Make CAT," *Wisconsin State Journal,* August 18, 1993; Mike Oliver, "Law Aimed at Drug Abuse Backfires," *Orlando Sentinel,* August 15, 1994; *Domestic Chemical Diversion Control Act of 1993: An Act to Amend the Comprehensive Drug Abuse Prevention and Control Act of 1970 to Control the Diversion of Certain Chemicals Used in the Illicit Production of Controlled Substances Such as Methcathinone and Methamphetamine, and for Other Purposes* (Washington, D.C.: GPO, 1993).

14. Jerry Moskal, "Clinton Signs Law Imposing Controls on Deadly Drug CAT, Gannett News Service, December 17, 1993; "a high school chemistry set," Representative Gary A. Condit, in *New Challenges Facing the DEA,* 2.

15. Material is taken from the NEXIS "ALLNEWS" database. Scott Bowles, "New Drug 'Cat' Is More Addictive Than Crack," *DN,* September 26, 1992.

16. "These labs leave behind dangerous chemical waste . . . ": *New Challenges Facing the DEA,* 12. McGivney, "The New and Potent Methcathinone"; Karen Cohen, "Feingold Says Wisconsin Needs Money to Fight CAT," *Wisconsin State Journal,* November 10, 1993; idem, "Wisconsin Would Win under Crime Bill," States News Service, March 9, 1994; idem, "Feingold Requests Anti-Drug Money," *Wisconsin State Journal,* September 3, 1994; Carol Stevens, "Levin, Stupak Push Bill to Stop Designer Drug,"

DN, November 19, 1993; "CAT Drug Slowed," *Wisconsin State Journal,* December 18, 1993; "Man Sentenced," *Wisconsin State Journal,* December 31, 1993.

17. "New Drug 'Cat' Is Giving Police Kittens," *Courier-Journal* (Louisville, KY), September 27, 1992; Richard F. Calkins, "Methcathinone: The Next Illicit Stimulant Epidemic?" *JPAD* 27 (1995): 277; Jim Schaefer, "CAT Attack: US Epidemic of New Drug Is Feared," *AR,* March 28, 1993; Mike Nichols, "New Drug Emerges in Midwest More Powerful Than Cocaine," *Houston Chronicle,* July 11, 1993 (story also appeared in *CT,* June 24, C2).

18. Connie Walker, "New, Readily Available Drug Sweeping the Midwest," Broadcast on NPR's *All Things Considered,* October 12, 1993; Paul Glastris, "The New Drug in Town," *USNWR,* April 26, 1993, 20–21; John Flesher, "Michigan Woods a War Zone against New Drug Epidemic," *LAT,* August 10, 1993; idem, "Drug CAT Is Clawing Up Michigan," *LAT,* August 22, 1993; Jack Anderson and Michael Binstein, "Home-Grown Drug Menace," *WP,* October 10, 1993.

19. "CAT Poses National Threat, Experts Say," *Alcoholism and Drug Abuse Week,* December 13, 1993; McGivney, "The New and Potent Methcathinone"; Walker, "New, Readily Available Drug Sweeping the Midwest"; Evelyn Petersen, "Highly Addictive Drug CAT Can Have Devastating Effects," *Houston Chronicle,* May 17, 1994. The quote "Put a pound of coke . . . " is from Anthony R. Lovett, "Wired in California," *RS,* May 5, 1994, 39–40. Schaefer, "CAT Attack: US Epidemic of New Drug is Feared"; Miles Oliver, "Law Aimed at Drug Abuse Backfires," *Orlando Sentinel,* August 15, 1994.

20. See for example *United States v. Vold and Cox,* 1995; "CAT Facts" (letter), *WP,* October 25, 1993. Norman E. Zinberg, *Drugs, Set and Setting* (Yale Univ. Press, 1984); compare John P. Morgan and Lynn Zimmer, "The Social Pharmacology of Smokeable Cocaine," in Craig Reinarman and Harry G. Levine, eds., *Crack in America* (Univ. of California Press, 1997), 135; Craig Reinarman, "The Social Construction of Drug Scares," in Patricia A. Adler and Peter Adler, eds., *Constructions of Deviance,* 2d ed., (Belmont, CA: Wadsworth, 1997), 97–108.

21. Webb, "Patent Office Lets CAT out of the Bag"; Flesher, "Drug CAT Is Clawing Up Michigan"; "Drug CAT Creeps across State," *Capital Times* (Madison, WI), September 21, 1993; Judy Pasternak, "Despite Crackdown, Drug CAT Is Spreading across Midwest," *LAT,* October 23, 1994; idem, "New Designer Drug CAT Creeps out of Midwest Home Labs," *LAT,* Octo-

ber 30, 1994; Schaefer, "CAT Attack" and idem, "Chemical Predator"; Glastris, "The New Drug in Town"; Chuck Shepherd, "News of the Weird," *Star Tribune* (Minneapolis), September 9, 1993.

22. Karen Cohen, "Feingold Says Wisconsin Needs Money to Fight CAT," *Wisconsin State Journal,* November 10, 1993; John Patrick Hunter, "Anti-CAT Legislation Awaits Clinton," *Capital Times* (Madison, WI), November 26, 1993; Brian Baron, "Levin Reflects on End of Year," States News Service, November 30, 1993; "Clinton Signs Bill Outlawing Home-Made Drug Called CAT," *NYT,* December 19, 1993.

23. *New Challenges Facing the DEA,* 2; Michael Kranish, "Elders Stirs a Furor with Legal-Drugs Suggestion," *BG,* December 8, 1993.

24. *New Challenges Facing the DEA,* 54–55.

25. *New Challenges Facing the DEA,* 1–2, 6–7, 11, 34–36.

26. William J. Bailey, "Methcathinone, aka CAT"; Cynthia L. Webb, "CAT Drug Suspected in Three Deaths," *Memphis Commercial-Appeal,* August 8, 1993; Pasternak, "Despite Crackdown, Drug CAT Is Spreading Across Midwest," and idem, "New Designer Drug CAT Creeps out of Midwest Home Labs."

27. Schaefer, "Chemical Predator" and idem, "Chemistry Student Unleashes Dangerous Drug."

28. Joe Mahr, "It's Crystal Clear," *State Journal Register* (Springfield, IL), April 28, 1996; Gary Borg, "A Victory in War on Drugs," *CT,* May 23, 1996.

Notes to Chapter 7

1. Anthony R. Lovett, "Wired in California," *RS,* May 5, 1994, 39–40. Hilary Klee, ed., *Amphetamine Misuse* (Amsterdam: Harwood, 1997).

2. "Drug Agents See Shift in Trafficking in Speed," *NYT,* September 4, 1994; Tom Gorman, "Two Men Arrested, 1,900 Pounds of Drugs Seized in Raid," *LAT,* September 30, 1994; Isaac Guzman, "Six Arrested in Raid on Large Drug Laboratory," *LAT,* October 27, 1994; Robert J. Lopez, "Seven Held in Raid on Methamphetamine Lab in Pomona," *LAT,* December 5, 1994; Mark Arax, "California's Illicit Farm Belt Export," *LAT,* March 13, 1995.

3. "High Level of Methamphetamine in Willits Mass Killer's Blood," *SFC,* September 9, 1993; "A Mother's Drug Use, an Infant's Death, and Then a Conviction," *NYT,* September 11, 1994; "Three Children Die in Blaze Linked to a Drug Lab," *NYT,* December 28, 1995; George Doane, "Methamphetamine: A Growing Domestic Threat," *Police Chief,* March

1996, 24–28; "Wife Likely to Join Husband on Death Row," *The Press-Enterprise* (Riverside, CA), May 21, 1998.

4. The quote is from defense lawyer Michael Tigar in "Kingman Mad at Lawyer," AP story printed in *Denver Post,* May 2, 1997; Mark Hamm, *Apocalypse in Oklahoma* (Northeastern Univ. Press, 1998), 167–69. Remarks about press coverage are based on a search of the NEXIS "ALLNEWS" database for references to the terms "methamphetamine" and "Arizona" located within eight words of each other.

5. Erin Hallissy, "Contra Costa Kids Stealing for Speed," *SFC,* May 19, 1995.

6. For "a startling rise" see Christopher S. Wren, "DEA Maps Plans to Fight Methamphetamine," *NYT,* February 14, 1996. For the explosion of news coverage from late 1995 onwards, see for example Henry K. Lee, "The Kiss of Meth," *SFC,* August 27, 1995; Sam Walker, "Drugs Speed West to East," *CSM,* October 27, 1995; Gordon Witkin, "A New Drug Gallops through the West," *USNWR,* November 13, 1995, 50–51; Thomas H. Maugh II, "Amphetamine Use Soars in California, Study Finds," *LAT,* November 29, 1995; Joe Holleman, "New Drug Is Cheap, Dangerous," *St. Louis Post-Dispatch,* December 23, 1995; Sam Dillon, "Mexican Drug Dealer Pushes Speed, Helping Set Off an Epidemic in U.S.," *NYT,* December 27, 1995; Susan Ferriss, "Fast Track to Nowhere," *SFC,* March 31, 1996; Anastasia Toufexis, "There Is No Safe Speed," *Time,* January 8, 1996, 37; Pierre Thomas, "Mexico Speed Trade Alarms DEA," *WP,* February 14, 1996; "In San Diego, An Old Drug Comes Back," *NYT,* February 22, 1996; "Meth Drug Returns to California, Death and Violence in Its Wake," *NYT,* February 22, 1996; "Methamphetamine's Cruel Comeback," *St. Louis Post-Dispatch,* March 9, 1996; Janice Frink Brown, "Crank Is New Drug of Choice," *Afro-American,* March 30, 1996; Lee Romney, "25 Arrested in Crackdown on Meth Makers," *LAT,* April 16, 1996; Mark Kleiman, "Meth Is Back and We're Not Ready," *LAT,* May 1, 1996; Henry K. Lee, "Police Arrest Sixteen in Twelve-City Drug Sting," *SFC,* May 30, 1996; Bill Wallace, "Speed Abusers Need More and More," *SFC,* May 31, 1996; Barbara Marsh, "Meth at Work," *LAT,* July 7, 1996; Tim Friend, "An Escalating Drug War," *USA Today,* July 17, 1996; V. Dion Haynes and John O'Brien, "Bad Blast from Past Back Again," *CT,* October 8, 1996; Daniel Sneider, "Sinister Drug Infiltrates Rural U.S." and "A Meth Addict Tells Her Story Of Dependence," both in *CSM,* February 3, 1997; Matt Bai, "White Storm Warning," *Newsweek,* March 31, 1997, 66–67; Marcia Kurop, "Bootlegged Chemicals for Poor Man's Cocaine," *CSM,* April 17, 1997; Roberto Suro, "Other Drugs Supplanting Cocaine Use," *WP,* June 25, 1997.

7. "Meth's Deadly High," Television program broadcast on A&E Network's *Investigative Reports,* August 16, 1997; Karen A. Joe, "Ice Is Strong Enough for a Man But Made for a Woman," *Crime, Law and Social Change* 22 (1994–95): 269–89, and idem, "The Lives and Times of Asian-Pacific American Women Drug Users," *Journal of Drug Issues,* 26 (1996): 199–218. For the notion of latency periods, see *The Re-Emergence of Methamphetamine: Hearings before the Subcommittee on Narcotics Abuse and Control,* House, 101st Cong., 1st sess., October 24, 1989 (Washington, D.C.: GPO, 1990), 111.

8. Daniel Sneider, "A Meth Addict Tells Her Story of Dependence," *CSM,* February 3, 1997; Carey Goldberg, "Way Out West and under the Influence," *NYT,* March 16, 1997. The quote about an epidemic of burned-out brains is from "Meth's Deadly High," as is "These home labs bring the war on drugs. . . . " For similar portrayals, compare "High in the Heartland," Segment on CNN's *Impact,* October 5, 1997. Elizabeth Karlsberg, "The Nightmare of Crystal Meth," *Teen,* February 1996, 44–47; Alicia Diaz, "Doing Drugs Trashed My Life," *YM Magazine,* October 1996, 60–63; Alexis Jetter, "She Had Four Weeks to Save Herself," *Redbook,* April 1998, 106–109+.

9. Both quotes are from "Meth's Deadly High"; compare "High in the Heartland."

10. Bill Wallace, "Case of Missing Girl Illustrates Small Towns' Drug Troubles," *SFC,* March 25, 1996; Randy Fitzgerald, "A Demon Stalks the Land," *Reader's Digest,* February 1994, 87–92. For the user as "paranoid, delusional and extremely violent," see "Meth's Deadly High." The Florida officer is quoted in Paulo Lima, "Meth Tide Rising in Region," *Tampa Tribune,* April 26, 1998; the Arizona officer in "Meth Country," Segment on CBS's *48 Hours,* May 23, 1996. Compare "Speed Trap," Segment on *48 Hours,* September 24, 1998.

11. "Methamphetamines," Broadcast on NPR's *All Things Considered,* September 18, 1996; Sharon Cohen, "Drug Craze Takes Foothold in Midwest," AP story published in *CDT,* March 9, 1997, and idem, "Methamphetamine Invading the Heartland," *CT,* March 21, 1997. Compare Angie Cannon, "Drug Probe Focuses on Midwest," AP story published in *CDT,* September 27, 1996; Sneider, "Sinister Drug Infiltrates Rural U.S."; Bai, "White Storm Warning"; and Carol Napolitano, "Recent Deaths Personalize Danger of Drug Crank," *Omaha World-Herald,* June 6, 1997.

12. Dirk Johnson, "Influx of New Drug Brings Crime and Violence to Midwest," *NYT,* February 22, 1996. The "perverse vision" is quoted from Christopher S. Wren, "The Illegal Home Business: Speed Manufacture,"

NYT, July 8, 1997. The Marshalltown case study is from Dan McGraw, "The Iowan Connection," *USNWR,* March 2, 1998, 33–36. Walter Kirn, "Crank," *Time,* June 22, 1998.

13. The reference to "a supernatural force" is from Cohen, "Drug Craze Takes Foothold in Midwest"; "David Lynch-ian violence" is from Peter Wilkinson, "America's Drug: Postcards from Tweakville," *RS,* February 19, 1998, 49–53+. The picture of the drug situation in Missouri is from Jason Piscia, "Meth Trend Heads East to Illinois," *State Journal Register* (Springfield, IL), March 30, 1998; Phil Stewart and Gita Sitaramiah, "America's Heartland Grapples with Rise of Dangerous Drug," *CSM,* November 13, 1997.

14. See for example "High in the Heartland"; and "Meth's Deadly High."

15. "Meth Country." Compare William Hermann and Paul Brinkley Rogers, "Meth Busts Risky Routine for Officers," *AR,* April 29, 1995.

16. Laura Gomez, *Misconceiving Mothers* (Philadelphia: Temple Univ. Press, 1997), 69; Ardi Carthane, "Will New Drug 'Ice' Freeze Hope in Black Communities?" *Jet,* December 18, 1989. The 1997 television program "Meth's Deadly High" was one of the very few treatments to focus on black users.

17. Both quotes are from Wilkinson, "America's Drug: Postcards from Tweakville."

18. Annalee Newitz, "White Savagery and Humiliation," in Matt Wray and Annalee Newitz, eds., *White Trash* (New York: Routledge, 1997), 133, 152.

19. Wilkinson, "America's Drug: Postcards from Tweakville"; Dale Brown, *The Tin Man* (New York: Bantam, 1998).

20. Robert Stone, *Bear and His Daughter* (New York: Houghton Mifflin, 1997), 204, 210, 217; Kathryn Harrison, *Exposure* (New York: Warner, 1994); Stewart O'Nan, *The Speed Queen* (New York: Doubleday, 1997), 82. These fictional accounts are echoed in the words of authentic meth users, including those interviewed in William Finnegan's *Cold New World: Growing Up in a Harder Country* (New York: Random House, 1998).

21. *Statement by Thomas A. Constantine before the Senate Foreign Relations Committee Regarding International Drug Trafficking Organizations in Mexico, August 8, 1995,* WWW site of the DEA, 1995. For earlier Mexican connections, compare *Psychotropic Substances Act of 1973: Hearing before the Subcommittee to Investigate Juvenile Delinquency, Judiciary Committee,* Senate, 93rd Cong., 2d sess., February 25, 1974 (Washington, D.C.: GPO, 1974), 140–90.

22. Wren, "DEA Maps Plans to Fight Methamphetamine"; *Rising Scourge*

of Methamphetamine in America: Hearing before the Subcommittee on Crime of the Committee on the Judiciary, House, 104th Cong., 1st sess., October 26, 1995 (Washington, D.C.: GPO, 1996); *Methamphetamine/Speed Abuse,* WWW site of the DEA, 1996; *Press Briefing by General Barry McCaffrey, Director of the Office of National Drug Control Policy, July 15, 1996,* WWW site of the White House, 1996.

23. *Statement by Thomas A. Constantine before the Senate Committee on Banking, Housing and Urban Affairs Regarding Drug Trafficking in Mexico, March 28, 1996,* WWW site of the DEA, 1996; *Methamphetamine Situation in the United States, March 1996,* WWW site of the DEA, 1996; R. Lamere, "Regarding Iowa," Statement to U.S. Senate Drug Caucus, April 14, 1998, WWW site of the DEA, 1998.

24. *White House Press Release: Memorandum for the Heads of Executive Departments and Agencies, April 8, 1996,* WWW site of the White House, 1996; William J. Clinton, *Statement on National Drug Control Strategy, Coral Gables, Florida, April 29, 1996,* WWW site of the White House, 1996; *Press Briefing by General Barry McCaffrey at the Biltmore Hotel, Coral Gables, Florida, April 29, 1996,* WWW site of the White House, 1996; "Clinton Launches Attack against Methamphetamine," *WSJ,* April 30, 1996.

25. *Statement by Thomas A. Constantine before the House Appropriations Committee, Subcommittee on Commerce, Justice, State, the Judiciary, and Related Agencies Regarding FY 1997 Appropriations, May 1, 1996,* WWW site of the DEA, 1996; *Statement by Harold D. Wankel, Chief of Operations, DEA, before the House Judiciary Committee, Subcommittee on Crime Regarding the Comprehensive Methamphetamine Control Act of 1996, HR 3852, on September 5, 1996,* WWW site of the DEA, 1996; Marc Sandalow, "Clinton Signs Bills to Fight Crime and Crank," *SFC,* October 4, 1996; *Comprehensive Methamphetamine Control Act of 1996: Hearing before the Subcommittee on Crime of the Committee on the Judiciary,* House, 104th Cong., 2d sess., September 5, 1996 (Washington, D.C.: GPO, 1997); *Statement by Thomas A. Constantine before the House Appropriations Committee, Subcommittee on Commerce, Justice, State and Related Agencies Regarding FY 1998 Appropriations, March 19, 1997,* WWW site of the DEA, 1997; Rick Ruggles, "Nation's Drug Experts Target Meth at Omaha Conference," *Omaha World-Herald,* May 30, 1997.

26. McGraw, "The Iowan Connection." *The National Methamphetamine Drug Conference, Proceedings: May 28–30, 1997, Omaha, Nebraska* (Washington, D.C.: Office of National Drug Control Policy, 1997); *Methamphetamine, A New Deadly Neighbor: Hearing Before the Subcommittee on Technology, Terrorism, and Government Information of the Committee on the Judiciary,* U.S.

Senate, 105th Cong., second sess., April 6, 1998. (Washington, D.C.: GPO, 1998).

27. *New Challenges Facing the DEA: Heroin, Methamphetamine, and Cat: Hearing before the Information, Justice, Transportation, and Agriculture Subcommittee of the Committee on Government Operations,* House, 103rd Cong., second sess., August 2, 1994. (Washington, D.C.: GPO, 1994), 40. Thomas E. Feucht and Gabrielle M. Kyle, *Methamphetamine Use among Adult Arrestees: Findings from the Drug Use Forecasting (DUF) Program.* (Washington, D.C.: Department of Justice, Office of Justice Programs, NIJ, 1996). For 1998 figures, see *1997 Arrestee Drug Abuse Monitoring (ADAM) Report,* NIJ (Washington, D.C.: GPO, 1998); Peter Baker, "Cocaine Use Continues to Decline; Methamphetamines Becoming More Prevalent," *WP,* July 12, 1998; Burt Hubbard, "Speed in the Suburbs," *Rocky Mountain News,* July 12, 1998.

28. *Statement by Thomas A. Constantine before the House Appropriations Committee, Subcommittee on Commerce, Justice, State and Related Agencies Regarding FY 1998 Appropriations, March 19, 1997.* For further discussion, see above, chapter 2.

29. *Preliminary Estimates from the Drug Abuse Warning Network, Substance Abuse and Mental Health Services Administration, Office of Applied Studies, Advance Report Number 11, November 1995,* DHHS/PHS (Washington, D.C.: GPO, 1995); compare V. A. Catanzarite, "Crystal and Pregnancy," *Western Journal of Medicine* 162 (May 1995): 454–; Erich Goode, *Drugs in American Society,* fourth ed. (New York: McGraw-Hill, 1993), 111–17. See the discussion in Craig Reinarman and Harry G. Levine, eds., *Crack in America* (Berkeley: Univ. of California Press, 1997), 25–26.

30. Compare Dianne Danis, "Increasing Incidence of Methamphetamine Abuse Sequelae," *Journal of Emergency Nursing* 22, no. 3 (1996): 244–; Thomas H. Maugh II, "Statistics Point to Surge in Use of Amphetamines," *LAT,* July 2, 1996; Sabin Russell, "Speed Hospitalizations Soar," *SFC,* July 2, 1996.

31. *Statement by Harold D. Wankel, Chief of Operations, DEA, before the House Judiciary Committee, Subcommittee on Crime Regarding the Comprehensive Methamphetamine Control Act of 1996, HR 3852, on September 5, 1996; Remarks by the President at U.S. Conference of Mayors, May 21, 1997,* WWW site of the White House, 1997.

32. *Methamphetamine/Speed Abuse,* January 1996, from the WWW site of the DEA. Compare "Increasing Morbidity and Mortality Associated with Abuse of Methamphetamine," *Morbidity and Mortality Weekly Report,* December 1, 1995: 882–86.

33. Johnson, "Influx of New Drug Brings Crime and Violence to Midwest"; Eric Brazil, "Deaths Rising from Meth Abuse," *San Francisco Examiner,* December 3, 1996.

34. John A. Newmeyer, "The Epidemiology of the Use of Amphetamine and Related Substances," *JPD* 10 (1978): 298; Edward M. Brecher, *Licit and Illicit Drugs* (Boston: Little Brown, 1972), 288–89; compare Harold Kalant and Orianna Josseau Kalant, "Death in Amphetamine Users," in Smith et al., eds., *Amphetamine Use, Misuse, and Abuse,* 169–88.

35. Reinarman and Levine, eds., *Crack in America,* 26.

36. Jason Lazarou, Bruce H. Pomeranz and Paul N. Corey, "Incidence of Adverse Drug Reactions in Hospitalized Patients," *JAMA* 279 (April 15, 1998): 1200–1205; Stephen Fried, *Bitter Pills* (New York: Bantam Doubleday Dell, 1998); Thomas J. Moore, *Prescription for Disaster* (New York: Simon and Schuster, 1998).

37. Compare Henry Brownstein, *The Rise and Fall of a Violent Crime Wave* (Guilderland, NY: Harrow and Heston, 1996).

38. *Uniform Crime Reports.*

39. *Press Briefing by General Barry McCaffrey at the Biltmore Hotel, Coral Gables, Florida, April 29, 1996;* Mark Kleiman and Sally Satel, "Methamphetamine Returns," *Drug Policy Analysis Bulletin* 1 (1997): 1–2.

40. *DEA Highlights—1995,* WWW site of the DEA, 1995.

41. *New Challenges Facing the DEA;* Lizette Alvarez, "The Middle Class Rediscovers Heroin," *NYT,* August 14, 1995.

42. Peter Applebome, *Dixie Rising* (New York: Harvest Books, 1997).

43. Kathy Marquardt and Judith A. Alsop, *Health, Heat, and Water Hazards Associated with Illegal Drug Manufacturing* (Sacramento, CA: State of California, Health and Welfare Agency, Emergency Medical Services Authority, 1991); Vicki M. Skeers, "Illegal Methamphetamine Drug Laboratories," *Journal of Environmental Health* 55, no. 3 (1992): 6–; Lee Romney, "Methamphetamine Labs Leave Growing Toxic Legacy," *LAT,* November 27, 1995; Ray Johnson, "Meth Labs—An Explosive Problem," *SFC,* January 6, 1997; Gary Fields, "Drug Labs Leave Dangerous Residue," *USA Today,* May 2, 1997; "Meth's Deadly High"; Mike McCloy, "Cost of Fighting Meth Labs Astounding," *AR,* April 7, 1998.

44. Erich Goode, *Between Politics and Reason* (New York: St. Martin's Press, 1997); "Methamphetamine's Cruel Comeback," 1996.

45. "Strange Bedfellows Surface in Midwest Methamphetamine Debate," *Alcoholism and Drug Abuse Weekly,* July 22, 1996, 3; Bai, "White Storm Warning."

Notes to Chapter 8

1. Jerome Beck and Marsha Rosenbaum, *In Pursuit of Ecstasy* (Albany, NY: State Univ. of New York Press, 1994); Richard S. Cohen, *The Love Drug* (Binghamton, NY: Haworth/Harrington Press, 1998).

2. The quote is from Matthew Collin, *Altered States* (London: Serpent's Tail, 1997), 4. See also Teri Randall, "Ecstacy-Fueled Rave Parties Become Dance of Death for English Youths" and "Rave Scene, Ecstacy Use, Leap Atlantic," both in *JAMA*, September 23, 1992, 1505–1506. (Though the standard English spelling is "ecstasy," the drug is occasionally described as "ecstacy" in the popular—and even, as here, the professional—literature). Nicholas Saunders, *E for Ecstasy* (London: N. Saunders, 1993); idem, *Ecstasy and the Dance Culture* (London: N. Saunders, 1995); and idem, *Ecstasy Reconsidered* (London: N. Saunders, 1997); Steve Redhead, *Rave Off* (Brookfield, VT: Avebury, 1993); Steve Redhead, *Subculture to Clubcultures* (Oxford: Blackwell's, 1997); Steve Redhead, Derek Wynne and Justin O'Connor, eds., *The Clubcultures Reader* (Oxford: Blackwell, 1997); Sheila Henderson, *Ecstasy: Case Unsolved* (Hammersmith, London: Pandora, 1997); Anthony Wayne, *Class of 1988* (London: Virgin, 1998).

3. Douglas Rushkoff, *The Ecstasy Club* (London: Scepter 1997); A. D. Atkins, *Ecstasy Sorted and On One* (London: A. D. Atkins, 1995); Irvine Welsh, "The Undefeated," in Irvine Welsh, *Ecstasy: Three Tales of Chemical Romance* (New York: W. W. Norton, 1996), 229, 230, 252. Compare Irvine Welsh, *The Acid House* (New York: W. W. Norton, 1995).

4. Randall, "Ecstacy-Fueled Rave Parties Become Dance of Death for English Youths"; David Concar, "After the Rave, the Ecstasy Hangover," *New Scientist*, June 21, 1997. For claims on the supposed slippery slope from Ecstasy to methamphetamine, see for example Paulo Lima, "Meth Tide Rising in Region" *Tampa Tribune*, April 26, 1998. For criminal subcultures in the British Isles, see Julian Madigan, *The Agony of Ecstasy* (Dublin, Ireland: Poolbeg, 1996) and Bernard O'Mahoney, *So This Is Ecstasy?* (Edinburgh, Scotland: Mainstream, 1997).

5. Quoted in Randall, "Ecstacy-Fueled Rave Parties Become Dance of Death for English Youths"; Pat Phillips, "Ecstasy Makes Clouded Comeback," *Medical World News*, March 13, 1989, 68–71; James W. Gibb, et al., "MDMA: Historical Perspectives," *Annals of the New York Academy of Science* 600 (1990): 601–12. EVE, or MDEA, is more properly N-ethyl-methylene-dioxy-amphetamine.

6. The "Cat in the Hat-hats" reference is quoted in Randall, "Rave Scene,

Ecstacy Use, Leap Atlantic," 1506; Michael J. Cuomo, "Increasing Use of Ecstasy (MDMA) and Other Hallucinogens on a College Campus," *Journal of American College Health* 42, no. 6 (1994): 271; Dan Levy, "Safe-Sex Drive Aimed at Users of Drug Ecstasy," *SFC,* April 9, 1993.

7. Michael Hernandez, Charles H. McDaniel, Christopher D. Costanza and Oscar J. Hernandez, "GHB-Induced Delirium," *American Journal of Drug and Alcohol Abuse* 24 (1998): 179–83; Samantha Miller, Ward Dean, John Morgenthaler and Steven W. Fowkes, *GHB: The Natural Mood Enhancer* (Smart Publications, 1998).

8. Alan Breier, Anil K. Malhotra, Debra A. Pinals, Neil I. Weisenfeld and David Pickar, "Association of Ketamine-Induced Psychosis with Focal Activation of the Prefrontal Cortex in Healthy Volunteers," *AJP* 154 (1997): 805–11; Gustav Hansen, Svend Boel Jensen, Lars Chandresh and Tonnes Hilden, "The Psychotropic Effect of Ketamine," *JPAD* 20 (1988): 419–25.

9. John C. Lilly, *The Scientist,* revised ed. (Berkeley, CA: Ronin, 1996). The quote about "the young, hip, up-for-anything set" is from Michelangelo Signorile, "A Troubling Double Standard," *NYT,* August 16, 1997. Richard Alleman, "From A-Gays to Young Hustlers," *Newsweek,* July 28, 1997. For the Limelight and the Tunnel, see Frank Owen, "The King of Ecstasy," *Village Voice,* April 1, 1997, 36–39; idem, "Nightclubs, Downtown and Dirty," *WP,* February 14, 1998.

10. Christopher S. Wren, "A Seductive Drug Culture Flourishes on the Internet," *NYT,* June 20, 1997.

11. Carrie Hedges, "Cheap, 'Safe' High Is Costing Lives," *USA Today,* February 16, 1998; *Ketamine Abuse Increasing,* WWW site of the DEA, 1997; James W. Dotson, "Ketamine Abuse," *Journal of Drug Issues* 25 (1995): 751–57.

12. Compare Breier et al., "Association of Ketamine-Induced Psychosis . . . "

13. Andrew A. Skolnick, "Beware the Tangled Web They Weave," *JAMA* 278 (December 3, 1997): 1724–.

14. For Ayahuasca and the world of "psychedelic shamanism," see for example Jonathan Ott, *Ayahuasca Analogs* (Kennewick, WA: Jonathan Ott Books, 1994) and Ralph Metzner, *Ayahuasca* (Thunder's Mouth Press, 1999).

15. Michael Valentine Smith [pseudo.], *Psychedelic Chemistry* (Port Townsend, WA: Loompanics Unlimited, 1984).

16. "LSD Return Trip," Segment on CBS's *48 Hours,* January 6, 1993; Robin Cross and Seth Jacobson, "Return of the Psychonauts," *Hot Air* (Virgin Atlantic inflight magazine), August 1997, 33–35.

17. Shawn Hubler, "Designer Drug Enters Hollywood's Fast Lane," *LAT,* November 3, 1993.

18. M. A. J. McKenna, "CDC Issues Warning on Date Rape Drug," *Atlanta Constitution,* April 4, 1997; "Date-Rape Drug Linked to a Death, 69 Poisonings," *WSJ,* April 4, 1997; Mike McPhee, "Doctors Warn of New Rave Drug," *Denver Post,* January 17, 1998; Karla Haworth, "The Growing Popularity of a New Drug Alarms Health Educators," *Chronicle of Higher Education,* July 10, 1998, A31–32.

19. Cindy Horswell, "The 'Mickey Finn of the Nineties' Labelled a Killer," *Houston Chronicle,* September 15, 1996; Christine Gorman, "Liquid X," *Time,* September 30, 1996, 64.

20. Ruth Rendon, "New Tests Have Family Asking If Date Rape Drug Really Killed Teen," *Houston Chronicle,* February 7, 1997; Bill Torpy, "Was 'Rape Drug' Cause of Coma?" *Atlanta Journal Constitution,* November 9, 1996; Doug Payne, "Father of Dead Teen Wants Sheriff Apology," *Atlanta Journal Constitution,* February 5, 1998. In other cases, users might have suffered harm or death through mistaking clear GHB for water and accidentally drinking a huge overdose: see for instance "Party-Drug Victim's Mom Crusades via Web Site," *Orange County Register,* June 29, 1998.

21. The quote is from "Daughters, Drugs and Death," Segment on CNN's *Impact,* June 22, 1997. "Trendy Drug Goes Club Hopping," CNN News, August 11, 1996.

22. ABC's *20/20,* February 20, 1998; John Cloud, "Is Your Kid on K?" *Time,* October 20, 1997, 90–91.

23. "Daughters, Drugs and Death." "Party-Drug Victim's Mom Crusades Via Web site," Associated Press story, *Orange County Register,* June 29, 1998; Greg McDonald, "Man Pleads To Have Date-Rape Drugs Outlawed," *Houston Chronicle,* July 31, 1998; Chris Krewson, "Recent Overdoses Key GHB's arrival," *CDT,* August 2, 1998; Chris Gosier, "Attorney-General Wants State to Outlaw Home-Brewed Drug GHB," *CDT,* August 22, 1998.

24. ABC News, December 22, 1997.

25. David J. Langum, *Crossing over the Line* (Chicago: Univ. of Chicago Press, 1994).

26. Dan Weikel, "Rape Drug Battle Rages," *LAT,* August 19, 1996.

27. Broadcast on NPR's *All Things Considered,* June 20, 1995; "You don't hear anything bad about it . . . " is quoted by Mireya Navarro, "A New Abused Drug in Florida Is Prescribed Abroad," *NYT,* December 9, 1995; "flunitrazepam is used widely in Texas . . . " is from *Flunitrazepam (Rohypnol/Roofies),* WWW site of the DEA, 1996; "The 'lunch money' high" is from Jean Seligmann and Patricia King, "Roofies: The Date-Rape Drug," *Newsweek,* February 26, 1996, 54.

28. The quote is from Seligmann and King, "Roofies: The Date-Rape Drug". Navarro, "A New Abused Drug in Florida Is Prescribed Abroad."

29. Sarah R. Calhoun, "Abuse of Flunitrazepam (Rohypnol) and Other Benzodiazepines in Austin and South Texas," *JPAD* 28, no. 2 (1996): 183–; Linda E. Ledray, "Date Rape Drug Alert," *Journal of Emergency Nursing,* February 22, 1996, 80; Wendi Hale, "Drug Alert: Date Rape Danger," *Sassy,* June 1996, 36–37; Beth Shuster, "Crackdown Sought on Date Rape Drug," *LAT,* June 8, 1996; "Rohypnol Moves through South Florida and Texas," *Alcoholism and Drug Abuse Weekly,* June 10, 1996, 7; Marshall Wilson, "Drug Zaps Memory of Rape Victims," *SFC,* June 11, 1996; Arthur Santana, "Banned Date Rape Drug Is Linked to Six Assaults in Area," *WP,* June 14, 1996; Kit Lively, "The Date-Rape Drug," *Chronicle of Higher Education,* June 28, 1996, A29; Julie Hirschfeld, "Rape Is Only Thing That This Drug Is For," *St. Louis Post-Dispatch,* July 17, 1996; Eunice Moscoso, "Panel Looks at Date-Rape Drug," *Atlanta Constitution,* July 17, 1996; Lewis Rice, "DEA Moving Against Rape Drug," *DN,* July 23, 1996; Marilyn Robinson, "Police Set Date-Rape Drug Tests," *Denver Post,* August 31, 1996; "Fighting the Date Rape Drug," *LAT,* October 8, 1996; Matea Gold, "New Rules Unveiled for Date Rape Drug Probes," *LAT,* December 12, 1996; Sara Glassman, "No Means No," *Seventeen,* February 1998, 60.

30. J. B. Dixson, "Slow DEA Action Gives Women No Relief from the Threat of New Date-Rape Drug," *DN,* June 29, 1996.

31. The episode of *Beverly Hills 90210* appeared on February 11, 1998; "Sex, Lies and Videotape" Segment on ABC's *Primetime Live,* December 3, 1997.

32. "Rape Drugs," Program on CBS's *Oprah Winfrey Show,* January 6, 1998. For a similar serial-rape case at about this time, see Julia Scheeres, "Trial Offers Look at Date Rape Drug," *LAT,* May 31, 1998.

33. The "Dear Abby" column appeared February 27–March 5, 1998.

34. Faye Flam and Marie McCullough, "Date-Rape Drug from Internet Puts Two Boys into Comas," *Philadelphia Inquirer,* March 27, 1998; compare the AP story, "Police Link Chemical to Date-Rape Drug," in *CDT,* April 18, 1998. For more on the movement against sexual predators in these years, see Philip Jenkins, *Moral Panic* (New Haven, CT: Yale Univ. Press, 1998).

Notes to Chapter 9

1. Compare Joel Best, *Threatened Children* (Chicago: Univ. Chicago Press, 1990).

2. The quote is from Lord Salisbury.

3. Jeff Leen, "A Shot in the Dark on Drug Use," *WP,* January 12, 1998, 32–33, weekly edition.

4. Paul De Kruif, "Demerol," in *JAMA,* September 7, 1946, 43. Among other achievements, De Kruif was the technical adviser for Sinclair Lewis' novel *Arrowsmith.*

5. Craig Reinarman and Harry G. Levine, eds., *Crack in America* (Berkeley: Univ. of California Press, 1997), 24.

6. Eric L. Jensen and Jurg Gerber, eds., *The New War on Drugs* (Cincinnati: Anderson, 1998); Michael Massing, *The Fix* (New York: Simon and Schuster 1998); Mike Gray, *Drug Crazy* (New York: Random House, 1998); Dan Baum, *Smoke and Mirrors* (Boston: Little Brown, 1996); Richard Lawrence Miller, *Drug Warriors and Their Prey* (Westport, CT: Praeger, 1996); Alfred W. McCoy and Alan A. Block, eds., *War on Drugs* (Boulder, CO: Westview, 1992); Sam Staley, *Drug Policy and the Decline of American Cities* (New Brunswick, NJ: Transaction, 1992). For the massive disproportion between the harmfulness of a substance and the official reaction, see also Lynn Zimmer and John P. Morgan, *Marijuana Myths, Marijuana Facts* (New York: Lindesmith Center, 1997).

7. Jeffrey Reiman, *The Rich Get Richer and the Poor Get Prison,* 5th ed. (Boston: Allyn and Bacon, 1997).

8. Arnold S. Trebach, *The Great Drug War* (New York: Macmillan, 1987); Erich Goode, *Between Politics and Reason* (New York: St. Martin's Press, 1997).

9. Sheryl Gay Stolberg, "President Decides against Financing Needle Programs," *NYT,* April 21, 1998.

10. Neil A. Lewis, "Reno Lifts Barrier to Oregon's Law on Aided Suicide," *NYT,* June 6, 1998.

11. These products include "Sudafed, Cenafed, Chlor-Trimeton Non-Drowsy Decongestant, Drixoral Non-Drowsy Formula, Efidac/24 and PediaCare Infants' Oral Decongestant Drops": Richard Winton and Nicholas Riccardi, "Meth War Hits Close to Home—at Local Pharmacy," *LAT,* January 31, 1998.

12. Aldous Huxley, *The Doors of Perception* (London: Penguin, 1959), 53; Siegel is quoted in M. M. Kirsch, *Designer Drugs* (Minneapolis: CompCare Publications, 1986), 96.

INDEX

Acetaminophen, 149

Acquired Immune Deficiency Syndrome (AIDS), 93, 103, 151, 186, 193

ADAM. *See* Ecstasy (MDMA, methylene-dioxy-methamphetamine)

Addiction, definition of, 4, 126–27, 136, 174, 188–89, 192

African-Americans, 13–14, 60–61, 68, 74, 140. *See also* Racial component in drug scares

AIDS. *See* Acquired Immune Deficiency Syndrome (AIDS)

Akaka, Daniel, 107–12

Alpha-methyl-fentanyl (AMF). *See* Fentanyl, alpha-methyl-fentanyl (AMF)

Amphetamines and related drugs: chemical description of, 204; history of, 30–32; 1960s panic concerning, 37–38; popularity of, 32–34; regulation of, 47–48. *See also* Benzedrine (amphetamine sulfate); Biphetamine; Dexedrine (Dextroamphetamine sulfate); Ecstasy (MDMA, methylene-dioxy-methamphetamine); EVE (MDEA, N-ethyl-methylene-dioxy-amphetamine); MDA (methylene-dioxy-amphetamine); Methamphetamine (d-Desoxy-ephedrine); Methamphetamine, smokable (ice); Methedrine

Anderson, Jack, 126

Angel dust. *See* PCP (phencyclidine)

Anslinger, Harry, 36, 168

Arizona: drug-related violence, 129–130, 137–138; electoral importance of, 156–57; illicit laboratories in, 134; methamphetamine use in, 14, 49, 135, 144. *See also* Kingman, Ariz.; Phoenix, Ariz.

Arkansas, 130

Asian-Americans, 109, 140

Asset forfeiture, 99–100

Atlanta, Ga., 19, 106, 164

Babies and drug addiction, 108–9, 137, 182, 188–89

Baby boomers: and amphetamine drugs, 32–34; as parents, 26, 160–61. *See also* Demographic factors

Baltimore, 64

Barbiturates: amphetamine-barbiturate mixture, 34–35, 44; dangers of, 66; illicit use, in 1960s, 34–37; legal restrictions on, 49, 59, 85; and suicide, 152; synthesis of, 6

Becker, Howard, 20

Belushi, John, 96

Bennett, William, 98, 108

Bent, Daniel, 107–9

Benzedrine (amphetamine sulfate), 30–31, 33–34, 49

Bias, Len, 96

Biden, Joseph, 166

Bikers. *See* Motorcycle gangs

Biphetamine, 34, 49

Blake, Robert, 72

BNE. *See* Bureau of Narcotics Enforcement (California)

Bowie, David, 85

Britain. *See* United Kingdom

Brown, Dale, 142

Bureau of Drug Abuse Control (BDAC), 38, 48

Bureau of Narcotics Enforcement (California), 84, 99, 102, 133, 185

Burroughs, William S., Jr, 38–39, 44

Bush, George, 98

California: drug legalization, 157; electoral importance, 156–57; methamphetamine in, 133–36, 147; methcathinone in, 121. *See also* Bureau of Narcotics Enforcement (California); Gates, Darryl F.; Humboldt County, Calif.; Los Angeles, Calif.; Pasadena, Calif.; San Diego, Calif.; San Francisco, Calif.; San Jose, Calif.; San Mateo, Calif.; Santa Monica, Calif.; Ukiah, Calif.
CAT. *See* Methcathinone (CAT)
Centers for Disease Control, 19, 171
Chemical Diversion and Trafficking Act (1988), 84–85, 123
Chicago, Ill., 58
Chiles, Lawton, 1, 81–84
China White. *See* Fentanyl
Chloral hydrate, 176
Cigarettes. *See* Nicotine
Cinema: *Airplane*, 56; *Altered States*, 10; *Cocaine Fiends*, 72; *Easy Rider*, 45; *Fargo*, 138; *Fort Apache, The Bronx*, 73; *French Connection*, 81; *Gorillas in the Mist*, 68; *Kalifornia*, 143; *Killing Zoe*, 94; *London Kills Me*, 162; *Pulp Fiction*, 94, 141; *Natural Born Killers*, 143; *Reefer Madness*, 72; *Rosewood*, 141; *Scream II*, 166; *Terminator*, 73–74; *Time to Kill*, 141; *Trading Places*, 73; *Trainspotting*, 94, 162; *Witness*, 49–50, 73. *See also* Television movies
Clinton, Bill, 94, 128, 132, 145, 149, 156–57, 193
Club culture. *See* Homosexuals, gay clubs; Raves
Cobain, Kurt, 177
Cocaine: boom in, 55–56, 187; changes in trafficking, 145–46; decline of use, 96–98; discovery of, 6. *See also* Crack cocaine
Cohen, Harvey, 31, 44
Colorado. *See* Denver, Colo.
Columbia, District of. *See* Washington, D.C.
Comprehensive Crime Control Act (1984), 80

Comprehensive Drug Abuse Prevention and Control Act (1970), 47
Comprehensive Methamphetamine Control Act (1996), 145
Computers. *See* Internet
Congressional investigations: amphetamines, 37, 46–47; designer drugs, 9, 81–84; GHB, 174; ice, 105–9; methamphetamine, 52–53, 143–45; methcathinone, 121–22, 128–30; PCP, 71–72; rape drugs, 178
Constantine, Thomas A., 130, 143–45, 193
Constructionism, social, 2–4, 27
Controlled Substances Act (1970), 47–50
Cook, Robin, 11
Coughlin, Lawrence, 52, 112
Crack babies. *See* Babies and drug addiction
Crack cocaine, 4, 61, 96–100, 129, 136, 143; media and, 16–17, 97; penalties for use, 13, 99. *See also* Cocaine
"Crack houses," 97, 100, 140
Crystal methamphetamine. *See* Methamphetamine (d-Desoxy-ephedrine); Methedrine
Currie, Elliott, 107
Cyberpunk, 162
Cyborg, 202

Dallas, Tex.: amphetamines in, 35–36; Ecstasy in, 16, 88, 90, 164; methamphetamine in, 36, 101–2, 147, 156
Date rape. *See* Rape-drugs
DAWN. *See* Drug Abuse Warning Network (DAWN)
Deaths, drug-related, 43, 64–71, 114, 150–54, 189–90
De Kruif, Paul, 188, 237
Demerol, 77
Demographic factors, 26, 160–61
Densen-Gerber, Judianne, 57
Denver, Colo., 102, 146–47
Designer Drug Act (1986), 84
"Designer drug" concept, 7, 76–79
Designer jeans, 7, 78

Detroit, Mich., 62
Dexedrine (Dextroamphetamine sulfate), 30, 33–34, 49
Dick, Philip K., 44
Dieting, and amphetamine drugs, 32, 103
Disco culture, 55–56, 72, 85
District of Columbia. *See* Washington, D.C.
Dizocilpine, 167
Dodd, Thomas J., 37, 48
DOM. *See* STP (2,5-dimethoxy-4-methy-lamphetamine)
Domestic Chemical Diversion Control Act (1993), 123
Doonesbury, 47, 89
Dornan, Robert, 67–69
Drug, meaning of term, ix–x
Drug Abuse Control Act (1965), 38
Drug Abuse Resistance Education (DARE), 97
Drug Abuse Warning Network (DAWN), 49, 60, 101, 147–50
Drug czar. *See* Bennett, William; McCaffrey, Barry
Drug Enforcement Administration (DEA): CAT and, 121, 129–30; funding of, 98–99, 114, 145; influence of, on media, 21, 144, 185; LSD and, 170; and methamphetamine, 133, 143–48, 150–57; origins of, 48; rape drugs, 179; and regulation of medicine, 192–94; and smokable methamphetamine, 114–15. *See also* Constantine, Thomas A.; Federal Bureau of Narcotics
Drug Use Forecasting system (DUF), 102, 146–47
Drug war, 96–100, 128, 191–92
DUF. *See* Drug Use Forecasting system (DUF)
Dukakis, Kitty, 32
Du Pont, Robert, 54

Ecstasy (MDMA, methylene-dioxy-methamphetamine), 3, 7, 24, 86–93, 160–70, 195–96

Elders, Joycelyn, 128
Emergency room visits. *See* Drug Abuse Warning Network (DAWN)
Environmental concerns, 128–29, 157
Ephedrine, 30, 84, 101, 107, 120–24, 128, 146, 194
Epidemic imagery, 71–72, 97, 114, 117, 125–26, 130, 133, 146, 170, 186
Eugene, Ore., 102
EVE (MDEA, N-ethyl-methylene-dioxy-amphetamine), 164

Fargo, N.Dak., 138, 147
Farias, Hillory Janean, 171–74, 182
FDA. *See* Food and Drug Administration (FDA)
Federal Bureau of Investigation (FBI), 36, 129
Federal Bureau of Narcotics (FBN), 20–21, 36, 188. *See also* Drug Enforcement Administration (DEA)
Feingold, Russell, 128
Fentanyl, 2, 77–80, 84, 90, 92–94, 170; alpha-methyl-fentanyl (AMF), 77; 3-methyl-fentanyl (3MF), 78, 80
Fiction. *See* Brown, Dale; Burroughs, William S., Jr.; Cook, Robin; Dick, Philip K.; Gibson, William; Harrison, Kathryn; Holleran, Andrew; Hucklenbroich, Frankie; Huxley, Aldous; O'Nan, Stewart; Rushkoff, Douglas; Stone, Robert; Strasser, Todd; Welsh, Irvine
Films. *See* Cinema; Television movies
Florida: barbiturates in, 35; electoral power of, 156; gay rights in, 57; marijuana in, 10; methamphetamine fears in, 107, 144–45; Quaaludes in, 85; rape drugs in, 177, 179. *See also* Chiles, Lawton; Miami, Fla.
Flunitrazepam. *See* Rohypnol (flunitrazepam)
Food and Drug Administration (FDA), 32, 36, 92, 165
Football. *See* Sport, drugs and
Frankenstein imagery, 1, 8, 43, 83

Gamma-hydroxy-butyrate. *See* GHB (Gamma-hydroxy-butyrate)

Gangs, 17, 57, 62, 108. *See also* Motorcycle gangs; Organized crime, and drug trafficking

Gates, Darryl F., 63, 69, 97–98

Gay subculture. *See* Homosexuals

Georgia, 16, 20, 144, 171–74. *See also* Atlanta, Ga.

GHB (Gamma-hydroxy-butyrate), ix, 16, 156, 160, 165–68, 170–76, 179, 181–82, 235

Gibb, Douglas, 106, 109

Gibson, William, 162

Ginsberg, Allen, 8, 43–44

Glue-sniffing, 4, 18

Griffiths, John, 35

Gusfield, Joseph, 13

Hall, Stuart, 4

Harkin, Tom, 158

Harrison Act (1914), 36

Harrison, Kathryn, 142

Hawaii: "ice" crisis, 16, 102–3, 105–9; politics in, 22–23, 109–12. *See also* Methamphetamine, smokable (ice)

Hayward, Calif., 62

Hell's Angels. *See* Motorcycle gangs

Henderson, Gary, 76, 81

Heroin, 6, 47, 77, 92–94, 149–50, 152, 155–56, 173. *See also* Fentanyl

Holleran, Andrew, 55

Homicides, drug-related, 17, 43, 65–69, 130, 137–38, 154–55, 189

Homosexuals: gay clubs, 55, 88, 103, 165–66, 190–91; gay rights movement, 57, 142; methamphetamine and, 103

Honolulu, Hawaii, 102, 105–6, 111, 114

Houston, Tex., 37, 171

Hucklenbroich, Frankie, 40, 44

Humboldt County, Calif., 140

Huxley, Aldous, 3, 9–10, 31, 183, 196

Ice. *See* Methamphetamine, smokable (ice)

Illinois, 37. *See also* Chicago, Ill.

Independence, Mo., 141–42

Indiana, 117, 120

Internet, 11, 86, 119–21, 165–69, 176

Iowa, 138–40, 144, 158. *See also* Marshalltown, Iowa

Jackson, Michael, 59

Japan, 35, 104–5, 111–13

Kansas, 158. *See also* Wichita, Kans.

Kentucky, 125

Ketamine hydrochloride ("Special K"), 156, 160, 165–67, 173–75

Kidston, Barry, 83

King, Rodney, 68–69

Kingman, Ariz., 135

Kramer, Peter, 24

Laboratories: CAT, 121–23; designer drug, 83–84; illicit, 39, 41; methamphetamine, 133–34; PCP, 66; products of, 94, 100; raids on, 97, 100, 139, 147, 149; scale of, 9, 123, 146

Langston, J. William, 83–84

Leary, Timothy, 43, 164

Levin, Carl, 128

Lewis, Tom, 107

Lilly, John, 10, 165

Lilly Corporation, 90–91

"Liquid Ecstasy." *See* GHB (Gamma-hydroxy-butyrate)

Look-alike drugs, 33–34

Los Angeles, Calif.: amphetamines in, 35; cocaine in, 16; drug trafficking, 158; gangs in, 57; methamphetamine in, 102–3, 144, 147, 151; methcathinone in, 125; PCP in, 19, 62–63, 65–71, 84; police, 67–69, 73; rapists, 180; raves, 164; riots, 68, 191. *See also* Gates, Darryl F.; King, Rodney; Phoenix, River; Press, *Los Angeles Times*

Louisiana. *See* New Orleans, La.

LSD: laboratories, 41; revival of popularity, 131, 160, 169–70; synthesis of, 7; vogue for, in 1960s, 30, 38, 43, 84, 87, 162, 164; violence and, 69

Lysergic Acid Diethylamide. *See* LSD

Mafia. *See* Organized crime, and drug trafficking
Mandell, Arnold, 46
Marijuana: boom in 1960s, 34, 38, 49, 59; deaths related to, 150–151; as drug, ix; legal status of, 47, 56, 71, 157; panic of 1930s, 4, 10, 20–21
Marshalltown, Iowa, 138–39
McCaffrey, Barry, 128, 145, 193
McVeigh, Timothy, 135
MDA (methylene-dioxy-amphetamine), 87
MDEA. *See* EVE (MDEA, N-ethyl-methylene-dioxy-amphetamine)
MDMA. *See* Ecstasy (MDMA, methylene-dioxy-methamphetamine)
Media. *See* Cinema; National Public Radio; Press; Syndication, news; Television news and documentary programs; Television programs
Meperidine. *See* Demerol
Merck corporation, 7, 87
Methamphetamine (d-Desoxyephedrine): boom of, in 1990s, 2, 132–40; deaths related to, 18; effects of, 8; illicit manufacture of, 49–52, 100–102; injection of, 33, 38–39, 103–4; as outlaw drug, 41–46; synthesis of, 7, 30; usage patterns of, 33, 100–104; violence and, 41–44, 129–30, 134–40. *See also* Methamphetamine, smokable (ice); Methedrine
Methamphetamine, smokable (ice), 19, 25, 95, 104; Asian product, 104–5; in Hawaii, 102–10; political furor over, 104–13
Methaqualone. *See* Quaaludes
Methcathinone (CAT): history of, 118–20; manufacture of, 120–23; panic over, 2, 25, 117–18, 123–31, 156; regional market for, 120, 125
Methedrine, 30, 38–40, 43, 46–49, 208. *See also* Methamphetamine
Methylene-dioxy-amphetamine. *See* MDA (methylene-dioxy-amphetamine)
Methylene-dioxy-methamphetamine. *See* Ecstasy (MDMA, methylene-dioxymethamphetamine)
Mexico and Mexicans, 13, 31, 99, 139, 143–46, 155
Miami, Fla., 58, 154, 165, 177
Michigan: CAT problem and, 16, 117–19, 123, 127–30; Upper Peninsula of, 20, 119
Mill, John Stuart, 194–95
Mineta, Norman, 71
Minnesota, 175
Missouri, 138–41, 158. *See also* Independence, Mo.; St. Louis, Mo.
Moral panics, 4–5
Morphine, 6, 11
Motorcycle gangs, 34–35, 41–42, 51–52, 60, 102, 142. *See also* Gangs; Organized crime, and drug trafficking
Movies. *See* Cinema; Television movies
MPTP, 79, 90, 92
Musto, David, 13

National Public Radio, 125, 138, 177
Nebraska, 140, 158. *See also* Omaha, Nebr.
Neurotransmitters, 10, 30, 90, 136
Nevada, 147, 157
Newitz, Annalee, 141
New Mexico, 134, 157
New Orleans, La., 16, 164
News media. *See* Press; Television news and documentary programs
Newspapers. *See* Press
New York city: cocaine in, 16; fentanyl in, 93; gangs, 106; methamphetamine in, 42; nightclubs, 166; PCP in, 58, 62, 74; raves, 164. *See also* Press, *New York Times*
Nicotine, x, 3, 151, 189
North Dakota. *See* Fargo, N.Dak.
Novels. *See* Fiction

Oklahoma City, Okla., 35–36, 135, 142, 147–48
Omaha, Nebr., 35, 146–47
O'Nan, Stewart, 132, 143

Oregon, 157, 193. *See also* Eugene, Ore.; Portland, Ore.
Organized crime, and drug trafficking, 49–53, 82, 104–5, 133, 164. *See also* Gangs; Motorcycle gangs

Pagans. *See* Motorcycle gangs
Parke-Davis, 36, 58, 118–19, 166
Parkinson's Disease, 79, 83, 86
Parris, Stan, 106
Pasadena, Calif., 67
PCP (phencyclidine): boom in, 2; in California, 19, 61–63; history of, 57–58; image of, 53, 63–71, 79, 90; regional markets for, 58–63, 147; violence and, 65–72, 134, 137
Pennsylvania, 52, 182. *See also* Philadelphia, Pa.
Pep-pills. *See* Amphetamines and related drugs
Perkin, William H., 6
Peters, Charles, 65–66
Pharmaceutical industry. *See* Food and Drug Administration (FDA); Lilly corporation; Merck corporation; Parke-Davis; Smith Kline French
Phencyclidine. *See* PCP (phencyclidine)
Phenyl-2-propanone (P2P), 50–51, 101
Philadelphia, Pa., 49–53, 58, 82, 101, 106, 112, 127
Phoenix, Ariz., 102, 134, 144, 146–47, 150, 153–56
Phoenix, River, 170
Police: corruption, 49–51; militarization of, 97–100, 139–40, 191; PCP and, 67–69. *See also* Bureau of Narcotics Enforcement (California); Drug Enforcement Administration (DEA); Federal Bureau of Investigation (FBI); Federal Bureau of Narcotics (FBN); Gates, Darryl F.; Gibb, Douglas
Popular culture. *See* Cinema; Fiction; Press; Raves; Rock music; Television movies; Television news and documentary programs; Television programs
Portland, Ore., 102, 147

Precursor chemicals, 71, 84–85, 122, 194. *See also* Ephedrine; Phenyl-2-propanone (P2P)
Press: *Arizona Republic*, 125; *Chicago Tribune*, 80, 105, 125; *Christian Science Monitor*, 107, 135; *Harper's Bazaar*, 89; *Journal of the American Medical Association*, 18–19, 164; *Life*, 39, 43; *Los Angeles Times*, 105, 125–26, 130, 178; *Newsweek*, 39, 55, 89, 97, 136, 178; *New York Times*, 55, 80, 105, 135–38, 150, 166; *Parents*, 46; *Philadelphia Inquirer*, 182; *Reader's Digest*, 39, 46, 137; *Rolling Stone*, 65–66, 106–7, 141; *San Francisco Chronicle*, 135; *Time*, 39, 64, 80, 89, 97, 136, 171–73; *U.S. News and World Report*, 2, 72, 80, 125, 135; *Village Voice*, 43; *Wall Street Journal*, 80; *Washington Post*, 64, 107, 178. *See also* Television news and documentary programs
Prozac, 3, 10–11, 90–92

Quaaludes, 39, 55, 85, 88

Racial component in drug scares, 5, 11–15, 57, 74–75, 173. *See also* African-Americans; Asian-Americans; Whiteness, concept of
Rangel, Charles, 22, 81, 95, 105, 107, 109–12
Rape. *See* Rape-drugs
Rape-drugs, 2, 26, 60, 171–72, 175–82, 194. *See also* GHB (Gamma-hydroxybutyrate); Rohypnol (flunitrazepam); Women
Raves, 160–66, 170, 177
Reagan, Ronald, 24, 96
Reiman, Jeffrey, 192
Reinarman, Craig, 126
Reno, Janet, 144
Ribicoff, Sarai, 65
Ritalin (methylphenidate), 31
Robertson, Robert J., 81
Rock music, 56, 135, 162. *See also* Raves

Rohypnol (flunitrazepam), 2, 20, 156, 161, 166, 177–82, 194
"Roofies." *See* Rohypnol (flunitrazepam)
Rossi, Randy, 84
Rushkoff, Douglas, 87, 162

Saiki, Patricia, 110–13
San Diego, Calif.: designer drugs in, 84; homicides, 154; methamphetamine labs in, 102, 105; methamphetamine-related deaths, 144, 151; methamphetamine use in, 102, 115, 134, 146–47, 156; naval presence in, 105; police, 102, 136
San Francisco, Calif.: fentanyl in, 78; LSD in, 162, 170; MDA in, 87; methamphetamine in, 39–42, 102–3, 115, 144; PCP in, 58; raves in, 164. *See also* Press, *San Francisco Chronicle*
San Jose, Calif., 60, 62, 66, 71, 74, 102, 147
San Mateo, Calif., 65
Santa Monica, Calif., 180
Seattle, Wash., 58, 102, 124
Serial murder, 65
Sex crimes. *See* Rape-drugs; Sexual effects of drugs
Sexual effects of drugs, 14, 39–40, 60, 85, 103, 163, 175–76. *See also* Rape-drugs
Sheehy, Gail, 29, 42, 44–45
Shulgin, Alexander, 86–87, 168
Siegel, Ronald, 196
Smith Kline French, 30, 36
Speed freak image, 8, 23–24, 41–45, 136–40
Spokane, Wash., 136
Sport, drugs and, 46–47, 140
St. Louis, Mo., 146
Stone, Robert, 142
STP (2,5-dimethoxy-4-methylamphetamine), 86
Strasser, Todd, 74
Stupak, Bart, 128–29
Sublimaze. *See* Fentanyl

Summer of Love (1967), 42, 86–87, 162
Syndication, news, 19, 124–25, 130

Television movies, 72–73. *See also* Cinema
Television news and documentary programs: *48 Hours,* 14, 140; *Primetime Live,* 179; *60 Minutes,* 65–66, 70; *20/20,* 173, 179
Television programs, 56: *Beverly Hills 90210,* 179; *Millennium,* 180; *Oprah Winfrey Show,* 180–81; *Phil Donahue Show,* 80; *South Park,* 180; *The X-Files,* 139, 166
Terrorism, 41–42, 135
Texas, 20, 84, 88, 156, 171, 177. *See also* Dallas, Tex.; Farias, Hillory Janean; Houston, Tex.; Waco, Tex.
Thompson, Hunter, 34–35, 47–49, 64
Tobacco. *See* Nicotine
"Trailer trash" stereotype, 14, 135, 140–43
Tryptamines, 86
Truck drivers, and stimulants, 31

Ukiah, Calif., 143
United Kingdom, 35, 162–64

Valium, 47, 177
Veterans, and drug use, 31, 39. *See also* Wars
Violence. *See* Deaths, drug-related; Homicides, drug-related; Organized crime, and drug trafficking
Virginia, 51, 106

Waco, Tex., 134
Walker, Robert S., 52
Wars: Gulf War, 115–16; Second World War, 31, 38; Vietnam war, 41, 45. *See also* Veterans, and drug use
Washington, D.C., 49, 60–62, 64, 147, 165
Washington state. *See* Seattle, Wash.; Spokane, Wash.
Web, World Wide. *See* Internet

Welsh, Irvine, 160, 162–63
Whiteness, concept of, 11–14, 141–42.
  See also Racial component in drug
  scares; "Trailer trash" stereotype
White trash. *See* "Trailer trash" stereo-
  type; Whiteness, concept of
Wichita, Kans., 93
Wisconsin, 119–20, 122–24, 128
Women: and amphetamine pills, 32, 46;

and methamphetamine, 26, 102–3,
  136–37; and PCP, 60. *See also* Babies
  and drug addiction; Rape-drugs
World Wide Web. *See* Internet

XTC. *See* Ecstasy (MDMA, methylene-
  dioxy-methamphetamine)

Zombie imagery, 8, 11–12, 83

ABOUT THE AUTHOR

Philip Jenkins was born in Wales, and since 1980 has taught at Penn State University, where he holds the position of Distinguished Professor of History and Religious Studies.

His main interests involve the means by which the media construct (and misconstruct) social problems, and how these perspectives are reflected in both policy-making and popular culture. His recent books include *Using Murder: The Social Construction of Serial Homicide* (Aldine de Gruyter, 1994), *Pedophiles and Priests: Anatomy of a Social Crisis* (Oxford University Press 1996), *Hoods and Shirts: The Extreme Right in Pennsylvania 1925–1950* (University of North Carolina Press 1997), *A History of the United States* (Macmillan, 1997), and *Moral Panic: Changing Concepts of the Child Molester in Modern America* (Yale University Press, 1998.) He is currently studying the development of cults, cult scares and anti-cult movements in American history.